The Producer's Business Handbook

The Producer's
Business Handbook

Second Edition

John J. Lee, Jr. and Rob Holt

ELSEVIER

AMSTERDAM BOSTON HEIDELBERG LONDON
NEW YORK OXFORD PARIS SAN DIEGO
SAN FRANCISCO SINGAPORE SYDNEY TOKYO
Focal Press is an imprint of Elsevier

Acquisitions Editor: Elinor Actipis
Senior Project Manager: Angela Dooley
Assistant Editor: Cara Anderson
Marketing Manager: Christine Degon

Focal Press is an imprint of Elsevier
30 Corporate Drive, Suite 400, Burlington, MA 01803, USA
Linacre House, Jordan Hill, Oxford OX2 8DP, UK

Library of Congress Cataloging-in-Publication Data
Application submitted.

British Library Cataloguing-in-Publication Data
A catalogue record for this book is available from the British Library.

ISBN 13: 978-0-240-807102
ISBN 10: 0-240-807103

For information on all Focal Press publications
visit our Web site at www.books.elsevier.com

05 06 07 08 09 10   10 9 8 7 6 5 4 3 2 1

Printed in the United States of America

Contents

Foreword _____ ix

Introduction _____ xi

Chapter 1 / How the Motion Picture Industry Functions _____ 1
    Major Participant Categories and Their Functions   *1*
    Chapter Postscript   *17*

Chapter 2 / U.S. Theatrical Distributors   *19*
    The Major and Minor Distributors   *19*
    Studio Integrity   *21*
    The Three Studio Arenas   *21*
    Studio Relationships with Independent Producers   *22*
    Producer Relationship Comparisons   *24*
    Share Analysis Review   *31*
    Split Negative Pickup Relationships   *33*
    Studio Acquisition of a Renegade Picture   *33*
    Chapter Postscript   *35*
    The Critical Effect of U.S. Studio Attachment   *35*

Chapter 3 / International Territories _____ 37
    The Global Popularity of American Motion Pictures   *37*
    Producer Relationships with International Distributors   *41*
    Establishing New International Distribution Relationships   *44*
    Nurturing the Relationship   *45*
    International Territory License Timing   *46*
    License Documentation   *47*
    Managing Global Relationships   *49*
    International Trends   *50*
    Chapter Postscript   *50*

Chapter 4 / Ancillary Markets and Rights _____ 51
    The Effect of Theatrically Released Motion
    Pictures on Other Windows   *51*
    Audience Sizes in Major Windows   *52*
    Ancillary Audience Characteristics   *53*
    Producers Rely on Ancillary Earnings   *56*

The First Ancillary Window: Video Distribution   57

The Second Ancillary Window: Premium Cable Television   58

The Third Ancillary Window: Network or Cable Television Premiere   59

The Fourth Ancillary Window: Free Television Syndication   61

Other Ancillary Rights   61

Chapter Postscript   65

Chapter 5 / Entertainment Banking   67

The Banking Business   67

Basis of Lending Decisions   68

The Loan Approval Process   71

Production Financing Worksheet   71

Types of Loans   74

Gap Financing   75

When to Approach the Bank   75

Chapter Postscript   76

Chapter 6 / Completion Guarantors   77

What Completion Guarantees Do   77

Producers' Perceived and Real Value of Completion Guarantors   78

Completion Insurance Relationships   79

The Completion Bond Package   79

Completion Insurance Cost   81

Chapter Postscript   81

Chapter 7 / Attorneys, Negotiations, and Entertainment Law   83

Attorneys and Their Firms   83

Producers Performing as Attorneys   84

Negotiating   86

Vital Legal Aspects Relating to the Story   87

Deal Memos, Letter Agreements, and Long Form Contracts   94

The Benefits Associated with the Producer Preparing
Deal Documentation   95

Deal Reviews   95

The Attorney as Counsel   96

Dispute Resolutions   97

Chapter Postscript   97

Chapter 8 / Talent, Agents, and Agencies   99

The Relationship Evolution   100

Meetings with Talent and Agents   101

Attorneys as Agents   102

Planning the Deal   102
Development Negotiation   103
Points Participation   104
Preparation of a Fair Deal   104
Agents as Creative Resources   105
Talent Reserve   105
The Participation of the Producer's Attorney   105
Chapter Postscript   105

Chapter 9 / Development, Production, and Producing Company Structures   107

The Power of Company Structure   107
The Companies   108
Company Interrelationships   110
Development Company Financing   110
Securities   111
Forms of Companies   111
Chapter Postscript   112

Chapter 10 / Development Financing   113

The Essential Power of Funded Development   113
Development Funding Sources   115
The Process of Securing Development Financing   118
Chapter Postscript   130

Chapter 11 / The Team   131

The Complete Team   131
Company Structure   133
The Production Company's Team   133
The Development Company's Team   135
Optimizing the Teams   136
Discovering, Negotiating, and Compensating   137
Chapter Postscript   138

Chapter 12 / Production Company Operation   139

Defining and Establishing the Production Company   140
The Story Search   140
Development Company Emphasis   142
Preparing the Investment Offering   142
Assembling the Team   143
Producing the Investment Memorandum   143
Raising the Development Financing   143

Investment Partner Communications   144
Working the Development Plan   145
Story Selection and Initial Greenlights   147
Predirector Picture Development   152
Director Attachment   153
The Producer/Director Relationship   154
Shooting Script   155
Lead Cast Attachment   156
Preparing for Physical Production   156
Maturing Marketing Materials   157
Preparing the Production Bank Financing Facility   157
The U.S. Studio Distribution Agreement   158
The Presales   158
Engaging the Completion Bond   159
Engaging the Production Bank Loan   159
Final Preproduction   160
Principal Photography   160
Post-Production   161
The Picture's U.S. Branding   161
The Global Territories and Ancillary Markets   162
Chapter Postscript   163

Chapter 13 / The Producer's Business   165
Multiple Picture Management   165
Time and Budget Economies   166
Establishing the Production Company Brand Presence   167
Sustaining Business, Artistic, and Personal Objective Balance   169
Managing Library Pictures   170
Advancing Team Vitality and Allegiance   171
Chapter Postscript   172

Chapter 14 / Reports, Data, and Producer's Principles 173
Entertainment Industry Statistics and Reports   173
Information Sources   182
Producer Success Principles   186

Index   189

Foreword

"The play's the thing," according to Shakespeare. Please note that the bard did not wax poetic about how the play was paid for or marketed, or whether, at the end of the day, the investors made a dime. If the play's the thing, the business part of the play is the "other thing." Understanding business ultimately determines if we get to stick around and enjoy a profitable career at the Dream Factory.

This new edition of John Lee's incomparable book is a sophisticated and practical guide for filmmakers and potential investors that reveals the unique business disciplines followed by a group of independent film companies that enables them to finance every picture they develop, distribute every picture they produce, assure each picture's profitability, retain creative autonomy, and enjoy the lion's share of the backend profits. Learn how these production companies take the risk out of filmmaking before filming even begins.

Each year, over $3 billion are invested in over 4,000 U.S. independent feature-length movies, the majority of which will never be seen by a paying audience. Most will be lucky to return ten cents on the dollar to their investors. Those of us who would like to avoid one of these disasters and return a profit to all involved need to read this book.

Show business is big money: billions of dollars invested and tens of billions returned annually. If you would like to know how the 100 percent successful Indies determine which pictures to invest in and which ones to pass, this is the book to study.

This new edition includes a presentation and thorough explanation of all the elements necessary for the reader to either "greenlight" or pass on each contemplated project. *The Producer's Business Handbook* will show how to apply hard-learned business lessons to your next production. Whether it's a multimillion dollar film or a small Indy movie, every filmmaker should go through this same exercise when deciding whether or not to make their next movie.

In clear, precise language, John Lee lays out a business model that has a 100 percent chance of recouping an investor's money before a single frame of film is shot. What's more, the creative team—those folks actually responsible for making the film—can retain a larger share of the profits from their labors.

There are many books about the "show" part of show business. *The Producer's Business Handbook* stands alone in describing the entire inner workings of the financial engines that keep the "business" part of the movie business humming. Only within the covers of this book will you find such a wealth of knowledge that removes the mysteries of financing, marketing, and distribution. The author provides another way of understanding the movie business that will change your thinking forever.

If you're planning to produce a movie or thinking about investing in a movie and want a realistic, in-depth look at the business of show business, you need to read *The Producer's Business Handbook*—and then you'll want to read it again.

Steve Ecclesine, Producer, President of Production, Brookwell McNamara Entertainment

Introduction

Most of the hundreds of active U.S. independent producers operate unstable, often unprofitable businesses. Yet at the same time, fewer than two dozen independent production organizations operate solid, consistently profitable companies. The success of these companies is not attained by accident, but rather through the application of sound business principles and practices that drive their ever-advancing motion picture production craft.

The purpose of this book is to assist producers in attaining this unquestionably preferable operating position. Specifically, it discusses how the global motion picture industry works and focuses on the processes used by these independent production companies, that enable them to almost exclusively use banks to provide their production financing, to release their pictures theatrically through major studios, and to consistently do so at a profit.

This book is a global orientation to the relationships that the most successful motion picture producers have with the various participants in the motion picture industry. This includes how these producers direct their relationships with domestic and international distributors, agencies, attorneys, talent, completion guarantors, banks, and private investors. As there is no natural relationship between the production cost of a motion picture and its earnings capacity, this book also presents a thorough orientation to each project's business evaluation. This process is each picture's *internal greenlight analysis* and is the discovery of the proportional relationship of the producer's share of global profits as compared to the picture's all-in production cost: its earnings-to-cost ratio. The results indicate the business feasibility of a picture and point to its likely funding, global distribution partners, optimal release time of year, distribution costs, target audiences, ancillary products, and marketing strategies. This volume also contains the producer's thorough orientation to planning, organizing, and operating development and producing companies, from solicitation of literary properties, through direct rights sales and the management of global distribution relationships. Also presented is an in-depth discussion of the team needed to operate the companies, as well as how to find and attach them. Additionally, there are worksheets and instructions for the business processes of development and production, which are used by many of the industry's consistently profitable production companies.

To assist readers in a deeper understanding, and for use within their own companies, a CD-ROM accompanies this book, containing, in Microsoft Excel:

1. The Producer's Share Analysis/Internal Greenlight Summary
2. The Bank Financing Worksheet
3. The Production and Development Companies' Organization Charts
4. The Multiple Picture Development and Production Activity Projection
5. The Multiple Picture Development and Production Cash Flow Projection

6. The Production Company Model
7. The Development Company Model
8. Most Successful Picture Analysis

and in Microsoft Word:

1. A Literary Release Sample
2. Target Audience Analysis

This book is written to provide both instruction and worksheet support to independent motion picture producers at all levels of industry experience. Specifically, it is written to:

1. Assist experienced producers (as well as directors, writers, and other entertainment professionals), and hone and sharpen their hard-won experience and knowledge into increasingly effective tools with which they can manage their resources. In this highly specialized field of motion picture production, often the difference between success and failure hinges on the producer's ability to dynamically engage and balance the full spectrum of business resources and relationships within his or her reach. This book opens for producers a full-aperture view of the entertainment business and provides them with the tools and instructions they need to engage all aspects of the film industry related to global production and exploitation. It opens the way to improved industry understanding and, more importantly, to the capacity to operate predictably profitable production organizations.

2. Assist entry-level producers in understanding how the motion picture industry operates, plot their most promising path to achieve their independent producing objectives, and provide them documentation, as well as relationship and operational support.

Independent Producers

This book focuses on *independent producers*. These are not to be confused with attached producers (who may be executive producers, financiers, line producers, executives with a studio deal, or a star's boy- or girlfriend). Independent producers, as they are referenced in this text, are those who are at the creative and business helm of each of their pictures from development inception.

Many studio production-unit pictures begin their film lives in development pools. These pictures have producers, but they are often attached to perform production services and are rarely these pictures' creative genesis. Development pool pictures often have a director and one or more actors attached before a producer is attached. Although these producers are typically seasoned motion picture makers, they do not have the same relationship with their pictures as do independent producers.

For instance, *Return of the Jedi* is appropriately regarded as George Lucas's picture, though it was directed by Richard Marquand. Although the director is the production chief during principal photography, and often is also the supervising editor, we can be assured that Mr. Lucas's fiercely independent creative participation permeated the entire production process. It is his picture. So although creative collaboration is a bedrock quality of the best independent producers, the independent producers referenced in this book are those who are their pictures' genesis and ultimate creative authority.

Similarly, John Hughes's production company produced *Home Alone* with 20th Century Fox. Hughes was the producer and writer. Although Hughes used Chris Columbus (a respected writer/director/producer) to direct the picture, giving him the creative freedom due a director of his stature, Hughes sustained the creative dominance of an independent producer throughout the picture's creation.

In a final example, though Steven Spielberg directs most of his pictures, he generally brings in producers or coproducers. Of course, if he chooses to produce only (as he did with *Goonies*), he delegates the direction duties to someone else. Regardless, on his pictures, Spielberg is the independent producer and consequently the ultimate creative authority.

The producer definition used in this book refers to those independent producers who choose to retain their pictures' development and production authority and creative genesis, regardless of the specific functions they select in each picture.

Investors

This book is also a breakthrough point-of-reference guide for investors. The original edition of this book was used widely by private and institutional investors, as well as banks and attorneys representing investors, as a business orientation to assist them in evaluating investment opportunities and assessing the business acumen of their related independent producers. Those with real estate development experience will find their orientation especially facilitated and this book beneficial in the process as there are many funding and business similarities between motion picture development and real estate development.

Workbook

This is also a workbook. Included are seven worksheets and several business forms. These will be most beneficial to learning and business when used with the CD-ROM that accompanies this book.

The worksheets are presented in Microsoft Excel software. Each worksheet is in live sample form, allowing the most detailed scrutiny and understanding, as well as in a blank template form for their broader use in the producer's production and development companies. Central to the worksheets are the Activity Projection and the Cash Flow Projection. The production forms are presented in Microsoft Word and can easily be customized for each producer's use.

Basis for the Principles

Like most principles worth learning, the principles set forth in this book are simple and are proven by experience, as they are used by many of the industry's most successful independent motion picture production companies. The core of these principles is discovered in the answers to three questions that should be applied to all works considered for development and production.

- Is the story worth being told?
- Who are the story's primary target audiences?
- What is the ratio between the story's production and costs and the producer's share of global, all-rights income?

Producers who make their decisions predicated on the analysis of the answers to these questions consistently guide each of their pictures through successful development, production, and distribution.

Though motion picture producers are the reader focus of this book and theatrical release motion pictures are the product focus, the application of this volume's principles will be as beneficial to seasoned feature producers' continuing pictures, as well as to a student's first film school productions.

Common Orientation

This information will likely cast some surprising light in a few dimly lit corners for seasoned producers and related motion picture professionals, and will be particularly illuminating for students of film who are preparing for careers in independent feature film production.

The following industry parable may help bring the reader to a common grounding with the information in this text.

The Forest

A squirrel and an otter agreed to confide with one another in an attempt to unravel the mysterious anomalies unique to the forest in which they lived— you know, the stuff they did not understand that frequently drove them a little crazy. The squirrel described what she saw from the trees and the otter described what he saw from the water and ground.

They met regularly to share their prevailing theories and enjoy the mutual therapy and camaraderie. This did not escape the attention of their contemporaries, and soon a broad cross section of them met, sharing new and often fascinating perspectives. Over time, the group became secure in their mutually affirmed understandings. They settled many matters: that forest fires were caused by the sun touching the tops of the trees, and—well, almost every other problem was caused by the forest's predators.

From time to time, eavesdropping eagles listened and were amazed at some of the forest animals' twisted conclusions. Pleased to dispel their bizarre notions, one of these eagles explained that he had soared over the entire forest, observing all its creations for decades, that he possessed a sound under- standing of how and why things happened in the forest, and was willing to share what he knew.

It was a novel resource never before available to them. The forest animals agonized over the offer among themselves and then finally declined the eagle's proposal. They determined that they were comfortable with their under-standing, and that they had the scoop from sparrows and robins. Besides, the eagle was a predator and obviously an unreliable source.

There are scores of cliques within the motion picture industry, each comfortable in its peculiar understanding of how the industry functions, and why seemingly irrational anomalies regularly occur. This condition is like that of Galileo, who was forced to renounce his published discoveries of astronomy and physics, among them the stunning reality that the world was actually turning. Pressed into a humiliating public renunciation by those who were not comfortable with how these discoveries affected their understanding of life, Galileo afterward calmly declared, "And yet the world turns."

So it was with the forest animals, and so it is with many of us in the business of creating motion pictures. This is an expansive, powerful industry, with dynamics that often vault participants to the top of the heap at a given time, then dash them to relative obscurity at another. Though we may have our notions that explain why it does or doesn't work the way we think it should, it can be instructive to remember that our personal perceptions do not affect how the motion picture industry actually functions.

This volume draws upon each of the authors' understandings, harvested primarily from serving as production and distribution business affairs executives for a combined 36 years, most recently as CEO and President, respectively, of Entertainment Business Group, a business affairs, funding, and global sales organization. This volume also employs the knowledge and experience of several film industry mavens to whom we are grateful for their help, and data from the most reliable industry sources, many of whom are referenced in this book's final chapter.

As an industry seminar speaker, I assumed that capacity, attendance, and aggressive participation at my presentations were a result of producers' ongoing panic about securing production funding. However, in preparation for a three-year film school commitment to teach business of film courses, I discovered that although most books were excellent in some regard, none presented a complete picture of how the industry functions from an independent producer's perspective, or most important, what the specific operating practices of the most successful production companies are. This book delivers the critical missing material.

How the Motion Picture Industry Functions

This chapter is a broad entertainment business overview and presents the motion picture industry by its 10 major participant categories. Further, it reveals independent production companies as creation and production businesses with distribution capacities. Finally and appropriately, it examines story as the critical core of the producer's universe.

Major Participant Categories and Their Functions

There are 10 participant categories, basic functions and interrelationships within the motion picture industry. The most prosperous companies in each category are successful, in large measure, because they sustain a perspective of how the whole industry operates and continually sharpen their individual participation within the entire entertainment universe.

This perspective includes the view that (1) the motion picture industry is a consumer-product business; (2) each participant contributes to and is reliant upon other participants and (3) the various target audiences are each picture's most important participants.

In their order of importance, the 10 categories of players are:

1. Audiences
2. Distributors
3. Producers
4. Retailers and licensed media

5. International territories
6. Financing participants
7. Distributor subcontractors
8. Production talent and subcontractors
9. Ancillary media and licensees
10. Major consumer brands

Participant Category 1: The Audiences

Each picture's target audiences are its sources of income. Audiences are the highest priority participants in the industry, because without them, there is no industry. Producers must know the specific target audiences for each of their pictures, evaluate each picture according to its audiences, and, after committing to a story creatively, make decisions to proceed on the picture based on its target audience dynamics.

After finding a story that interests them, producers should ask two questions regarding its audiences:

1. By order of dominance, who are this picture's target audiences? This answer prepares the producer to research the leading 54 U.S. major metropolitan areas (metros), and discover the size, entertainment consumption, and media-use profile of each of the picture's target audiences. (These leading 54 are the focus of the more than 200 U.S. metros, since each of these 54 have a half-million television households or more and together spend over two-thirds of total U.S. entertainment dollars.)

2. How have these audiences responded to at least five pictures released in the most recent five years that are most similar in story, anticipated above-the-line creatives (director and lead cast), and anticipated television marketing campaign? The answer to this question enables the producer to project gross receipts, and the producer's share of those gross receipts, for the story being considered. Pictures with similar audiences are identified by comparing the proposed picture's dominant campaign elements and above-the-line participants with the campaign elements and above-the-line participants of previously released pictures.

Initial Feasibility Analysis of Internal Greenlight

The answers to these two questions, weighed against a picture's estimated production and distribution costs, determine whether that picture will be greenlit by the producer. This is a picture's initial feasibility analysis.

If the audience profiles and picture comparisons are positive, and the income-to-cost ratio is at least two-to-one (in other words, the projected distributor's net income is at least twice the projected production costs), the producer should proceed with the next step in the development of most pictures. If a picture's target audiences lack dynamic consumer profiles, or are too small or difficult to reach in comparison to the picture's costs, the producer should pass rather than proceed.

The specific methods of obtaining and analyzing this information, and a complete explanation of obtaining a picture's internal greenlight, are presented in later chapters, especially Chapters 2 and 12. The following diagram demonstrates the economics of this process.

The Picture's Initial Feasibility Analysis
(in millions)

(Ratios are from recent historical comparisons)

Global projected gross income	$188
Less theatrical participations, distributor's fees, and expenses	$131
Distributor's net	$57
Negative cost and production financing expenses (actual estimated budget)	$20
Ratio of distributor's net income to production costs	2.85:1
Feasibility	Recommend proceeding

Audience Orientation

Producers should understand and use the consumer terms used by Madison Avenue and the reporting agencies such as Nielsen Media Research, as these are the audience semantics of the entertainment industry. Utilizing this language is an especially effective tool in the producer's relationships with international and domestic distributors, licensees of international and domestic rights, product placement and premium tie-in brand representatives, advertising agencies, and public relations and promotion companies.

Audiences are categorized demographically by age as follows:

Primary Audience Age Demographic Categories

Audience Terms	*Age Demographic*
Kids	5–11
Youth	12–17
Adults	18+
Youth and single adults	12–24
Older youth and single adults	16–24

Adults are separated into several categories, by gender, most significantly in the motion picture business by ages 18 to 24, 18 to 34, 25 to 34, 25 to 44, 25 to 54, 45-plus, and 55-plus.

Audiences also are identified and evaluated by lifestyles, such as active adults, affluent adults, educated adults, inner-city youth, working women, and so on.

There are excellent, easy-to-use consumer databases available to producers at reasonable costs, or accessible through major advertising agencies, media buying companies, and the television networks. These consumer databases allow target audiences to be identified by an extensive array of demographic and lifestyle search criteria. The lifestyle options are broad, the data is reliable, and the reports are exceptionally useful in audience quantifying and qualifying.

For example, you can sort the major metros by men 18 to 34 who are college graduates, watch a movie at a theater at least twice a month, and own a mountain bike. The requested report can reveal how many are in this audience, where their population concentrations are, what their consumption profiles for the various media are, which TV programs they watch, and so on.

Becoming conversant with this information and the databases it is derived from is crucially important, as the application of this data becomes a very powerful tool for producers who will be originating promotions, reviewing media buys, and projecting their pictures' earnings.

Distributor Pitch Preparation

Many producers are skilled in preparing the creative aspects of their pictures to pitch to distributors. However, they are not ready to pitch until they also have prepared and can present information about their pictures' audiences in the full spectrum of the distributors' interest.

Pitching their pictures to distributors, after having first fulfilled their internal green-lights, empowers producers to present information that is essential for distribution executives to evaluate their interest. This information includes these pictures' audiences and projected gross receipts. Producers armed with this information are in the strongest presentation position possible, to both present and negotiate from the distributors' perspectives. The appropriate presentation of this information in order to receive optimal positive distributor responses is reviewed in Chapter 2.

Participant Category 2: The Distributors

The major distributors are the motion picture marketing and sales companies in the global territories that establish the brand presence of each picture to their respective target audiences, and are wholesalers of motion pictures to their various media.

In the U.S., the major distributors are 20th Century Fox, Universal, Buena Vista, Paramount, Sony, Warner Bros., Miramax, DreamWorks, and New Line. Each of these is a full-service studio in the traditional definition, with the exception of Miramax, DreamWorks, and New Line, which lack only a studio lot. These nine majors are all-rights distributors, globally distributing every theatrical, nontheatrical, and ancillary right associated with their motion pictures. And they are the prominent U.S. theatrical and home entertainment distributors for major U.S. independent producers.

In addition to the major studios there are:

1. Twenty minor theatrical distributors, five of which are owned by major distributors (Sony Pictures Classics, Fox Searchlight, Warner Independent, Paramount Classics, and Focus Features). Some of the largest and best operated of the remaining minors include Lions Gate and New Market. The largest of these 20 minors are all-rights distributors.

2. Direct international territory distributors. The largest of these are studios within their respective international territories, which produce and direct-distribute to all their territories' major media, and who also sell their pictures' rights globally. These are presented in Chapter 3.

3. International rights sales companies. The largest of these organizations produce and coproduce some of their own pictures, in addition to acquiring motion pictures and performing international market sales and distribution services for their independent producers' pictures. These include Summit Entertainment and Icon Entertainment International.

4. Producers representative organizations. These organizations plan and execute sales to distributors in international territories, and may also plan and engage U.S. distribution, as well as plan and engage all global rights liquidation of their independent producer clients' pictures and related rights. Among these are Entertainment Business Group and Kathy Morgan International.

5. Television syndication companies. These companies plan and carry out sales to television stations and cable companies.

6. Product placement. These companies plan, negotiate, and manage the use, borrowing, giving, or fee earned by their producer clients for products appearing in their pictures.

7. Promotional tie-in companies. These companies originate, plan, negotiate, and manage relationships in advertising or promoting the release of producers' motion pictures with other consumer brands. The most prolific brand categories that participate in the motion picture industry are soft drinks and fast food.

8. Publishers. These entities are discussed in more detail in Chapter 4, and primarily include (1) book publishers either republishing novels associated with pictures being released, or publishing new novels based on original screenplays; (2) comic book, coloring book, and workbook publishers who create and release books coordinated with picture releases; and (3) paper-based role playing and other game publishers who create and distribute their respective products timed with picture releases.

9. Ancillary rights sales companies. These organizations, examined in Chapter 4, include companies specializing in merchandising, in-flight, scholastic, ships-at-sea, and other sales and marketing.

Establishing Each Picture's Brand and the Studio Operating Perspective

The operations and functions of U.S. theatrical distributors are presented in Chapter 2. The following section introduces both the distribution phenomenon of establishing a picture's brand as well as the distributors' operating perspective.

Brand Presence. Each picture's value for every other U.S. rights area is primarily established during its U.S. theatrical release. American audiences are introduced to each picture during this premiere distribution window. This is where the brand, the audience perspective, and the picture's entertainment value are established.

As is thoroughly reviewed in Chapter 2, though this is the most important release window, media expenses for brand establishment are so costly that most motion pictures do not earn sufficient income to equal their media outlay alone.

The physical aspects of theatrical distribution are highly sophisticated. These functions include theater circuit bidding, booking the multiplexes and the screens within them that are best matched with each picture, negotiating favorable film rental terms with the circuits, and staging the physical release of the picture through film exchanges, and, finally, the actual settlements that are negotiated with each theater circuit after each picture's play. These operations substantially affect the success of each picture. For example, audiences expect the finest pictures to be on the largest screens at the best theaters. A good picture booked at a questionable multiplex or playing on a smaller screen sends a message to the target audiences that it may be a poor picture, potentially overturning other well-executed distribution moves.

As complex and crucial as physical distribution is, however, the peerless genius in the art of distribution lies in establishing the public's opinion of each picture through paid advertising, publicity, and promotion. This is the process through which motion pictures become major brands to their target audiences.

A brand is the name by which consumers identify a product or group of products. Pepsi, Levi Strauss, and Quaker Oats have the luxury of fighting for sustained brand dominance. Theirs is a continuing and absolutely rugged battle, but it pales in comparison with motion picture brand establishment.

Every motion picture released is a separate brand. Each picture must come from absolute obscurity (with the exception of novels and sequels) to become top-of-mind with each picture's target audiences. This typically is begun 9 to 12 months before a picture opens, but is substantially accomplished in a major media blitz three to five weeks prior to each picture's opening. A television campaign may have a reach and frequency performance as high as 12 impressions (advertising viewings) by 80 percent of that picture's target audiences before the picture opens. Depending on the target audience and time of year, the cost of media alone is typically $20 to $35 million, *before* a picture's initial street date. Brand presence is so fundamental to a picture's earnings performance in every distribution category that distributors' projections of the picture's gross earnings are based on a percentage of each picture's opening weekend theatrical receipts.

Typically the distributor originates and directs the entire campaign, and it is the campaign, its media buys, and promotions that drive each picture's initial audiences. In fact, even with prescreenings, the picture itself usually has little effect on the theatrical opening weekend gross, and only limited effect on the first week's earnings. Though critical reviews have little opening weekend effect on pictures with kids, youth, and young adults as primary audiences, these audiences are highly affected by Internet reviews posted by their contemporaries. These posted reviews significantly affect their attendance after opening weekend. However, a powerful media campaign with strong television commercials that delivers well over the minimum necessary to form a critical mass will still overcome word of mouth during the opening two weeks, even among these savvy and tightly connected audiences.

The two major campaign elements that determine each picture's opening two weeks' theatrical gross are (1) how motivating the television spots are to the picture's unique target audiences, and (2) the reach and frequency of the campaign's television schedule for these target audiences. Television is the hammer media for all audiences, though radio, outdoor, and print advertising are important, especially during the summer.

Consequently, producers benefit most when they focus on heightening the impact of their pictures' campaigns and assuring that the aggregate media buys are significantly beyond critical mass and are optimized for their targets, as these largely determine each picture's opening weekend performance.

The picture's brand presence established during its theatrical release predicates the picture's earnings capacity in all subsequent distribution release windows. These other earnings windows, especially home entertainment (video/DVD and soon, Internet downloading and pay-per-view), premium cable, and network television, are the producer's highest earnings sources. Often those distributors who have established a strong positive brand with their picture's target audiences during the theatrical release, but have seen competing pictures, weather, or other factors keep theatrical audiences low, find that they experience a substantial audience increase during the home video/DVD release.

Distributors Operating Perspective

Each theatrical screen is a unique retail environment. It accommodates only one product at a time. Consequently, distributors closely examine the earnings performance of each picture on each screen. When gross receipts fall below a screen's house-nut (the exhibitor's attributed cost to provide and operate that screen), the picture is soon replaced with another. For example, if an exhibitor's house-nut is $3,200 and that week's gross was $2,800, the distributor knows the picture will soon be replaced by a picture with greater grossing potential.

As discussed earlier, each picture's opening two weeks of theatrical earnings are largely predicated on the effectiveness of its campaign. After the opening two weeks, audience opinion largely determines a picture's theatrical life. This being the case, distributors create and refine the after-opening campaigns to drive target audiences' peak attendance.

Again, campaigns are the central reason audiences buy tickets, and TV commercials are the most convincing campaign elements. This is largely so because they allow target audiences to actually sample the movie before buying a ticket. This sampling is sufficiently powerful to initially overpower negative reviews and even word of mouth. When viewing the campaign, the audience sees and hears evidence that a picture is indeed funny, exciting, romantic, scary, or contains other emotional connections that motivate them to see the picture or not. When making their ticket-buying decisions, audiences lean to their own experience, even when that experience is limited to 30-second commercials and 2- to 3-minute trailers.

These market realities motivate motion picture distributors to focus first on each picture's campaign, for this is what substantially drives each picture's earnings. Every distributor's first responsibility is to get its pictures' target audiences to theaters. Campaigns drive audiences; audiences drive box office receipts; distributors focus on campaigns.

It should be no surprise, then, that in deciding whether they will distribute a picture, distributors look first to a picture's campaign elements, then to its overall entertainment power. *Accordingly, producers should anticipate that distributors will assess their interest in distributing each picture based on a formula of 70 percent campaign integrity and 30 percent entertainment power.* That is to say, 70 percent of the decision will be based on the audience sales dynamics of the picture's story and the emotional (drama, comedy, action/adventure, romance, etc.) intensity of the picture's elements that will be used in its 30-second TV commercials and theatrical trailers (the picture's campaign), and 30 percent will be based on how the audience will feel as they leave the theater (the picture's entertainment power).

Therefore, even in predevelopment, when producers make picture presentations to distributors, they should weigh their presentations according to this formula. The distributor must be convinced of the salability of the picture before they will seriously consider its production and overall entertainment values.

Participant Category 3: Independent Producers

Independent producers are the creators and manufacturers of the motion picture products. The industry's leading producers also plan and manage all their pictures sales and distribution, and directly conduct some sales.

The final five chapters of this text present independent production company operations. This section presents the two main independent producer operating profiles: creative protectionist producers and balanced producers.

Considering the two prior participant categories (audiences and distributors), we can now confidently embrace a fresh independent producer orientation. Audiences pay for the producer's goods, and distributors create and motivate a market for them. Though uncomfortable to some producers, these simple realities render these audiences and distributors preeminent to the producer in every aspect of decision making. In all their operations, producers will make the most sound and profitable decisions for their pictures and their companies if they hold themselves accountable to these two categories. Audiences and distributors are the producer's most beneficial and crucial sources of business checks and balances.

Creative Protectionist Producers

Creative protectionist producers comprise the greatest number of independent producers in the film industry. In the United States, there are more than 800 of these production companies, operating chiefly from New York or Los Angeles.

The characteristic unique to these producers is their arm's-length, creative protectionist attitude toward distributors. These producers are so intensely focused on the creative purity of the vision they have for each picture that any other opinion, especially those of distributors who must focus on the commercial success of each picture, appear to represent a threat to the artistic integrity of their pictures and are commonly blamed if their pictures financially underperform. This attitude often creates a love-hate relationship with their distributors.

If you ask these producers about their experience with the distributors of their pictures, they frequently assume a crazed expression and say, "I could tell you stories!" And they can. But so can their distributors. No matter the stories, this separatist operating style (1) promotes strained production financing, which then must come partially or wholly from private sources; (2) results in their pictures underearning for lack of market preparation; and (3) causes some of their theatrical feature films to receive no U.S. theatrical release at all.

Most creative protectionist producers fall well within the purview of the sage commentary, "They were often filled with the exhilaration of their progress up the ladder, only to find when they neared the top, it was leaning against the wrong wall."

Some of these producers are highly skilled and have industry and audience reputations for creative wizardry. Often, their pictures are released through major studios, and some even win Academy Awards. At the same time, this high-risk operating style yields high attrition among these producers, and unfortunately creates a substantial disparity between their numbers of produced pictures, distributed pictures, and profitable pictures.

The exhilaration of "climbing the ladder" occurs during production. The producer actually is producing the aspired movie, using and expanding production talents, and hopefully fulfilling his or her highest vision of the picture. The "wrong wall" revelation comes as the producer realizes that the film's audiences are too limited and the campaign elements too light to justify the distributors' production advances. In the case of too many of these pictures, they never play to a paying audience.

In most industries, this trend would correct itself, but not in the motion picture industry. Though there are far too many casualties, especially among first-time producers, the lure of fame engendered by the one success among the thousands of failed such attempts each year is sufficient to attract new and even experienced producers back to climbing the ladder that leans against the wall that will not bring the distribution and consequently neither the audiences nor the profits necessary for the picture to succeed.

To those producing their first picture, this path is sometimes referred to as the "festival" or "Sundance path." The prescription to follow the festival path reads something like this (this is an actual encapsulation from a current private-film-school text):

> *Once you have found or written a screenplay that you are passionate about, then employ all your filmmaking craft, engage production associates willing to be paid chiefly from the picture's profits, pool all the money you have, borrow from relatives and any other sources who are willing to lend, run up your credit cards for the balance of the budget, and make the film. When it is complete, enter it in as many festivals as you can, and see how you fare.*

Following this counsel, thousands of motion pictures are completed each year by well-intending producers and submitted to one or more of the approximately 2,500 annual film festivals. In 2004, the highest profile of the events, the Sundance Festival, considered over 2,613 motion picture submissions and selected just 120 that were screened during the festival, in all categories. Of these entrants, the industry trade papers (which rarely miss a transaction of substance) recorded 14 distributor pickups. These were huge wins for the 14 producers, their financier, and creative associates, but what of the 106 producers who didn't obtain a distribution relationship for their pictures? Even more telling, consider the 2,493 producers who didn't even get the opportunity to screen their films.

Wracked by the conflict between the thrill of producing their first feature-length picture and the reality of severe debt and disappointed, if not angry, investor-relatives and friends, many of these producers eventually approach distributors directly to screen their films, or continue along the festival path until their hopes abate.

Distributors are unquestionably willing to help new producers but are loath to receive calls from those with completed pictures to be screened, as these pictures usually, even if clever, are simply not sufficiently marketable to warrant the substantial, essential, distribution investment.

Over the course of our careers, we have screened far too many of these films for distributor clients. After the screening (and typical pass on behalf of the distributor), if the producer is interested, we meet with him or her and ask the difficult, but vital question that can open the way to a more productive approach to filmmaking. The question is, "Before you poured your talent and resources into this film, why didn't you contact a distributor to find out if they were interested in your vision of the picture?"

At this point in the process, it is tough for producers to come up with an answer. Those who do offer an explanation generally fall into the creative protectionist category, and enthusiastically defend their position, asserting that distributor involvement would have threatened their picture's creative integrity.

Perhaps from a purely artistic point of view, this may be true. The question is, then, are producers motivated only by their opportunity to express their vision of the story—or would they also like their vision to be shared with audiences and earn a profit?

Fundamentally, most producers want their films to fulfill three major objectives:

1. Creation: to powerfully reveal the producer's vision of the story.
2. Audience: to play the picture to as extensive an audience possible.
3. Profits: to recoup production costs and receive a fair participation of the picture's earnings.

Balanced Producers

Balanced producers are simply that. They understand and sustain a balance between their pictures' creative, audience, and income aspects. As of this writing, there exists a small group of just under two dozen balanced producers, operating principally from New York or Los Angeles. These include Imagine Entertainment, Beacon Pictures, New Regency, Icon, Working Title Films, and Morgan Creek. The pictures that come from these producers and their production companies consistently receive global distribution, are profitable, and attain their producers' creative visions.

Balanced producers understand the essential importance of both preparing their pictures for the global marketplace and preparing the global marketplace for their pictures. Consequently, their creation and production decisions are wholly knit together with their global distribution and rights-sales decisions.

As a result of this operating style, most of these producers are able to primarily, if not exclusively, use bank-provided production financing, release their pictures through major distributors, and extract the maximum possible media and rights earnings from the various global territories.

To become a Castle Rock or Lakeshore Entertainment, producers must employ the sound, balanced approach to production that will lead them to such success. Producers must do the work that engenders the broad, global industry relationships that these companies enjoy. Such an operating style is the result of a consistent, disciplined approach to the creation and distribution of a producer's motion pictures.

Because the operating style of these companies is low-risk, their pictures are principally released by major studios (more than 90 percent), their pictures are generally profitable (more than 80 percent), and accordingly their organizations build value, some of them becoming publicly traded.

Before committing to a picture's production, in most cases even prior to acquiring a literary property or idea (with the exception of bidding frenzies, which rarely serve even the winner well), balanced producers proceed only when they become convinced that the producer's potential gross profits are sufficiently high compared with the picture's approximate production and distribution costs. If these numbers do not proof out, balanced producers pass on the picture, even if the producer is wild to do it. Sometimes referred to as "therapy pictures," even creative triumphs are shallow victories if few ever see them and they do not earn more income than that necessary to clear production and distribution costs.

Balanced Producer's Development and Production Approach. To receive the greatest creative freedom and highest earnings, producers must sustain a balance among each picture's story, audiences (as affirmed by major territory distributors from earliest development), and margin between cost of production and the producer's share of profits (presented in Chapter 2). This is the success wall for serious producers to lean their ladders against.

Just as balanced producers' production analyses for their pictures include script breakdowns, production boards, schedules, and budgets, so should they include liquidation breakdowns, global rights analysis, distribution window schedules, potential premium tie-in lists, and cover-shot recommendations from the major international territories. These processes are presented in subsequent chapters and the worksheet CD.

Understanding the intricate business of motion picture rights liquidation, for example, allows producers to plan and perform the distribution of their pictures with the same predictability as they perform the production of these films. Just as there is only one opportunity to produce a picture, there is only one opportunity to liquidate its rights.

For instance, knowing that a picture lends itself to merchandising products, in-flight and novelization allows a producer, while still in development, the advantage of including product development and cover shots (necessary for some in-flight as well as international versions) in the picture's production plans and budgets. At the same time, the novelization of the screenplay can be planned and a publishing relationship put in play. With sufficient lead time the paperback can feature the picture's one-sheet (poster art) on its covers at retail check-out stands two to four weeks before the picture's U.S. theatrical premiere and the merchandisable goods can further cross-promote the picture and be released in its optimal timing to benefit the picture's release. Without the producer's involvement in these processes, the marketing and income benefits from them would be lost or seriously compromised.

Independent production is inherently intense. Embracing the practices of balanced producers not only assures producers the greatest possible success in marketing their pictures, but also delivers all those who are committed to the producer's success the greatest possible infusion of stability and sanity.

Even producers working under a studio umbrella are well served to remember that while most producers create one picture every six months to two years (many of these pictures passing through a before-funded development gestation of several years), each major U.S. studio releases one to three pictures a month!

The studios are masters at evaluating and extracting the greatest income from their pictures. However, producers should not expect a distributor to plan and prepare as early or as comprehensively as the producer. If the producer is the picture's parent, consider the distributors as aunts and uncles. Although a crucial part of the family, they will never care for the picture like the producer will.

Before a producer commits to a project, he or she should process it through his or her own in-house tests, as presented in later chapters, and summarily in Chapter 12. After a producer internally greenlights a picture, then it's time to bring in the rest of the family.

To sustain sanity and balance in their companies and careers, independent producers must establish and follow these basic creative and business processes to experience the artistic, operational, and compensatory benefits. When producers (the third-tier participants) develop, produce, and distribute their pictures, deeply meshed with their audiences and distributors (the first- and second-tier participants), all other industry participants (tiers 4 through 10), will respect and confidently participate with them.

Participant Category 4: Retailers and Licensed Media

These are the theater circuits, video outlet rental chains, and home entertainment sell-through retailers, premium cable networks, major free television networks, and free television syndication participants, including cable networks and independent television stations. The producer's relationships with each of these are presented in subsequent chapters. This section focuses on the larger view of how these motion picture retailers impact and contribute to the motion picture arena.

It is important to realize that each of these represents a massive, sophisticated, and separate industry. Each has separate associations and conventions and each makes its own crucial and very specialized contributions in selling to its specific and unique audiences. They are similar, however, in that they all rely on producers to deliver dynamically entertaining pictures and theatrical distributors to initially establish a powerfully motivating brand for each picture.

Distribution Windows

Though each picture's liquidation schedule is singular to its audiences, marketing power, time of year and date of initial theatrical release, financing, and distribution agreements, the typical U.S. distribution windows are as follows:

Traditional U.S. Distribution Windows

Distribution window	Time from prior window	Cumulative months
Electronic Games	6–12 weeks prior to theatrical release	
Paperback	3–7 weeks prior to theatrical release	
Theatrical	Opening day	
Video rental/sell-through	4 to 6 months later	6 months
Premium cable	6 months later	12 months
Video sell-through rerelease (if not originally at lowest release price)	6 months later	18 months
Network television	6 months later	24 months
Syndicated television	12–24 months later	36–48 months

In addition to the substantial and sophisticated campaigns mounted by theatrical distributors, each of these participants makes the following contributions:

1. Theatrical exhibitors (theater chains) plan and purchase print (newspaper) advertising in their theaters' markets. Most exhibitors have their own in-house ad agencies that manage this process. They also show trailers (movie previews) of upcoming releases and display one-sheets (movie posters) of current and upcoming pictures. Both trailers and one-sheets are provided by the distributors. Unquestionably the most motivating contribution that exhibitors make to each picture's success is providing a high-profile exhibition environment with large screens, superior sound, comfortable seating, and a theater staff who are informed about the picture and anxious to make patrons happy that they chose to come to their theater to see it.

2. Video outlet chains rely primarily on video distributors (who are most often also the theatrical distributor for each picture) to motivate their audiences. In addition, video outlets display one-sheets, may run picture trailers on video screens in each outlet (this is really more miss than hit for most stores), and may place local newspaper advertising, and in the case of the largest chains, even use television campaigns. As with exhibitors, most video outlets

provide customers with a high-tech film industry environment that advances each picture's video audience and earnings. Further, ordering an adequate copy depth (volume of copies) of each picture satisfies the early heavy audience demands and also crucially extends each picture's video audiences and earnings.

3. The sell-through video retail category is notably expansive and continuing to expand. This category returns greater profits to picture participants than any other single category. The highest volume of these participants are mass merchandisers, supermarkets, and music stores. These participants sell the dominant share of videocassettes and DVDs, and for many titles, serve larger audiences and earn greater income than any other domestic partner. Even with the stunning evolution of home downloadability, these retail participants are expected to sustain the lion's share of audiences and earnings until about 2010. They will continue to be energized by the new generations of consumer hardware that offer superior performance while becoming less expensive over time. These retailers have the substantial advantage of high-volume consumer traffic. The most effective retail marketers place motion picture products in high-traffic areas, some screening the product on a television monitor. Many use print ads as part of their newspaper campaigns and some use direct mail. For the stronger titles, many retailers actually sell pictures at or below their cost as promotions to draw traffic into their stores.

4. Premium cable networks are uniquely important licensees, because producers often license directly with them. These licensees use the brand power of the most popular pictures to expand their subscriber base by advertising on cable systems and in a variety of magazine, newspaper, and direct-mail media.

5. Free television networks also license directly with producers. Though it continues to grow, just under half of U.S. TV households subscribe to a premium cable network. Consequently, the television network premiere often attracts the largest single viewing audience during a picture's life. The networks are masters at drawing audiences, by using their networks as the primary source to advertise motion pictures with theatrical release status.

6. Free television syndication participants, including cable networks and independent stations, deliver long-term audiences and income. Licensing to these participants is sophisticated, complex, and typically sold and managed by a television syndication company. These stations and station groups, like the networks, primarily advertise motion pictures via their stations.

Participant Category 5: International Territories

These are the audiences, distributors, retail media, and other rights purchasers in territories outside the United States. International territories yield well over half the earnings of most motion pictures created by U.S.-based producers. The seven leading international territories and producers' relationships with them are reviewed in Chapters 3 and 12.

Participant Category 6: Financing Participants

These include banks that provide production and distribution financing, studios and distributors that function as "commercial lenders" for many independent producers, governments that provide production tax and/or cash incentive programs, as well as private and institutional investors who provide development, distribution, and in some cases, partial production funding, some motivated by tax-sheltered programs. Other participants in this category include law firms, private attorneys, and accounting firms and accountants, who advise, author, and assist in the management of securities. The roles of these participants are explained fully in Chapters 2, 5, 9, 10, and 12.

Participant Category 7: Distribution Subcontractors

This category includes sales and licensing specialists, media planning and buying companies, and campaign creators and producers as well as advertising agencies (some of which contribute to all three of the just-listed items). These are also manufacturers and duplicators of products including CD, DVD, and new generations of consumer technology. Distribution subcontractors are discussed in Chapters 4, 12, and 13.

Participant Category 8: Production Talent and Subcontractors

These include a diverse and stunning array of above- and below-the-line performers and craft imagineers, producers, and suppliers. Especially included in this category are agencies, agents, managers, and attorneys who represent talent. Producer relationships with participants in this category are reviewed in Chapters 8, 11, and 12.

Participant Category 9: Ancillary Media and Licensees

These are additional retail media including pay-per-view, hotels and motels, in-flight and ships-at-sea, and other licensed free audiences, including prison systems, Indian reservations, and schools. This category also includes licensed rights, such as electronic games, publishing, printing, merchandising, sound tracks and music publishing, clothing, and Internet applications. Though these are each growing in earnings and promotion importance, and occasionally out-earn conventional income categories, these markets typically represent a modest portion of a picture's income. These participants are reviewed in Chapter 4.

Participant Category 10: Major Consumer Brands

These are brands that link their products or name to a motion picture and advance that picture and their brand by nature of the relationship. Consumer brand relationships may take a number of forms, but generally fall into two categories.

The first and most common is the brand exposure of products used in the picture. For this, the brand either pays for the exposure or gives or lends its products to the producer.

The second relationship is a brand's use of a picture to advertise or promote its name or products. Fast food chains are the most active participants in these relationships. These relationships often substantially assure the success and increase the income of their pictures through escalating their advertising campaigns during its theatrical release.

These complementary brand relationships lend authenticity to pictures by using brands that create a sense of reality for the film's audiences. Such relationships often offset production costs and may even become a revenue source or powerful advertising alliance for the producer. Consumer brand relationships are reviewed in greater depth in Chapter 4.

Participant Category Summary

Having reviewed these motion picture industry participants, reconsider their order of importance.

1. Audiences
2. Distributors
3. Producers
4. Retailers and licensed media
5. International territories
6. Financing participants
7. Distribution subcontractors
8. Production talent and subcontractors
9. Ancillary media and licensees
10. Major consumer brands

Although traditionally viewed primarily as creatives, independent producers who operate their own development and production companies are also *business owners*. In large measure, their creative and financial success is reliant upon their understanding of, empathy for, and relationships with the industry participants above them on this hierarchical scale (audiences and distributors), as well as with those below them.

Story

If the creative categories were listed in priority, as the business categories have been, one creative category would clearly stand above the others. This is the ultimate art of creative genius. It is where the picture is first produced. It is the screenplay.

Story is the most essential and important, and therefore the most powerful creative asset in the motion picture industry. It is more powerful than money. Too many people with deep pockets have entered this industry to establish a motion picture production empire, only to leave months or, in some insufferable cases, years later, with a monument of odd and underperforming pictures to show for their substantial investments.

Story is even more important than star power or a great director. Even "A-list" actors and directors, for money or career politics, occasionally allow themselves to be attached to pictures that should never have been made. Fine direction and acting may lift a picture somewhat, but ultimately can never redeem a weak story.

An audience-pleasing, entertaining story is the most powerful and essential asset in the motion picture business. Talent with story sense always gravitate to these pictures and want to participate in their creation.

Business operating technique, organization, planning, excellent relationships with studios and great artists, or the availability of any other assets will never offset the essential need for producers to discover, develop, and produce stories that deserve to be told. The greatest independent producers recognize great stories.

Excellence in all other producer characteristics will not compensate for failure in this one. Call it story sense, having a nose for the audience, or what you may, this is the single essential attribute, if all the other producer qualities are to even matter.

At the same time, in order to sustain the whole perspective, it's important to remember that a great story alone is not sufficient justification for a producer to greenlight its production. Great stories without sufficient audience power as compared to their production and distribution costs should not be made. But great stories are always the germ, the genesis, the foundation of every consummate picture. If the story isn't worth being told, then none of the producer's other considerations matter.

Chapter Postscript

If there is no picture, nothing can be delivered. However, one of the oldest business adages is: "Nothing happens until somebody sells something." Audiences and sales/distribution are more preeminent than production.

As in all industries, marketing and distribution is the single largest determinate of each motion picture's success or failure. Distribution is also where the greatest profits are earned. Consequently, the most successful producers

- Have strategic relationships with global distributors
- Set up each picture's distribution in advance of its production, confirming the picture's basic global earnings value and assuring its release
- Are very involved in the initial brand establishment strategy, as well as release and marketing course-correction of their pictures
- Retain some sales and distribution rights in each picture
- Either makes or participates in these sales

The motion picture industry is expansive, robust, and intense. Operating satisfaction and success is largely reliant upon well-served strategic business relationships with leading entities in every major category.

U.S. Theatrical Distributors

This chapter reviews how major U.S. distributors function, and more particularly, looks at the three traditional relationship categories these studios engage in with independent producers:

- In-house studio production
- Negative pickup
- Distribution agreement

Motion picture distributors, especially the major studio distributors, are the greatest advocates of independent producers. The more producers understand how studios operate, the various relationships they may have with them, and why studios function the way they do, the more producers will be able to appreciate these studios and forge more productive relationships with them.

The Major and Minor Distributors

The nine major distributor/studios are 20th Century Fox, Universal, Buena Vista, Paramount, Sony, Warner Bros. (WB), Miramax, DreamWorks, and New Line. There are 20 minor U.S. distributors. Most of these companies release narrow target audience exploitation pictures, including those produced in international territories. Relationships with these distributors are essential for balanced, profitable production and release of narrow target-audience pictures. (These distributors are not the subject of these volumes.) Each of the major studios is a massive, sophisticated media conglomerate. Most earn billions of revenue dollars each year.

These distributors rigorously compete with each other in all markets and every media and right, with the exception of the natural sister relationships between Buena Vista, which owns Miramax, and Time-Warner, which owns New Line.

The major studios are the ultimate motion picture entities. They have evolved both to operate completely self-contained, as distributor and producer, as well as to facilitate multiple independent producer relationships. Each studio has the advantages of global theatrical and ancillary sales power, global media alliances, availability of sophisticated bank, commercial, and public funds, and sophisticated creative and operational checks and balances. They each have their individual committee operating styles, which in the main benefit marketing and distribution, but typically cripple motion picture development and production, often sucking the creative life from stories through slow decision making and dulled or incongruous creative vision.

The ultimate definition of a motion picture studio is *a global distribution entity with in-house production*. Within the studio, every department and all operations in their best form are geared toward stabilizing and optimizing motion picture marketing and distribution. The brief history of the motion picture industry reveals the tragic flaw of studios that become in-house production dominant, or fit the definition of *a production entity with global distribution capacity*. Studios are distribution-focused primarily because

- Distribution yields higher profits per picture than production.
- Distribution accommodates a greater volume of pictures.
- Distribution connects directly with the marketplace and is consequently more stable and business powerful.

With a distribution focus, studios are naturally driven to accommodate independent producer relationships to deliver most of the motion pictures they will distribute. Studio executives enter many more picture relationships than do producers, are excellent negotiators, and are consequently exceptionally well prepared to set up relationships with producers.

Knowing this, prior to meeting with a studio, producers should thoroughly prepare, understand what they want, have *in writing* the deal points of a fair relationship for both sides, and should have reviewed the deal points with their entertainment legal counsel.

Producers are classically underprepared and underexperienced. They too often leave the negotiating table without obtaining the benefits and power they should have, and with a substantially different understanding of their relationship than the documented deal points define. Contract language is precise—it is enforced in its ultimate interpretation by contract law, not by dictionary; and though most of the language is stable, definitions can literally change daily. Producers must be prepared in every creative, business, and legal aspect relative to the production and distribution relationships they negotiate. They should expect and respect that studio executives will be excellent negotiators and impeccably well prepared.

Studio Integrity

Having entered into a major studio relationship, producers may be confident that the studio—yes, all the majors listed earlier (we haven't audited DreamWorks, but their executives are notorious for their integrity in this area)—will deliver an honest, complete, and timely accounting for each picture. Auditing on behalf of producers, we have found posting errors, but typically as many in favor of the producer as not. Because of the high volume of entries, allocation errors will occur, but they are honest mistakes and will be corrected readily when presented. Producer and talent participant comments implying accounting dishonesty by the majors are clearly undeserved slander. A review of the theatrical performance example later in this chapter reveals that producers and other profit participants who complain that their picture has a box office of $50 million, but cost only $20 million, may conclude that the studio must have a creative accounting method. But they simply do not understand how the money flows, commonly referred to as the profit participant waterfall.

The Three Studio Arenas

Each studio has its own unique organization structure. However, it is important that producers be familiar with the three basic operational arenas the studios have in common:

- The *executive arena*, which consists of the ultimate studio chiefs
- The *distribution arena*, which is a combination of each of the distribution organizations within the studio (the most powerful are theatrical and home entertainment)
- The *production arena*, which consists of each studio's production organizations

Each of these arenas has its individual presidents. Some studios have multiple presidents within each of their distribution and production arenas.

Studio Executives

Studio executives are the studio chiefs and corporate level directors of each studio, and at the time of this writing, include Marc Shmuger and Stacey Snider at Universal, Alan Horn at Warner Bros., Yair Landau, Amy Pascal, and Jeff Blake at Sony, Dick Cook at Disney, and Harvey Weinstein at Miramax, along with their teams.

Only the largest of the independent producers play in this arena. The studio chiefs make decisions relative to conglomerate studio direction, studio assets, media alliances, global market positioning, and the leaders, direction, and disposition of the various studio operating units. Studio chiefs are also responsible for the forest view and vigilantly adjusting their empire's inner and industry participation.

All leaders of studio units report to and are evaluated by the studio chiefs, including all financial, accounting, and legal departments.

This is the arena that ratifies, and, if appropriate, negotiates contracts with premium cable organizations, networks, the larger video chains, international studios, and ancillary media, among other powerful earnings sources. These relationships deliver a wonderful stability to each studio. Understanding these relationships substantially affects the deal and negotiating perception of independent producers in their dealings with the studios. These relationships will be reviewed later in this chapter.

The Distribution Unit

Distribution units include both the global distribution executives and their staffs, as well as each of the sales organizations for theatrical and home entertainment, which are the heart of most major independent producer's studio relationships. They also include every other international and domestic sales organization, and their advertising, promotion, and publicity units.

This arena relys on obtaining pictures to distribute. The majority of these pictures come from independent producers, the rest from the production units within the studio.

The Production Arena

In most studios these are multiple organizations (such as Fox, Fox 2000, and Fox Searchlight at 20th Century Fox). These organizations are directed by production executives and their teams. The production arena manages a large motion picture development pool, fulfills all the production processes for in-house pictures, and participates in the development and production of independent productions that are wholly or partially financed by the studio.

Studio Relationships with Independent Producers

The studios engage in three conventional relationships with independent producers: in-house studio production, negative pickup, and distribution only. Many independent producers progress in their studio relationships by evolving from studio pictures, to negative pickup productions, and then to strictly distribution relationships.

There are many crucial deal points in each of these relationships. The central deal point categories common to all these relationships are:

- Creative control
- Film negative and copyright ownership
- The specifics of the theatrical distribution commitment (especially minimums for advertising and opening number of screens)
- The distribution fees, studio charges and burdens, studio participation and, for in-house producer relationships, the producer's profit participation
- The Profits Definition (this is often a 15 to 30 page portion of the agreement that most crucially determines even if the producer will receive any profits) and assignment of the film's distribution rights between the producer and distributor

In-House Studio Production

This relationship is typically engaged through the studio's production operations. The producer provides an acceptable story, plus the capacity to complete development and deliver a finished picture. The studio provides all the development and production support, financial and business (legal and accounting) resources to complete the picture, and all the distribution resources to liquidate its rights.

Though the producer has creative freedom, the ultimate creative control typically resides with the studio. Also, the negative, copyright, and all distribution rights are owned by the studio. The producer is paid a production fee and typically has a net or gross-profits participation in the film, commonly called *points*.

Studio production is a good place for producers to start if their understanding is limited to the physical aspects of motion picture production. Some producers make all their pictures throughout their careers in this category, are creatively satisfied, and achieve excellent earnings.

A good example of this relationship is the early producing career experience of Andrew Davis, who brought Warner Bros. *Above the Law* and attached Steven Segal. He entered a studio production relationship with WB that allowed him to make the picture using the support of the production department, yet giving him the flexibility even to rough-cut the picture in his home. The picture received WB's formidable marketing muscle and was successful enough to make a sequel and launch Mr. Davis's subsequently prolific career.

Negative Pickup

This relationship is substantially more independent than studio production, and typically it is entered through a studio production unit. The producer provides an acceptable story and the capacity to complete development and deliver a finished picture and the picture's production financing. The studio provides production support, a bankable contract for all or a substantial portion of the needed production funds, and typically global, U.S., or international distribution, as negotiated. Negative pickup relationships commonly allow the producer almost complete creative freedom during the production process, though the studio may have the right to the picture's final cut.

Though it is a negotiable point, the picture's copyright typically is owned by the producer, and the distribution rights (as negotiated, either global, U.S., or international) are owned by the studio. From the gross receipts collected by the studio, the studio is paid its distribution fee for all rights it sells, recoups its direct distribution expenses, and may also have points in the picture.

An entertainment bank provides the producer with the negative pickup production financing, which necessitates that the producer have bank and completion bond relationships. The collateral provided to the bank for the production loan is one or more studio negative pickups. This collateral equals or exceeds the picture's negative cost, as well as loan interest and a loan contingency. Contingency elements in the negative pickup contract are primarily that the producer will deliver the studio access to the picture's negative or a CRI (color reverse internegative, created to make release prints) and campaign materials, on or before the contract delivery date, and that the picture contain basic above-the-line representations, including director and principal cast.

An insurance company provides the bank a guarantee (referred to as a completion guarantee or completion bond) that the picture will be delivered by the contracted delivery date with the specified creative elements intact. (Obtaining the production funding from the bank is reviewed thoroughly in Chapter 5; completion guarantees are discussed in Chapter 6.)

Distribution-Only Relationship

This relationship typically is entered through the studio's distribution arena. This is the most sophisticated relationship for producers to enter, and it delivers them the greatest overall benefits. This relationship naturally motivates the creation of the finest motion pictures, better prepares the various rights areas in the major markets, grants producers the greatest autonomy, earns the most revenues for each picture, and delivers the highest participation to the producer. Typically this is the most beneficial relationship globally for audiences, studios, producers, and licensees.

The distribution-only relationship takes many forms. Generally, the producer engages a U.S. studio to distribute U.S. theatrical and video. In this relationship the studio does not provide negative pickup, other financing collateral, or advance fees. The producer provides the finished picture, developed, produced, and financed, and in some relationships, part or all of the direct distribution expenses. The studio's distribution unit provides production and campaign consulting from the picture's earliest development, along with U.S. theatrical distribution, and most commonly, U.S. home entertainment distribution.

Though the producer consults with major market distributors throughout the development and production of the picture, and is license-bound to deliver the picture represented to presale participants, the producer has complete creative freedom during the production process.

The picture's copyright and distribution rights are owned by the producer. Distribution rights are licensed by the producer to U.S. and international studios and global media. From the gross receipts, collected by the U.S. studio, the studio is paid its distribution fee for all rights it sells, recoups its direct distribution expenses, and may also have points in the picture.

Producer Relationship Comparisons

To understand more fundamentally the three primary relationships just discussed, let us examine the individual and comparative financial performance of each, as shown in the example in Table 2.1.

The example in Table 2.1 is included and analyzed on the CD-ROM that accompanies this text. Instructions for using this file are with the CD. The cells are formula driven, allowing the user to perform "what-ifs" and to analyze specific pictures. As you move the cursor to each cell, the formula reveals its performance

Table 2.1 Worksheet for the Text "The Business of Producing Motion Pictures for the Major Studios"

Description	Studio Relationship Comparisons		
	Studio Producer	Negative Pickup	Distribution Only
N. American Theatrical Gross Box Office	50,000,000	50,000,000	50,000,000
Film Rental (at 50%)	25,000,000	25,000,000	25,000,000
Studio Distribution Fee (at 35%)	8,750,000	8,750,000	8,750,000
Direct Distribution Expense	28,000,000	28,000,000	28,000,000
N. American Theatrical Distributor's Net	(11,750,000)	(11,750,000)	(11,750,000)
N. American Home Entertainment Rental Gross Income	8,383,320	8,383,320	8,383,320
Home Video/DVD Distribution Fee (at 35%)	2,934,162	2,934,162	2,934,162
Video Duplication & Distribution Expenses	2,044,000	2,044,000	2,044,000
Distributors Video Net	3,405,158	3,405,158	3,405,158
N. American Home Entertainment S-Through Gross Income	51,386,850	51,386,850	51,386,850
Home Video/DVD Distribution Fee (at 35%)	17,985,398	17,985,398	17,985,398
Video Duplication & Distribution Expenses	12,560,000	12,560,000	12,560,000
Distributors Home Entertainment Net	20,841,453	20,841,453	20,841,453
N. American Theatrical & Home Entertainment Distributor's Net	12,496,611	12,496,611	12,496,611
Sales Agent Fee (at 5%)	—	—	624,831
N. American Theatrical & Home Entertainment Distributor's Net	12,496,611	12,496,611	11,871,780
N. American Premium Cable Gross	5,500,000	5,500,000	5,500,000
Premium Cable Distribution Fee (at 35%/35%/0%)	1,925,000	1,925,000	—
Direct Distribution Expenses	150,000	150,000	150,000
Sales Agent Fee (at 15%)	—	—	802,500
N. American Premium Cable Distributor's Net	3,425,000	3,425,000	4,547,500
N. American Network Gross	7,000,000	7,000,000	7,000,000
Network Distribution Fee (at 35%/35%/0%)	2,450,000	2,450,000	—

(continued)

Table 2.1 Continued

Studio Relationship Comparisons

Description	Studio Producer	Negative Pickup	Distribution Only
Direct Distribution Expenses	200,000	200,000	200,000
Sales Agent Fee (at 15%)	—	—	1,020,000
N. American Network Distributor's Net	4,350,000	4,350,000	5,780,000
N. American Syndicated Television	12,500,000	12,500,000	12,500,000
Syndicated TV Distribution Fee (at 35%)	4,375,000	4,375,000	—
Direct Distribution Expenses	200,000	200,000	200,000
Sales Agent Fee (at 5%)	—	—	615,000
N. American Syndicated TV Distributor's Net	7,925,000	7,925,000	11,685,000
International Theatrical Gross Box Office	75,000,000	75,000,000	75,000,000
International Theatrical Film Rental (at 50%)	37,500,000	37,500,000	37,500,000
International Distribution Fee (at 45%/35%/35%)	16,875,000	13,125,000	13,125,000
International Direct Distribution Expenses	42,000,000	42,000,000	42,000,000
Distributors International Theatrical Net	(21,375,000)	(17,625,000)	(17,625,000)
International Home Entertainment Gross Income	89,655,255	89,655,255	89,655,255
International Home Entertainment Distribution Fee (at 45%/35%/35%)	40,344,865	31,379,339	31,379,339
Home Video/DVD Duplication & Distribution Expenses	21,906,000	21,906,000	21,906,000
International Territory Distributors Home Entertainment Net	27,404,390	36,369,916	36,369,916
International Theatrical & Home Entertainment Distributor's Net	6,029,390	18,744,916	18,744,916
Sales Agent Fee (at 15%)	—	2,811,737	2,811,737
International Theatrical & Home Entertainment Distributor's Net	6,029,390	15,933,178	15,933,178
International Premium Cable Gross	6,750,000	6,750,000	6,750,000
International PC Distribution Fee (at 45%/35%/35%)	3,037,500	2,362,500	2,362,500
Direct Distribution Expenses	150,000	150,000	150,000
Sales Agent Fee (at 15%)	—	635,625	635,625
International Premium Cable Distributor's Net	3,562,500	3,601,875	3,601,875
International Network Gross	10,500,000	10,500,000	10,500,000

International Network Distribution Fee (at 45%/35%/35%)	4,725,000	3,675,000	3,675,000
Direct Distribution Expenses	200,000	200,000	200,000
Sales Agent Fee (at 15%)	—	993,750	993,750
International Network Distributor's Net	5,575,000	5,631,250	5,631,250
International Syndicated TV Gross	18,750,000	18,750,000	18,750,000
International Syndicated TV Distribution Fee (at 45%/35%/35%)	8,437,500	6,562,500	6,562,500
Direct Distribution Expenses	200,000	200,000	200,000
Sales Agent Fee (at 15%)	—	1,798,125	1,798,125
International Syndicated TV Distributor's Net	10,112,500	10,189,375	10,189,375
Global Consumer Product Royalties Gross	2,000,000	2,000,000	2,000,000
Merchandising Distribution Fee (at 45%/16.5/0%)	900,000	330,000	—
Sales Agent Fee (at 9%/15%)	—	180,000	300,000
Global Consumer Products Distributor's Net	1,100,000	1,490,000	1,700,000
Total Distributor's Net	63,213,501	73,602,914	79,500,583
Production Financing Expense @ 12%/6% (16 months)	4,000,000	2,000,000	2,000,000
Negative Cost	25,000,000	25,000,000	25,000,000
Studio Burden	18,750,000	—	—
Talent Residuals	10,000,000	10,000,000	10,000,000
Sales Agent Direct Sales Expenses	—	250,000	500,000
Producer's Gross	5,463,501	36,352,914	42,000,583
Talent Participation (if any, at 7%)	—	2,544,704	2,940,041
Producer's Net	5,463,501	33,808,210	39,060,543
Studio's Share	4,917,151	16,904,105	—
Producer's Share	546,350	16,904,105	39,060,543
Distributor's Net Earnings to Cost Ratio	1.6:1	2:1	2.1:1

relationship to other cells. Each relationship example is for the same picture, earning the same from each distribution and rights area.

The following definitions will help those unfamiliar with the terminology used in this example.

Theatrical Distribution

Gross box office is the total box office receipts collected from theater attendees for a particular picture. This example uses $50 million. Oh, that this were typical! Of the leading 50 pictures released in the summer of 2004 (May through August), only the leading 29 earned $50 million or more. More telling is that only five of the remaining pictures topped $20 million.

Film rental is the share of the gross box office due the distributor. The *film rental agreement* is the document setting forth the terms between the exhibitor and the distributor. The terms of these agreements commonly allow for higher earnings for the distributor early in the picture's run, when the box office is highest, and lower as exhibition continues and the receipts are lower. The example uses the commonly applied percentage of 50 percent each for exhibitor and distributor.

The *theatrical distribution fee* is earned by the distributor and calculated as a percentage of the film rental. The percentage is typically 35 percent of film rental, unless the producer provides most or all of the direct distribution expenses and negotiates a lesser fee. Producers are comfortable with the fairness of this fee if they consider (1) the distribution fees charged manufacturers in other industries, (2) the high distribution costs the distributor advances in behalf of the producer, (3) the sophisticated process and organization the distributor delivers and must sustain, and (4) the low probability that the picture will be theatrically profitable.

Direct distribution expenses (DDE) are the expenses incurred by the distributor in the process of distributing a picture, which are recoupable by the distributor from the picture's gross receipts remaining after deducting distribution fees. These expenses are principally advertising (often $25 to $35 million) and prints (for example, $3.8 million for 2,000 prints at $1,900 each). Together these are commonly referred to as P&A (prints and advertising). However, direct distribution expenses also include campaign creation and production, promotion and publicity, film exchange costs and festival expenses, among many other out-of-pocket expenses.

The *distributor's theatrical net* is the film rental less the distribution fee and direct distribution expenses. The application of fees and expenses are the same for all three distributor relationships, yielding the same amounts each. Consider how difficult it is for pictures even to recoup their distribution expenses from just North American theatrical distribution. With a $50 million gross box office, the typical picture is eight figures away from even recouping its distribution expenses.

Home Entertainment Distribution

Home entertainment gross income. For most pictures, home video and DVD is the single most profitable earnings category. Each picture has its own earning dynamics in each category and changes substantially, depending on the success of the theatrical campaign. Many pictures are nevertheless served conservatively well when their picture's projected video earnings are configured by using a ratio of 2½ to 3 times the picture's film rental. For the example, the units volume for both home video and DVD rental as well as home video and DVD sell-through were calculated on a ratio basis with the theatrical box office. Home video rental wholesale prices are estimated at $12.55; DVD wholesale rental prices are $16.16; home video sell-through wholesale prices are $12.63; and DVD sell-through prices are $16.17.

Home entertainment distribution is very sophisticated, but not nearly as much as theatrical distribution. Home video and DVDs are marketed at either a rental or sell-through price. Because the studios now share video rental revenue with the major rental chains, most motion pictures are released at sell-through wholesale costs.

Although home entertainment rental income remains a substantial revenue source, home entertainment sell-through is a larger revenue source, and continues at a steady pace. This growth is intended to slow considerably as consumers purchase home entertainment through their cable and satellite services on an on-demand or pay-per-view basis. The home entertainment release window continues to be incrementally dissected and shared with the on-demand/pay-per-view release window. Aspects of this area, including price-point and every facet of marketing, continue their escalating evolution. The *video distribution fee* is negotiable, but for all three relationships shown in the example, it is 35 percent.

Video duplication and distribution expenses. Video duplication is very competitive. If the duplicator performs all aspects of printing the sleeve, duplicates the product, and manages the inventory and shipping, the typical 120 minute movie in DVD or VHS is still not more than about $2 each. The additional advertising, promotion, publicity, and other expenses vary widely picture to picture, with the ad budgets of major sell-through titles rivaling their theatrical budgets. The projection in the example uses $3 per VHS unit sold and $4 per DVD unit sold, a conservative estimate that will be higher than most actual expenses, but lower than higher titles with larger theatrical grosses.

Distributor's home entertainment net. This is the home entertainment gross income less the distribution fee and duplication and distribution expenses. The application of fees and expenses is the same for all three distributor relationships, yielding the same amounts to each of these categories. The home entertainment gross income exceeds all other domestic earnings categories. Even more impressive is that the distributor's home entertainment net is 40 percent of the gross. Again, a picture's brand power is established in its theatrical release, but the greatest U.S. earnings and profits area is in the home entertainment release.

Premium Cable Gross

Premium cable gross. Premium cable companies are those television networks that are commercial-free and earn their income principally through viewer subscriptions. The major premium cable networks are HBO/Cinemax, Showtime/The Movie Channel, and Starz/Encore.

This category's primary income follows the greatest audience tune-in, which occurs during the picture's premium cable premiere period. The license for the premier of a picture with a $50 million gross should be about 11 percent.

The *premium cable distribution fee* should not exceed the 35 percent used in the projections. Because the market for these rights is limited, and the licensing is comparatively unsophisticated, it is common for balanced producers to sell these rights direct from their production companies, and preserve the distribution fee expense.

The *premium cable direct distribution expenses* are primarily legal fees, travel, and trade-show representation. They should not exceed the $150,000 indicated in the projections.

The *distributor's premium cable net* is the premium cable gross income less the distribution fee and direct distribution expenses. The application of fees and expenses is the same for all three distributor relationships, except the distribution fee retention for the distribution-only category.

Network Television Gross

Network television gross. The networks that purchase motion picture premiere free-television motion picture rights are those television networks that do not charge a separate subscription fee and are broadcast in every market where television programming is available. These networks are principally NBC, CBS, ABC, and Fox, as well as major new "netlets" including UPN and WB, and major cable networks including TNT, USA, TBS, Lifetime, and Spike.

The *license income* for the free television network premiere of a picture with a $50 million gross should be approximately 14 percent of the picture's U.S. theatrical gross, or the $7 million used in the projections.

The *free network television distribution fee* should not exceed the 35 percent used in the projections. Because the market for these rights is limited, and the licensing is comparatively unsophisticated, balanced producers frequently also sell these rights direct from their production companies and preserve the distribution fee expense.

The *free network television direct distribution expenses* are primarily legal fees, travel, and trade-show representation. They should not exceed the $200,000 indicated in the projections.

Distributors free television network net is the network gross income less the distribution fee and direct distribution expenses. The application of fees and expenses is the same for all three distributor relationships, except the distribution fee retention for the distribution-only category.

Sales Agent Fees

For producers who directly manage their pictures' distribution rights, the use of either a sales agent or an in-house sales division will be utilized to liquidate sales rights. Typically, the negative pick-up producer performs all or some of the international sales independent of the North American releasing studio, and the distribution-only producer performs all sales direct, even those within North America that do not become a part of the studio distribution agreement.

International Territory Gross

Most American-produced pictures have higher earnings from all the international territories combined, compared with U.S. earnings. Chapter 3 reviews international territories in depth. The projections use an international territory earnings figure equal to 60 percent, compared with a U.S. theatrical gross of 40 percent. The simplest equation that can be used to arrive at this international earnings amount is 150 percent of the U.S. theatrical gross.

The *international distribution fee* used in the projection is 45 percent. Because balanced producers sustain a close working relationship with the primary distributors in each of the seven major international territories, many of them have an international sales department as part of their organizations, and negotiate a distribution fee that is in proportion with the production advance provided by the distributor. The greater the production advance as a percent of expected distributor's net from that territory, the greater the distribution fee applied for that distributor to recoup the production advance and DDE (direct distribution expenses).

International direct distribution expenses are similar to those accounted from the domestic distributor. These are substantially advertising, promotion, and print expenditures for theatrical releases; and advertising, promotion, duplication, and distribution expenses for home entertainment. In the event that the international distributor has acquired all rights, the international distributor typically, in turn, will resell these rights to subdistributors within their territory. The picture's direct distribution expenses will be accounted and deducted from the picture's earnings by the subdistributor prior to the primary distributor's receipt of earnings from those sublicenses.

Distributor's international net is the international gross income less the distribution fee and direct distribution expenses. The application of fees and expenses is the same for all three distributor relationships.

Share Analysis Review

Total Distributors Net

This is an accumulation of the net income from all major earnings categories.

Production Financing Expense

This is the producer's cost of the money used to produce the motion picture. Because the studio is a commercial lender rather than a bank, the financing is more expensive, typically 3 to 5 percent over the prime rate. Further, because the distributor allocates all the funding at the time the motion picture documentation is engaged, it is common for interest to be charged on the entire amount from the first day of this relationship. Depending on the producer's credit history with the bank, the ratio between the collateral pledged and the loan amount, among other factors, the bank may charge an interest fee of one-half to 3 percent. It's important to note that most of these bank financings are lines of credit, drawn down by the producer in increments as needed, and accumulating interest only on the total amount drawn rather than the whole loan. The example is for a motion picture costing $25 million.

In this example, the two advantages of bank interest and charges on only the amount actually in use save the negative pickup and distribution-only relationships' half of this expense.

Negative Cost

The negative cost is the actual total costs of creating the picture. This picture's cost is $25 million. Though such expenses are not reflected here, studio relationships sometimes make it mandatory for producers to use their costlier studio facilities, equipment, and departments.

Producer's Gross

This is typically the distributor's net less the production financing expense and the picture's negative cost.

Studio Burden

This is a common expense for studio pictures. This expense is a portion of the studio's total distribution arena overhead (this does include direct distribution expenses). Each picture's expense formula is set forth in the agreement. It may be a picture's percentage of the studio's total earnings for the year. (Considering theatrical earnings only, if a studio earned $750 million during the year and your picture earned $25 million, your studio burden expense would be 3.3 percent of the total.) This example assumes the studio earned $400 million for the year with operating expenditures of $150 million.

Talent Participations

These are those points in the film's profits that are owned by key participants, possibly the director and one or more key cast members. This projection applies 7 percent of the producer's gross to talent participations.

Producer's Net

This is the producer's gross less any other distribution, production, or profit participant expenses.

Studio Share

This is that amount of the producer's net in which the studio participates for its share as a partner of the producer in making the production and distribution of the picture a reality. For the in-house producer, this is the whole remaining amount except for the producer's points—in this example 90 percent. For the negative pickup producer this is 50 percent for the studio. For the distribution-only producer, the studio is not a further participant.

Producer's Share

This is the amount remaining for the producer after all production, distribution, and financing expenses and participants have received their portions.

The in-house and negative pickup producer's shares are 1.4 percent and 43 percent, respectively, of the distribution-only producer's share. This substantially greater profit share is chiefly why balanced producers have the capacity to establish major businesses with greater creative and financial freedom than many of their creative contemporaries.

As you become familiar with the performance of these three studio relationships, it will become clear that there are, in fact, no poor studio relationships. It's easy to see why producers spend their entire careers in studio/producer relationships. They produce motion pictures in the powerfully sophisticated and immensely savvy confines of the studio, receive excellent producer fees, share in the pictures' profits, and have none of the operational distractions of a full service independent production company.

Split Negative Pickup Relationships

Negative pickup relationships are traditionally with one studio, for all rights, globally. However, occasionally, there are U.S./international split negative pickup relationships. An example of this is Icon's (Mel Gibson and Bruce Davey's independent production company) financing for *Braveheart*. Though they covered a portion of their budget from Ireland's Section 35 funds, their financing substantially came from Paramount (the lead studio), for acquiring U.S. rights and 20th Century Fox for international rights.

Studio Acquisition of a Renegade Picture

Let us now explore more deeply the studio's common economies and operating styles by examining how they respond to an independent producer's freshly completed motion picture offered them for pickup. *Renegade pictures* are those pictures developed and produced without studio participation or knowledge; these are almost exclusively privately financed. The picture in this example was produced for a trim $12 million. As is common, the picture's investors are now anxiously looking for their investment's return.

The studio screens the picture and discovers that it has strong crossover target audiences and motivating campaign elements, and is studio quality. The studio is interested (and amazed, as this is, unfortunately, a rare experience) and asks for a meeting with the producer.

Typically the producer comes to the meeting motivated to seek the return of the $12 million production cost and to obtain a distribution commitment. But the meeting is a little different from what the producer anticipates. The studio admits it likes the picture and that it is considering making a substantial distribution investment in it. It then reveals that if the campaign elements come together and the test audiences respond well to the campaign and the picture, it could invest $8 to $12 million or more in prints and advertising in the film, an investment close to or even exceeding the picture's production cost.

At this point it may not seem fair to the producer to ask the studio to return part or all of the production cost, as well as commit to such substantial distribution expenses. In this case, however, the producer explains that the investors are leaping up and down for their capital, and asks the studio for help.

Three business days later the studio and producer meet again. The studio presents an agreement granting the producer a $12 to $16 million deal. It sounds, and in many respects is, a dream come true for the producer. The studio executive explains that the studio is committing to the major theatrical release of the picture it had discussed, and may advance $8 to $12 million in theatrical distribution expenses alone. Plus the studio will pay the producer an advance against the producer's earnings of $4 million, and 50 percent of the picture's net profits. For this, the studio will receive all the picture's distribution rights globally and the other 50 percent of the picture's net profits. The producer typically is pleased with this offer, for the advance is sufficient to sate the investors' return-of-capital appetite, especially when it is combined with the good news of the studio's distribution commitment.

Before examining the studio's perspective, it is crucial to understand that most renegade pictures offered to the studios do not have sufficient earnings potential to warrant a distribution investment. Distribution is expensive, and these pictures are classically out of audience focus.

Motion Picture Output Relationships

Every studio (even studios that own or are media sisters with international, premium cable, television network, and video rental chain entities) has motion picture output contracts with premium cable entities, the major networks, major video rental chains, and international entertainment entities. To simplify yet keep this transaction well within the bounds of current studio media relationships, let's consider that this picture meets this distributor's premium cable contract criteria.

The studio's output deal criteria are typically simple, driven principally by a minimum television media expenditure during the picture's theatrical release and the potential of the picture to earn a minimum theatrical gross. For this example we will use a studio output base license fee of $5 million for each picture the studio delivers and assume that the studio will deliver at least, but not exceed without mutual consent, 10 pictures per year. These agreements typically have escalator clauses that allow higher license fees to be paid for pictures exceeding a minimum gross box office. For instance, if a picture's gross box office exceeds $30 million, an additional fee will be paid, for example, $100,000 for each additional $10 million in box office, not to exceed a total license amount, for instance, of $12 million.

Studios may also have multipicture license relationships with the major television networks. For this example we will use a base per picture amount of $3 million.

The video rental chain relationship, though substantially different, is fairly predictable. For instance, for a given picture, it may be apparent that it will be rental priced and sold to the leading three rental retailers in at least a 25,000-unit quantity. If the wholesale per unit price is $63 (or comparable income if this is the typical revenue sharing model), this is $1,575,000 from each retailer.

If the picture in consideration lends itself to be exercised in these output relationships, the studio will earn these revenues as it becomes the distributor of the picture:

Premium cable	$5 million
Network	$3 million
Video (after duplication cost)	$4.5 million
Output Total	$12.5 million

If the picture is strong enough to generate theater circuit bids, most or all of the direct distribution expenses may be advanced by the major circuits from the bidding process. Though it varies dramatically from picture to picture, consider that the average picture earns more than half its revenues from international territories.

Given this studio perspective, let us revisit the motion picture in review. If the studio is able to offset most of its theatrical direct distribution expenses from circuit bids, that leaves $12.5 million in ancillary output income to offset the producer's advance of $4 million. It should be remembered that the studio's primary deal motivation is the distribution fees it will earn off the top from all income, including the rest of the U.S. video market (the three leading chains represent less than one-third of the total U.S. video rental revenues), international territories, and all other ancillary rights.

By nature of its media and theatrical relationships, the studio could have acquired this picture for a $4 million advance and hefty distribution commitment to the producer, and actually started its relationship with this picture substantially in the black. Renegade picture pickups typically are negotiated through a studio's distribution unit.

Chapter Postscript

The Critical Effect of U.S. Studio Attachment

For the producer, the studio's U.S. theatrical or network commitment is the central element that affects the picture's preproduction sales, financing, and global earnings power.

For global licensees and major brand tie-in partners, their first query is: "Is a studio or television network attached?" U.S. studios and networks have powerful reputations for releasing pictures with substantial earnings power and related marketplace brand impact. Though every licensee internally assesses each picture, they are substantially attracted to or wary of each picture, depending on the picture's U.S. studio or television network relationship.

For prospective equity financers, a studio and/or television network relationship is mandatory, as most independent pictures that are produced are never distributed and consequently receive no income. Production is a shallow accomplishment without distribution and its associated income. Producers should ally each of their pictures, early in their development, with the releasing studio they believe will be optimal for that picture.

Chapter 3

International Territories

Immediately following each picture's internal greenlight, producers should begin comprehensive coordination of each picture's international creative, marketing, and sales planning. Just as producers identify each picture's U.S. distribution windows and liquidation breakdowns, they should also prepare each picture's unique major international territory marketing and releases with the support of their international territory distributors.

This chapter presents:

- The seven dominant international territories
- How to initiate and sustain the relationships within each of these territories that are necessary for pictures to perform at their global peak
- The process of negotiating and licensing these territories

The Global Popularity of American Motion Pictures

U.S. gross box office earnings exceed $9 billion annually. Even though pictures created by U.S. producers account for over half of the box office income in the largest international territories, all the international-territory produced pictures as a group barely approach 5 percent of the annual U.S. gross box office. This includes the international-territory produced motion pictures that are English language. Consequently, U.S. producers who have not done their research may not appreciate the pervasive popularity of U.S. pictures in the major international, English, and non-English speaking territories.

With the relaxation of international government import regulations of media and commerce, U.S. motion pictures continue to expand their global consumption dominance. It isn't the quantity of motion pictures coming from America that appeals to global audiences; producers in some international territories produce more feature films per year than those produced in the United States. The international popularity of U.S. productions is due more to either one or a combination of these reasons:

- The entertaining presentation of great stories
- The ever-increasing spectacle
- A broad fascination with American culture

Global and International Box Office Statistics

Because the global box office reports best demonstrate U.S. dominance in international markets, we will review the performance of the top 10 box office hits in each of the largest entertainment-consuming international territories and compare the global to the international-territory box office earnings of the top 30 motion pictures ever released.

A review of the chart in Figure 3.1 reveals that there are an average of six U.S. pictures of the top 10 grossing pictures in these six dominant global territories, and U.S. pictures earned 60 percent of the theatrical gross revenues in these territories in 1997. Though final scores are not all in, 1998 earnings in these territories exceeded 70 percent from U.S. pictures, as they also did in 1996. U.S.-produced motion pictures dominate international-territory motion picture releases and earnings.

A broader view of American films in the global market is revealed in Figure 3.2. These statistics clearly indicate the broad spectrum of motion pictures that capture audiences globally, the picture preference similarities between U.S. and international audiences, and the earnings dominance of U.S. films in international territories.

This analysis is prepared by EBG for *The Producer's Business Handbook*.

The top 30 pictures earned $23.3 billion in global box office receipts, with $14.2 billion of this income earned from international audiences. Although the single largest earnings territory for U.S. pictures is the United States, it is crucial for producers to understand that approximately 60 percent (and growing) of their pictures' income is earned from international audiences, and that well over half the international audience income comes from the seven territories shown in Figure 3.1, which are the United Kingdom, Japan, Australia, Germany, France, Italy, and Spain. Producers should include the leading studios and distributors within these territories in their motion picture development and production marketing and major creative planning decisions.

Current global consumption of American motion pictures contrasts sharply with that of international territory audiences of 20 years ago. International

Figure 3.1

Leading International Territory Motion Picture Theatrical Grosses 2003

Territory	Picture	$ or Admissions	% U.S.
Australia In U.S. Dollars In Millions	Star Wars: Attack of the Clones	18.39	
	The Fellowship of the Ring	17.35	
	Spider-Man	16.86	
	The Chamber of Secrets	16.48	
	My Big Fat Greek Wedding	13.00	
	Ocean's Eleven	12.08	
	Ice Age	11.10	
	A Beautiful Mind	10.72	
	Austin Powers in Goldmember	10.50	
	Scooby-Doo	9.90	
Total Gross		$136.38	100%
Territory	Picture	$ or Admissions	% U.S.
France In U.S. Dollars In Millions	Asterix & Obelisk (Fr/Ger)	14.22	
	The Chamber of Secrets	6.94	
	Spider-Man	6.32	
	Star Wars: Attack of the Clones	5.58	
	Men in Black II	4.52	
	Ocean's Eleven	4.45	
	The Two Towers	4.25	
	Die Another Day	3.57	
	8 Women (France)	3.54	
	Minority Report	3.46	
Total Gross		$56.85	69%
Territory	Picture	$ or Admissions	% U.S.
Germany In U.S. Dollars In Millions	The Chamber of Secrets	51.31	
	The Two Towers	38.57	
	Ice Age	36.38	
	Star Wars: Attack of the Clones	35.65	
	Spider-Man	28.70	
	Men in Black II	27.08	
	Die Another Day	26.73	
	Oceans Eleven	25.22	
	Minority Report	16.40	
	Monsters, Inc.	16.28	
Total Gross		$302.32	100%
Territory	Picture	$ or Admissions	% U.S.
Italy In U.S. Dollars In Millions	Christmas on the Nile (Italy/Spain)	26.60	
	Pinocchio (Italy)	24.62	
	Legend of Al, John & Jack (Italy)	20.94	
	The Chamber of Secrets	19.62	
	The Two Towers	19.34	
	My Big Fat Greek Wedding	13.02	
	Signs	10.47	
	Facing Window (IT/UK/Turkey/Port)	9.72	
	Minority Report	9.62	
	Remember Me (Italy/UK)	9.53	
Total Gross		$163.48	44%

Figure 3.1 *continued*
Leading International Territory Motion Picture Theatrical Grosses 2003

Territory	Picture	$ or Admissions	% U.S.
Japan	H. P. The Philosophers Stone	172.0	
In U.S. Dollars	H.P. The Chamber of Secrets	152.5	
In Millions	Monsters, Inc.	79.4	
	Star Wars: Attack of the Clones	79.2	
	The Fellowship of the Ring	76.9	
	Spider-Man	63.6	
	Ocean's Eleven	59.3	
	The Cat Returns (Japan)	54.7	
	Men in Black II	33.9	
	I Am Sam	29.3	
Total Gross		$800.80	93%

Territory	Picture	$ or Admissions	% U.S.
Spain	Spider-Man	21.32	
In U.S. Dollars	The Chamber of Secrets	18.39	
In Millions	The Fellowship of the Ring	16.14	
	Star Wars: Attack of the Clones	15.84	
	The Two Towers	15.29	
	Monsters, Inc.	15.04	
	Ocean's Eleven	13.23	
	Ice Age	11.66	
	The Other Side of the Bed (Spain)	11.48	
	A Beautiful Mind	11.32	
Total Gross		$149.71	85%

Territory	Picture	$ or Admissions	% U.S.
UK	The Chamber of Secrets	78.74	
In U.S. Dollars	The Two Towers	59.52	
In Millions	Monsters, Inc.	58.41	
	Star Wars: Attack of the Clones	58.01	
	Die Another Day	52.37	
	Spider-Man	44.53	
	Ocean's Eleven	40.86	
	Austin Powers in Goldmember	36.31	
	Men in Black II	34.35	
	Scooby-Doo	33.41	
Total Gross		$496.51	100%

Average Number of U.S. Pictures of the Top 10: 87%
Average Gross Box Office of U.S. Pictures of the Top 10: 84%

income of U.S. pictures has more than doubled in the last 10 years, and international audiences are currently growing at 18 percent annually. At a compound annual growth rate, this is almost doubling every four years. This is audience (as measured by tickets sold) rather than income growth, but income will continue to increase substantially in the highest audience-growth territories as their infrastructures develop, import restrictions are relaxed, and copyright protection is enforced, especially in territories such as mainland China, India, and Latin America.

Figure 3.2
Leading 30 Motion Pictures in International Territories

All amounts in USD Millions
Leading 30 Motion Pictures in International Territories
and the International Share of Global Box Office

International Earnings Rank	Motion Picture	Released	Gross Box Office		International Share
			International	Global	
1	Titanic (1997)	1997	$1,244.2	$1,845.0	67%
2	The Lord of the Rings: The Return of the King	2003	$741.9	$1,118.9	66%
3	Harry Potter & the Sorcerer's Stone	2001	$658.9	$976.5	67%
4	Harry Potter & the Chamber of Secrets	2002	$614.7	$876.7	70%
5	The Lord of the Rings: The Two Towers	2002	$584.5	$926.3	63%
6	Jurassic Park	1993	$557.6	$914.7	61%
7	The Lord of the Rings: The Fellowship of the Ring	2001	$556.6	$871.4	64%
8	Harry Potter and the Prisoner of Azkaban	2004	$540.3	$789.8	68%
9	Finding Nemo	2003	$525.0	$864.6	61%
10	Independence Day	1996	$510.8	$817.0	63%
11	Star Wars: Episode I — The Phantom Menace	1999	$493.4	$924.5	53%
12	Shrek 2	2004	$477.5	$918.5	52%
13	The Matrix Reloaded	2003	$457.0	$738.6	62%
14	The Lion King	1994	$455.3	$783.8	58%
15	Spider-Man	2002	$418.0	$821.7	51%
16	Spider-Man II	2004	$410.2	$784.0	52%
17	The Lost World: Jurassic Park	1997	$389.6	$618.6	63%
18	The Sixth Sense	1999	$379.3	$672.8	56%
19	Troy	2004	$364.0	$497.4	73%
20	E.T. the Extra-Terrestrial	1982	$357.8	$792.9	45%
21	The Day After Tomorrow	2004	$355.8	$542.8	66%
22	Armageddon	1998	$352.1	$553.7	64%
23	Pirates of the Caribbean: The Curse of the Black Pearl	2003	$348.5	$653.9	53%
24	Forrest Gump	1994	$347.7	$677.4	51%
25	The Last Samurai	2003	$344.3	$456.8	75%
26	The Incredibles	2004	$343.0	$617.2	56%
27	Star Wars: Episode II — Attack of the Clones	2002	$338.8	$649.5	52%
28	Men in Black	1997	$338.7	$589.4	57%
29	Mission: Impossible II	2000	$330.5	$545.9	61%
30	Terminator 2: Judgment Day	1991	$315.0	$519.8	61%
	Totals		**$14,151.0**	**$23,360.0**	**60%**

Producer Relationships with International Distributors

Producers should attend the major motion picture international markets:

- The American Film Market, held in Santa Monica, California, USA, in November, for one very focused week of picture rights sales, that also accommodates the full spectrum of international studio relationship activities
- The Cannes Film Festival, held in Cannes, France, in May, the most relaxed of the festivals, focusing more on production packaging and promotion than rights sales

Producers should begin their major international territory relationships for each of their pictures early in each picture's development. License relationships in these major territories should occur naturally as part of development for some territories and as part of production for others. Consequently, these two events are highly productive sales markets that expedite international territory relationships, but they are not the beginning or heart of these alliances.

Balanced producers most often use these markets:

- To centralize their meetings with major international territory distributors, studio heads, and other studio chiefs. The distribution top executives may attend meetings in London before Cannes, or may stay in Cannes for a few days, attending meetings, and leave actual market attendance to their staffs. This is also true of the American Film Market (AFM). International studio heads often travel to Los Angeles just prior to AFM's opening and stay perhaps into its first week or longer. But they often exclusively conduct their business outside the market.

- To pursue and consummate all nonmajor international territory sales. The major territories should be sold in the manner introduced in the preceding chapters, which is reviewed in Chapter 12.

For pictures to flourish in international territories, producers should do the following:

1. Manage relationships with international studios and distributors much as they manage and value their U.S. studio relationships, applying the relationship principles presented in Chapter 2.

2. Recognize that the best international studios are distribution centered, and as such, focus on target audiences and the power of each picture's campaign, and do everything reasonable to optimize each picture's exploitation and profits within their territory.

3. Recognize that international distributors have their various marketing strengths, just as U.S. studios do. One studio may have greater capacities and successful experiences distributing romantic comedies; another may be stronger in releasing action-adventure pictures. These relative strengths in marketing and releasing different types of pictures is a reflection of each distributor's familiarity with preparing campaigns, buying media, and creating promotion for these unique target audiences. It is important that producers develop an understanding of, and eventually relationships with, all the leading studios in every market, so that each picture will have the benefit of the greatest earnings power, matched with its particular audience dynamics.

4. Consider that though each of the largest territories has the four major distribution windows, the window timings vary in each territory, and all of them are different from those in the United States.

5. Anticipate that territories entering license agreements prior to a picture's production completion commonly purchase all that picture's distribution rights within their territory. Territories that purchase distribution rights after a picture's completion, however, may license theatrical, video/DVD,

premium cable/satellite television, free television, and the other rights separately or in combination with other rights.

Each major territory distributor allied with a picture should participate in the production of that picture from its earliest development. The producer's mantra to international studios is the same as it is to those in the United States: "We will neither develop nor produce a motion picture that you are not committed to distribute." This commitment and performance, on a global basis, allows producers to evaluate clearly the whole global dynamic of each picture before financially significant development begins. It also allows the producer to sustain global marketplace integrity throughout development and production.

When a producer is on fire for a picture, there is a natural reluctance to accept negative comments about it. However, with over half the audience and income coming from outside the United States, American producers receive crucially important creative and business insights about their global audiences if they seek and receive counsel from their international distributor partners. Producers must at least understand each major territory's response to every picture's creative, audience, and earnings performance profile. Only when producers approach and receive responses from these major territory distributors can they make accurate and informed judgments on "go" or "pass," talent, and other creative decisions for their pictures.

It is important to note that rarely will a producer gain unanimous consensus from all their international territory distributors relative to a picture's creative, audience, or earnings ability. However, knowing each distributor's position informs the producer as to which distributors are potential presale licensees and to adjust their license forecasts for those distributors who will be licensing after the picture has commenced production.

Each international territory has language and cultural peculiarities. It's a little frightening to see how pervasive American culture has become and is advancing within global cultures. Entertainment is the dominant source of this impact. Its influence escalates not only as governments relax import and programming restrictions, allowing people to decide what they will watch, but also through satellite and other new technologies, which deliver a more direct entertainment link between the provider and the audience. Producers demonstrate integrity and receive significant business benefits when they are sensitive to the major cultures and peoples who are their largest combined audiences. The American entertainment community substantially feeds the hearts, minds, and civilizations of the world. U.S. producers should review the numbers on the charts and accept the responsibility for affecting more people in international nations than do these nations' own producers.

At a recent Los Angeles industry event, motion picture line producer, James Dennett, said to an attentive audience, "Television is the church and religion of our day." I wrote it down. It is a scary notion. We may not openly acknowledge that motion pictures and television have such an influence on who we are, but regardless of our position, its effect remains. We certainly have a responsibility to consider the social impact of our productions in the lives of U.S. audiences. This sensitivity should be even greater for those global cultures in which we are guests.

Through dubbing or subtitling, producers and distributors substantially mold and shape each picture to better mesh with international audience cultures. In addition, creative suggestions should also be sought from each territory's distributor, and if they do not compromise the creative integrity of the picture, these suggestions ought to be used to prepare cover-shots, captured during principal photography, that will be used in the pictures released in these markets. The intent is to be empathetic to each culture and magnify each picture's creative, audience, and revenue performance.

Establishing New International Distribution Relationships

Engaging new relationships with each of the major international distributors is a natural part of the balanced producer's operations. Chapter 12 discusses in detail a producer's earliest development plan, which most often precedes even the literary property acquisition and includes meetings with at least one studio in each of the leading international territories. This may be a producer's first meeting with these distributors, but usually the producer and distributor have already met during film industry events. Meetings with international distributors should be set four to six weeks in advance, as these executives are important people with tight schedules.

In the first meeting, distributors expect the customary producer presentation. This presentation is creative focused, leaving the distributor to perform most of the picture's research and analysis work. Knowing this, producers should not be offended by distributors' first-contact skepticism or lack of enthusiasm.

Be prepared and confident by doing the work discussed in Chapters 1, 2, and 12. In almost every situation, as soon as the executives with whom you are meeting realize how you do business, they will be grateful and receptive to the presentation.

As distributors realize you understand and value their position, they will become earnest meeting participants. Present them with three to five pictures comparable to yours, including these pictures' earnings from the major distribution windows in their market, with the income adjusted to show today's value. Disclose your picture's target audiences, campaign elements, and projected grosses in the distributor's territory.

The distributor's reaction to this presentation determines if the pitch continues. If they respond positively to their review and your discussion, then present the story and the perceived audience satisfaction with the picture.

If the international distributor is enthusiastic about the picture, summarize the information already presented, demonstrate that you are fully funded to proceed with the development of the picture, and, if they are preliminarily committed to distributing this picture in their territory, you will immediately begin the picture's development, following a schedule that will allow you to deliver it to them during a specific predisclosed release time, typically 18 to 24 months in the future (after development and production).

The objective of this meeting is not to have the distributor sign an agreement or even provide an unbinding letter of intent. You simply are establishing the parameters of the relationship. These basic parameters are:

1. We (the producer) are convinced that you (the international distributor) are the ultimate distributor to release our picture in your territory.
2. We are going to perform as your fully funded development and production unit for this picture.
3. If you are not interested in distributing this picture, we are not inclined to proceed with its development. (In fact, if this studio is not interested in releasing the picture because they have a similar one already scheduled during that period, or for any other reason, you might approach a competing studio in that territory. However, this studio is your first choice because of their abilities demonstrated in successful releases of other pictures that have similar target audiences, campaigns, and above-the-line characteristics.)
4. We are proposing a best efforts, good faith, no obligation relationship.
5. We will include you, and you will assist us, in validating our continuing audience and marketing research for this picture in your territory.
6. We will continue to request your creative consultation throughout the major steps of this film's development and production.
7. We will exclusively communicate with you for all matters relating to this picture in your territory.
8. We will exclusively coordinate with you the press and advertising for this picture in your territory.
9. We will provide you copies of all this picture's promotion and advertising material for your use in promoting this picture during the various trade events in your territory.

These parameters may seem simple and undynamic, but they are impressively strong compared with the more common approach of saying, "This is our script, this is our budget, these are the creative elements we have attached so far, and we would like a production investment or distribution commitment." Sometimes such offers make sense, but after the producer leaves, the distributor is still left having to research similar pictures, identify and evaluate the target audiences, break down the script for the strongest campaign elements, and so forth. Following this analysis, if the distributor is still interested in the picture, he or she is faced with the formidable relationship deterrent of premature deal engagement. From the distributor's perspective, this is the difficult phenomenon of their beginning to invest in a picture both before development and preproduction are complete, and before the producer has demonstrated that he or she will closely correlate the picture's creative and marketing aspects with the distributor as the producer prepares for and proceeds with production. Considering the most common prior-to-production relationship offered to distributors, producers should expect distributors to be wary when they approach them for the first time.

Nurturing the Relationship

This process is wonderfully straightforward, though to the uninitiated, it may seem sophisticated. Each time producers meet with their international distribution partners, they fulfill a mutual objective and begin a mutual next-step target. These objectives and targets weave integrity into the deepening relationship.

The objective following the first meeting is to successfully negotiate the rights to the motion picture's literary property. The next target is to assemble the proposed list of the picture's directors.

If the producer successfully acquires rights to the literary property, each of the participating international territory distributors and the U.S. distributor are immediately and confidentially notified of this progress, and of the dates and methods for the producer's trade press release and advertising. Within a week, the press announcement, and soon thereafter, the first trade ad with the picture's initial look, appear in the entertainment trade papers.

In the next meeting with each distributor, the producer reviews the list of proposed directors. Again, the producer leads this meeting with an overview of how the proposed directors' pictures have performed in the distributor's particular territory. A producer rarely chooses a director who is the unanimous first choice of all the territories. The producer's target after the second meeting is to successfully negotiate the director. The next objective is to prepare, with the director, the ultimate leading cast.

After the producer successfully attaches the director, each of the distributors is immediately and confidentially notified and given promotion and advertising plans. Within a week the promotion and advertising appear in global trade papers.

As this process continues throughout development and initial preproduction, the distributor becomes increasingly confident in the producer's competence and delivery. In addition to development and production meetings, and other communication, the producer is meeting with this picture's distributors during the two annual international markets.

International Territory License Timing

License timing is categorized in two ways: (1) licenses that are part of the producer's presale plan and (2) licenses that are outside the producer's presale plan.

Producers should principally use bank financing to fund the production of their pictures. Presale licenses are the central and often the primary collateral for these bank loans, which are thoroughly reviewed in Chapter 5.

As part of the final preproduction process, the producer performs a final participating distributor analysis, and prepares a presale plan that by this time will have become obvious. This plan lists the fewest possible participants, including international territories and possibly premium cable or network television. Presale participants are in a separate category because they receive motivations unique to their presale participation.

Presale participants typically are approached about nine months before the picture is delivered. By this time they have been closely associated with the picture for several months during its development and are comfortable with the producer and their own territory's advance response to the picture. These participants are given two substantial incentives to participate: First, the picture becomes officially theirs and is no longer subject to competitive bidding. Second, the advance is discounted by as much as 20 percent. The producer usually knows, before approaching the proposed prebuy licensees, if the financial and inventory incentives will be sufficient to engage the licensees in the picture.

The prebuy licensees typically advance the producer 10 percent of the license fee and guarantee to remit the balance when they are delivered access to the completed picture's elements or they are delivered to them.

The remaining licensees are approached much differently. Though the producer exclusively matures specific distributors in each territory, the final license negotiation is affected by the natural existence of competition for the picture within each respective territory. This competition often prompts the distributors remaining after the presale to seek to license the picture before it is ready for delivery. Though predelivery licensing may occur, the discounts associated with presale participants are not available.

License Documentation

The Independent Film & Television Alliance (I.F.T.A. or "the Alliance") operates the American Film Market (AFM). The Alliance has developed and continues to refine effective and high-demand international license resources for global producers and distributors. They have standardized international rights sales *deal memos, licensing agreements,* and *delivery documentation.*

The Alliance is a singularly responsible resource for independent producers. Most of the forms and instructions essential for carrying out the operational aspects of documenting and fulfilling international territory rights sales and delivery are available through this universally recognized organization.

Licenses' terms are most often agreed to during a meeting of the parties representing the picture (Licensor) and the distributor (Licensee) and confirmed in the form of a *deal memo* soon thereafter. Deal memos are generally letters that set forth the basic agreed terms and typically provide for the other party's confirming signature.

Though there are license relationships that are bound without additional documentation, most sales are further documented by an actual *license agreement* that fully addresses all the terms and conditions relative to the license relationship.

The Alliance has created widely used licensing deal memos and fulfillments that are broadly used by producers and distributors. These documents are available from the Alliance at 10850 Wilshire Blvd., 9th Floor, Los Angeles, CA, 90024, USA; by phone at 310-446-1000; or through their Web site at www.info@ifta-online.org.

My first international sales event was the 1976 MIFED, in Milan, which at the time was the most productive international sales event. I was stunned by the number of international territories represented and how extensive global distribution was even then. Hundreds of small villages and hamlets without utilities have paying audiences. Some of these local audiences are served by exhibitors that travel to their locals with their film reels and sometimes just a single projector, often mounted on a truck bed. The picture is either shown against a wall, or on a screen drawn between poles. Weather permitting, after the sun goes down, the generator is fired up, and the picture is screened one reel at a time, if there is only one projector.

These remote areas are often licensed for a flat fee, using one or more previously used prints, rarely in their audience's language.

The deal memo identifies the parties, the project or series being licensed, the territory or territories the license covers, the particular rights covered by the license, and the window length for each.

License income. Earnings may come to the licensor from two sources: an advance/ guarantee or profit participation. One direct distribution expense difference unique to international territories is the often substantial post-production expenses related to talent and dubbing or subtitling. One unique income category from international territories is that of payments from the distributor for elements provided by the producer. These elements include mechanicals or color separations for printed promotion and advertising materials along with tangible film and video elements of the picture and its related video and film advertising, promotion, and publicity products.

Guarantee. The guarantee amount initially performs as payment "binder" to the agreement. The guarantee amount may be paid in installments as indicated on the deal memo and is most often 10 percent of the total minimum guaranteed payment, or *minimum guarantee.*

The minimum guarantee balance payment is most often triggered by delivery of the picture, or by access to specific elements of the picture by the licensee. To delay payment, the licensee may not accept immediate delivery of the elements, though they have been delivered to a freight forwarder within the territory, on the licensee's behalf. To regulate this, there may be language in the deal memo stating that the licensee will take delivery within a certain period, for instance two months of notification that the materials have been received.

Letters of Credit (LC) are occasionally required from smaller, more remote, newer, or less stable licensees. LCs are reviewed in Chapter 5. An example of a new release picture payment language and terms is "10 percent on agreement execution, via wire transfer, 90 percent within 14 calendar days from agreement execution, by letter of credit."

The license guarantee is advanced against the specific licensed rights. The percentage of the advance applied to each right is specified in the deal memo. This amount may be deducted from the licensor's share before the licensor participates in the profits of the picture earned from that specific right.

Disposition of gross receipts. In a "costs-off deal," income accounting with international distributors is very similar to the accounting with U.S. distributors. Distribution fees are paid on first receipts, direct distribution expenses are recouped next, then the guarantee is recouped, and then, typically, the producer participates in the picture's remaining profits. "Distribution deal" accounting is most commonly used in licenses with little or no advance guarantee.

Cross-collateralization may be used to bind the terms of a deal memo, including the distributor's advance recoupment, with the specific license rights to other pictures.

Using the Alliance's deal memo has many advantages. Because it is widely used, it is widely understood, accepted, and litigation interpreted. Further, its menu form allows easy selection, and it compels the parties to consider all the major points of the license.

However, the deal memo is a general form, and as such, may have wasted spaces and limitations for some licenses. It is also often too rigid to accommodate sophisticated license terms that may end up scribbled in the margins. This being so, many companies use the letter form of deal memo. Regardless of what you use, the Alliance deal memo remains an excellent guide for those less accustomed to the international licensing process.

Territory Differences

Each territory's earnings value is not defined so much by its size and population as by the territory's media sophistication, which is principally gauged by the presence and availability of all four major distribution windows, as well as by concentration of television households among its total population. This value is also defined by the strength of the economy, measured substantially by the audience sizes per capita, for each media, and by ticket cost, home video/DVD rental cost, and premium cable service subscription cost, along with average consumer discretionary spending and currency exchange value.

Strengths vary greatly between territories. For instance, Mexico has a land mass about five times that of Japan, but only a fraction of Japan's population. Further, Mexico has comparatively underdeveloped media and, though a high percentage of the population attend theaters, the admission price in Mexico is several times lower than in Japan. The most effective territory financial comparisons are drawn by examining each territory's box office and four major media category earnings records.

Managing Global Relationships

Though the producer will engage and sustain first-person relationships with the leading territories, this will not be possible for most other international territories. These other valuable relationships typically are managed by a small, very busy, in-house international sales staff. This is a powerful and increasingly important area, worthy of each producer's focus, accountability, and generous investment. With the same picture inventory, the only difference being the dynamics of the international department operating team, revenues can shift in either direction by one-third. The international sales department deserves the placement of a highly skilled, focused, wired, and genial team.

Though a producer may not pitch the major territory distributors on pictures they have yet to place in earnest development, distributors hope their independent producers will become regular suppliers of significant films. It is important for these distributors to understand their producers' five-year plans and the scope of pictures they intend to produce. Whether it is three pictures a year or two every three years, distributors need to know. Knowledge of production plans significantly affects the value distributors attribute to each production company relationship.

As a producer's inventory of motion pictures increases, so does the power to trade all pictures, both new and library releases. It is good business for producers to consider the library they are building, not just picture by picture, but by the effect each new film has on those in their libraries.

International Trends

International territories are a continually changing landscape that producers ought to keep their eyes on. Consider the following two trends.

International Production of American Style Pictures

In 1997, Gaumont, a studio based in France with multiple European media business interests, produced a very American motion picture, *The Fifth Element*. This creatively and financially bold experiment was extremely successful, with U.S. and international audiences responding equally to the American motion pictures after which it was styled. This picture was both an indication of the aggressive and culturally wired status of international studios for U.S. coproduction relationships, and a precursor of many pictures that have been produced and released from other major international studios since then.

Global Leading Territory Day and Date Theatrical Releases

The very savvy distribution team at DreamWorks released *The Prince of Egypt* on December 18, 1998. This was the first time in motion picture history that a film was released in all major global markets on the same day. Global theatrical day and date releasing requires massive creative (especially dubbing and subtitling) and distribution coordination. The success of *The Prince of Egypt*'s global release has led the way to a growing number of global day and date release motion pictures that satisfy the demands of international audiences who resent having to wait for pictures until after their U.S. openings. In addition to each of *The Lord of the Rings* pictures, *Spider-Man*, *Shrek* 1 and 2, and *Star Wars III— Revenge of the Sith* opened in 105 territories day and date with the United States, earning $253.2 million opening week, $108.5 million in the United States and $144.7 million internationally.

Chapter Postscript

As a group, U.S. consumers outspend every other global audience in every distribution window. However, the global growth area for American motion pictures is the international territories.

With over half of the average American motion picture's earnings coming from international territories, and an average ratio of 8 to 1 international to U.S. audiences viewing these pictures, producing for international audiences should carry (for American producers) a weight of focus at least equal to that of U.S. audiences, for most pictures.

Producers should understand the play and earnings dynamics of their pictures globally, and develop and produce them to maximize their performance in at least the leading international territories. Motion pictures created by these producers are better received by international audiences and consistently turn in substantially higher earnings.

Ancillary Markets and Rights

This chapter presents the ancillary markets and rights for theatrically released motion pictures; reviews their audiences, income, and license relationships; and details how producers should manage them.

The Effect of Theatrically Released Motion Pictures on Other Windows

For a motion picture to warrant beginning its distribution in theaters, it must meet the theatrical audience's expectations. This audience expects these pictures to be substantive entertainment. Theatrical feature films should create an emotional fire in their audiences. This quality ought to be the "event" in event motion pictures. Special-effects driven films may generate a respectable gross in the first or second film in which a new effect is used, but effects quickly lose an audience's respect if they are a picture's centerpiece.

One of the finest expressions of this was made by motion picture industry living legend Peter Guber, as he addressed independent producers during a session of the American Film Market:

> So is there a specific ingredient that's essential for [a picture's] success? My instinct, my curiosity, and my experience tell me that the key component is emotion. The story must have resonance and emotion. It must reside in the story . . . Watch your audience come out of a movie and see their state. Ask them to tell you about the film . . . When they tell you, or better yet show you,

the impact it has on them, the emotion generated, then you better buckle your seat belt because you have a hit, even if the reviews aren't good. That doesn't mean a film can't be thoughtful, it means the emotion must carry the information, not the other way around. What you have to move are not boxes of popcorn, or subs on a cable system, but people's hearts and spirits.

Audience reactions are the ultimate measure of a picture's entertainment power. Audiences look to theatrically released pictures to entertain and move them more than any other pictures made.

Theatrically released motion picture campaigns create an event aura that continues with these pictures through all distribution windows. If they deliver the emotion-packed entertainment they promise, audiences will view them again as these pictures pass through subsequent release windows.

Audience Sizes in Major Windows

In Chapter 2, we reviewed how difficult it is for pictures to become profitable in their theatrical distribution alone. But for most pictures, the larger their theatrical audience and earnings, the greater will be their ancillary audiences and earnings.

Though the following audience statistics are for the United States, the leading international territories perform similarly, and they are consistently moving closer to matching the U.S. ratios. In the United States, there are approximately 110 million television households and a potential audience of 1.8 per household (anyone between the ages of 5 and 80 is considered a potential audience). This creates a total potential audience of approximately 200 million people for each picture's several distribution windows. Each picture's audience varies depending on the target audiences the picture appeals to, the dynamics of the film's campaign, and the heat of its media buy and promotion.

According to the National Association of Theater Owners (NATO), the average picture's U.S. theatrical gross box office revenues among all pictures released in 2004 was approximately $16.1 million; the average gross box office per picture for major studio releases alone was closer to $31 million. Most pictures are considered successful if they attain a U.S. box office gross of $50 million. At the 2004 approximate average ticket price of $6.25, a picture with a U.S. theatrical gross of $50 million (about three times greater than the average picture) will have played to a theatrical audience of only approximately eight million people. Picture titles attaining such success become household names to most consumers, but will have been seen by only about 4 percent of the total potential U.S. audiences during their theatrical play. As most pictures that (U.S.) theatrically gross $50 million or more will be seen by at least 50 percent of all U.S. audiences by the time they have completed their initial U.S. television syndication, their theatrical audiences may represent only one-twentieth of their total audience reach. Whether measuring each picture by its audience or income, though the theatrical window is crucially important and literally determines the audiences and incomes in subsequent ancillary release windows, the theatrical audiences and income are the lowest of all release windows.

During its video release, the average picture earning $50 million in U.S. theatrical box office should earn an additional $75 million in video income. (This varies substantially depending on each picture's target audiences. For instance, a kids' dominated audience picture—ages 5 to 11—may have a U.S. video gross closer to $125 million.) With an estimated division of approximately 40 percent of this income from rental and 60 percent from sell-through, using an average rental rate of $3.20 and a retail sell-through price of $20,15, and using an estimated first-viewing audience of 1.7 people, this picture will reach a video audience of about 20 million viewers, which is more than double the U.S. theatrical audience.

One year after its theatrical premiere, the picture is released on premium cable, and this household-name picture still has not been seen by 85 percent of its potential audience. U.S. premium cable audience penetration in 2004 was 52 million homes. An ample premium cable allowance for a picture with a U.S. theatrical gross of $50 million will deliver another 30 million viewers. This increases the total U.S. audience reach to 58 million, still just over half its eventual total U.S. audience, leaving about 42 million new viewers who will see the picture during its network television premiere, which traditionally occurs about 30 months after the theatrical release and its original television syndication release. Though theatrical release motion pictures often win the dominant network audience share, the networks typically broadcast a picture only once, leaving a substantial audience for television syndication.

In every distribution window there are repeat viewers, which are not represented in the previous figures. These are especially important revenue-building audiences for network and syndicated television.

Many theatrically released motion pictures become important social references that are a must-see-early for their target audiences and a free television curiosity tune-in for their distant fringe audiences. Whether it is *The Fellowship of the Rings*, *Toy Story, Gladiator, Secondhand Lions*, or *Big Daddy*, most of the 200 million potential U.S. audience will eventually experience theatrically released motion pictures, even if it is at home on their surround-sound, big-screen television where they must sit through ads or channel-surf during a few commercials. Theatrically released motion pictures are often powerful, culture-shifting audience attractions that uniquely sustain their value, substantially because of their entertainment power and their status as a major theatrical event.

Ancillary Audience Characteristics

Each of the major four ancillary windows (home video/DVD, premium cable, network television, and syndicated television) has unique audience characteristics, which are defined more by their audiences' lifestyles than by their economics. Although audiences spend more of their entertainment time in their particular favorite distribution window, most consumers have purchased the equipment, are prepared, and want to experience each motion picture in the distribution windows they determine the motion picture warrants.

Consumers are passionate about making merchandise decisions, and motion pictures carry unique social importance. Pictures are exotic merchandise, universally known and talked about, and our opinions about them and their impact upon us make them one of the most high-profile and talked-about consumer product categories.

Consuming motion pictures is all about emotions, and most people make up their minds about how they will view a picture by the time they have seen a picture's third commercial. Typically, emotions rule over financial considerations. Choosing among a $9 theater ticket, a $20 video/DVD purchase, a $3 video/DVD rental, a $5 monthly premium cable subscription, or free network television, is rarely as important as wanting to see it now, or with a friend, or on a theater screen, or in its full uninterrupted length.

Some pictures are so compelling that they override our viewing preferences and habits. Many people who never see a movie at a theater, or never buy or rent a video/DVD, or who never see a movie twice, do so with certain pictures. This is demonstrated by especially audience-motivating entertainment like *Titanic*, *Harry Potter*, *Forrest Gump*, *E.T.*, and *Finding Nemo*, all of which drew uncommonly high audiences in all distribution windows.

In addition to our emotional connections with pictures, capriciousness often sways a person's viewing choice. Consumers may just *feel* like seeing a picture at a theater, buying one, or renting one from the video outlet, and so go to the local multiplex, retailer, or video store and seek a title. If there isn't one they have made a previous theatrical or video decision about, they most often buy a ticket, video/DVD, or rent a picture anyway. It may even be a picture that they have already relegated to a later ancillary window, but they take a chance.

Because of this phenomenon, producers and distributors often stage their release windows during the summer or the Christmas and New Year holidays. These are the dominant seasons during which consumers seek more movie experiences, often making their picture selection while they are in the marketplace. This tendency is largely the motivation behind the industries' six-month window structure; the holidays and summer are six months apart. Many of the strongest pictures are released in their two most critical distribution windows (theatrical and video) during the seasons when audiences are most aggressively seeking entertainment.

U.S. audiences consume more entertainment than any other territory's audiences, but Western European and Japanese audiences are close behind. According to Nielsen Media Research, more than 99 percent of all U.S. households own at least one television and receive one or more major network television signals. Ninety percent of these television households have at least one DVD or VCR, and according to the Motion Picture Association of America (MPAA), annually purchase more than 1.4 billion copies of prerecorded DVDs and videocassettes. Sixty-eight percent have basic cable, 20 percent have digital satellite, and according to the MPAA, 48 percent of television households subscribe to at least one premium cable network.

Despite the increasing availability and audience acquisition of sophisticated home entertainment equipment, theater audiences have sustained or steadily increased over the past 10 years. The MPAA reported a 2004 total U.S. box office of $9.3 billion, up from $5.4 billion in 1994.

During this same period, the entertainment consumption rate has increased proportionally higher in every major ancillary window, with audiences averaging over an annual 1 percent increase during the past 10 years.

The following theater audience statistics closely mirror each of the major ancillary (video, premium cable, network, and syndication) audience profiles.

Total Admissions by Audience Category

Age	12–17	18+	18–29	30–39	40–49	50–59	60+
Percentage of Yearly Admissions	19%	81%	29%	19%	14%	11%	8%

Frequency of Audience Attendance by Age

	12–17	18+	All audiences 12 and over
At least 1x/month	44%	23%	25%
2x/year	48%	35%	36%
1x/year	5%	12%	11%
Never	3%	30%	27%

As these NATO-prepared statistics indicate, 18- to 29-year old adults are the most important single demographically categorized audience, buying 29 percent of all tickets purchased. However, for sheer entertainment consumption aggressiveness, by each participant in a demographic category, 12- to 17-year-olds are way out front, with 44 percent buying a ticket at least once a month, demonstrating that youth are both easier to please and will accommodate a greater quantity of pictures than any other category.

Youth are the greatest consumers of motion pictures in *all* media. As a group, they attend the theater more often, rent more videos, and watch more premium cable, network, and syndicated television. They are also easier to sell to because they view and listen to more advertisements and are less influenced by critical reviews than older audiences as to what they will buy and watch.

Another interesting analysis of audience preferences is shown in the following chart; couples with children at home attend the theater more often than couples without children at home. Not surprisingly, single adults attend the theater more than married adults, but not by much.

Frequency of Audience Attendance by Family Status

	Single	Married w/Kids	Married No Kids
1x/month	25%	28%	21%
1x/6 months	32%	41%	37%
1x/year	11%	11%	12%
Never	31%	19%	30%

Although a decade ago there was a significantly male attendance dominance, MPAA statistics reveal it is now less than 2 percent.

Statistics are important indicators that are worthy of analysis by those who produce, distribute, and license motion pictures. However, statistics are easily misinterpreted. For instance, has the gap between men and women motion picture viewers closed because women have become more aggressive entertainment consumers, or because there are more pictures being produced and distributed that interest them? The consensus of the best industry analyzers supports the latter conclusion. Responding to the demand of women to view theatrically released motion pictures in all media, producers and studios are increasing their delivery to this powerful audience.

Regarding family movie viewing, there is a fairly even split among industry mavens, between those who believe families don't attend theaters more regularly because they spend less discretionary money than other audience categories, and those who believe that there are simply fewer motion pictures that are targeted to couples with children at home.

Motion pictures such as *Nightmare on Elm Street* and *The Princess Diaries* have almost exclusive single audience skews, whereas films like *Shrek*, *Bruce Almighty*, and *Spider-Man* are made for multiple target audiences. All these pictures were successful, and targeting for a specific audience often ensures a solid response; however, pictures with a strong appeal to multiple target audiences have a higher potential income in all distribution windows and rights sales.

Producers Rely on Ancillary Earnings

For U.S. and all major international territories, the theatrical release is unquestionably the most important distribution window through which each motion picture passes. This is almost exclusively so, because this is where audience perception of each picture's entertainment value is established. As discussed in previous chapters, producers rarely forecast any producer profits from the theatrical distribution of their pictures; however, producers should be keenly aware that, though their largest audiences and substantially all their income will come from their pictures' ancillary windows, the size of these audiences and earnings will be determined by the pictures' performances during the theatrical release.

It is important that producers take into account the whole performance and earnings dynamics of each motion picture. A picture may have a projected $20 million gross box office, offset by a theatrical television campaign of almost that amount. If it performs to its projection, this picture may conclude its theatrical run with a distributor's net loss of approximately $13.5 million, without any offset to its negative (production) cost. Examine these numbers.

Theatrical Release Earnings Analysis

Source	Amount (in millions)	Balance (in millions)
Gross box office earnings	$24	$24
Film rental	$12	$12
Distribution fee	$4.2	$7.8
Direct distribution	$27	($19.2)
Expenses (advertising $24 million; 1,600 Prints @ $1,900 each; other expenses $3 million)		
Distribution Net Loss	($19.2)	($19.2)

If the theatrical window is analyzed alone, neither the producer nor the distributor would release the picture. But when the ancillary windows are also considered, pictures often become sound business. For instance, if the $24 million in advertising and associated promotion and publicity for the picture sufficiently motivates the picture's audiences, then its first ancillary audience—the video audience—may even be larger than traditional ratios by drawing in theatrical audiences who did not get a chance to see the picture during its short theatrical run. As the following example indicates, even at the traditional "three times film rental" performance, the picture is almost at a break-even status ($800,000 loss) as it moves through its video ancillary window.

Video Release Earnings

Source	Amount (in millions)	Balance (in millions)
Video gross	$36	$36
Distribution fee	$12.6	$ 23.4
Direct distribution expenses	$5	$18.4
Distributor's net	$18.4	$18.4
Theatrical loss forward	($19.2)	($.80)

After analyzing these earnings, you might wonder why more movies don't begin distribution with video, spending the $20 million in advertising there. This would be the logical choice, save for the "theatrical dimension" it would never be able to gain, no matter how much video release advertising is done. If the project is made for the small screen first, it will never shake its small-screen stigma. The only motion picture exceptions are children's audience animation sequels, which perform in a uniquely "toy-like" manner for this particular audience.

The First Ancillary Window: Video Distribution

This window traditionally opens six months after a picture's theatrical premiere. When these pictures open in video, they still carry their theatrical marketing power and sometimes are still playing in theatrical situations (usually second-run theaters). As indicated previously, most of the potential audience (96 percent for an average picture) still have not seen this picture; having missed seeing the picture while it was in theaters, they are either waiting for its release on video or for a later ancillary window.

Using the customary video gross revenue projection formula of three times a picture's theatrical film rental is sufficient for a rough estimate of the film's success, but hardly touches on understanding how to manage this window.

Traditionally, a picture is released into its video life as a rental product, converting to a sell-through product after its first year of video release. Or, if the picture performed well enough in its theatrical release, typically grossing at least $80 million, it may commence at a sell-through price.

As a rental product, a picture is released at a wholesale price of about $65, paid by the video outlet. The substantial margin between this wholesale cost and an actual video production cost of about $3 leaves the studio and the producer with a built-in rental revenues share. The studios have an actual revenue sharing system with the larger rental chains.

For the majority of pictures theatrically grossing under $80 million, after their primary video rental life of about one year, if justified, these pictures are video released again at a wholesale sell-through price of between $10 and $17. This second release motivates consumer purchases—the highest purchase volumes generated by mass merchandise retailers.

For breakout pictures with box office earnings of at least $120 million, the video strategy is especially well crafted. Most of these titles have the capacity to earn five times or more than their film rental and typically are released at lower sell-through prices, to optimize volume and overall profits.

Since video earnings represent the highest single income category for most pictures, every studio's video distribution department configures a separate release strategy, including price variance for each picture, which keeps the studios, as well as video outlets and mass merchandisers, on their toes. The only change that may be apparent to consumers is that now more pictures are offered initially at sell-through prices, and because of rental sharing, there is a better chance for them to find the movie they want at their local mass merchandiser and video outlet.

Each of the major studios has excellent video distribution units and they video release most motion pictures that they theatrically distribute. They also are the primary marketing source for both video rental and sell-through. Video outlets advertise in their stores, some of them by direct mail, and larger chains advertise on television. The studios provide video retailers co-op advertising support (paying for a portion of their advertising media costs) to encourage their campaigns. Each video outlet's co-op amount usually is based on a percentage of its purchases.

The producer's video distribution agreement with the studio typically is associated with the theatrical distribution agreement. Terms vary, but the traditional relationship pays the studio a 25 to 35 percent distribution fee, recoups the studio's direct distribution expenses, then the studio's loss-carry-forward from theatrical distribution, if there is any. An operating reserve is then deducted to continue the video sales process, and finally, the balance goes to the producer.

The Second Ancillary Window: Premium Cable Television ____

Consumers eagerly embraced this release window, and it experienced aggressive growth during the early 1980s. The premium cable window provides solid consumer motion picture delivery, and subscriber growth continues in mostly single-digit annual percentages.

Premium cable networks provide an important audience and earnings window, delivering a far less complicated arena for producers to work in. There is a short list of potential licensees, which includes HBO/Cinemax and their sister channels; Showtime/The Movie Channel and their sister networks; and Starz/Encore and their sister networks.

These networks are very competitive for pictures because of the stability and growth of their subscriber bases, which are determined by the popularity and quantity of the pictures they broadcast. These networks gain subscribers almost exclusively by delivering major theatrically released motion pictures. There is no revenue sharing on this playing field. The license fees paid are the total income from this release category.

In this window, the exclusive premiere license is the greatest single income tier. The premiere license provides for a limited number of airings for a limited period of time. The fee is determined by each picture's theatrical release success. For pictures performing poorly, they may receive a license fee of five or six figures, if at all. For moderately and better performing pictures, they may engage license fees from $22 million to $6 million. For licenses engaged prior to a picture's theatrical release, they should include an escalator clause. This clause calls for the license fee to increase if the picture's gross box office earnings exceed a certain minimum (for instance, $40 million) and then increases it again for every additional gross box office increment attained (for instance, each $10 million), but not to exceed a total license amount (for instance, $20 million).

The nonexclusive premium cable license tier allows for a greater number of airings for a substantially reduced license fee, and is most often included in the premiere license agreement. This tier continues until the free television network premiere occurs. Following the network premiere, the picture may still be licensed by premium cable networks, but for lesser amounts.

Consumer marketing in this window is accomplished by the licensee network, primarily through network promotional spots, crossover network advertising through cable systems, and print ads.

Larger producers engage and manage these licenses directly. The producer must know each picture's value to the network. Producers discover this as they research each picture during the preparation of the picture's first draft global liquidation breakdown. This was discussed in Chapter 1 and will be reviewed in Chapter 12. Basically, this is the process of identifying recently released pictures with very similar target audiences, campaign emotion signatures, and media buys. Then producers identify these pictures' audience and financial performance in the United States and leading international territories. This information allows the producer to more accurately forecast earnings as well as confidently prepare and negotiate these and other rights.

To assist them in securing and managing these licenses, producers often use an independent producer sales representative, hire an employee experienced in ancillary sales management, or use an industry attorney well exercised in this process.

The Third Ancillary Window: Network or Cable Television Premiere

Licensing network television is similar in most respects to licensing premium cable networks, although the marketplace is quite different. The economy, the networks' broadcast time allotment and content constraints, and their average 30-month window from theatrical premiere to network premiere make for very different chemistry.

The network premiere of motion pictures is one of the most important distribution windows for two reasons: The network premiere is the first opportunity for audiences to view the picture without cost, and more importantly, it is the first opportunity for almost every person in the United States to watch the picture at the same time.

At a time when network executives are challenged more than ever to capture high audience shares for their respective network, motion pictures consistently deliver dominant audience shares. In some respects, the time from a picture's theatrical release to its network premiere works to build its audience. Many viewers who have seen the picture before and enjoyed it will tune in again. Pictures that have been aired so heavily through the three prior windows (such as *Forest Gump*, *Independence Day*, and many others) pull massive audiences, both new and repeat, to their network premiere.

Though the license sale approach is similar to premium cable, there are a greater number of potential licensees in the premiere television market. These primarily include NBC, ABC, CBS, Fox, and Paramount broadcast networks, and the major cable television networks, including TNT, TBS, USA, Discovery, A&E, and Lifetime, in this expanding license arena. Unlike premium cable, this typical license calls for a single broadcast and a window length of 12 to 24 months.

Since each picture's audience share draw determines its value to the network, there is a broad range of potential license fees. Pictures with U.S. box office of at least $25 million will garner license fees from $2.2 million to as high as $40 million for break-out pictures. Most licenses are $4 million to $7 million.

As with premium cable, larger producers license premiere television directly. The preparation for this license is a natural part of the whole development and production process. Prior to earnest development, producers should have identified the most likely network license candidate and the value of the picture to this network, if it meets its box office forecast. By preparing thoroughly, producers can explore entering pretheatrical release licenses with a network that can accommodate a tie-in "film-about-the-film," which could provide programming to the network and additional marketing heat for the picture during its theatrical release. The network provides promotion and advertising for the picture principally via tune-in promotional spots over its own network.

Most producers use either in-house ancillary sales talent or a producer's representative to fulfill and maintain these relationships, and the producer's attorney typically is essential in this process.

Occasionally producers license directly to network television, collapsing the premium cable window altogether, which substantially washes out premium cable premiere earnings. Producers electing to do this are motivated by aggressive networks willing to pay license fees equal to the combined traditional premium and free television premiere fees.

The Fourth Ancillary Window: Free Television Syndication ___

Television syndication is the evergreen audience and earnings television window. Syndication opens 12 to 24 months following the network premiere and continues to license-renew as long as people care to be entertained.

This window is sophisticated because it deals with many television station groups and independent stations. It requires continual sales, license management, and physical delivery maintenance. This window usually is managed by a television syndication organization, which is compensated through distribution fees and expense recoupment.

License fees vary widely in this window, depending substantially on the number of airings allowed, the audience reach, the number of stations, and the length of license.

Other Ancillary Rights ___

Producers should examine, identify, plan, and exploit every rights area that may be applicable to each of their pictures. Some nontraditional ancillary rights actually may exceed the producer's share of the picture's traditional earnings areas. In the case of electronic games, this category alone can generate a nine-figure income for some pictures. Their closely correlated marketing campaigns can also substantially increase income from the primary release windows.

Novelization

There are profits for producers from novelizing a screenplay or rereleasing an existing novel upon which the picture is based. Typically, the greatest benefits to these licenses are realized by having the novel released four to six weeks prior to a picture's theatrical premiere, with the picture's one-sheet (poster) on its front cover. Producers are best served if they negotiate first with publishers for the quantity of the run and retail placement, then for profit participation. Having the novel at most mass merchandise, supermarket, drugstore, bookstore, and airport checkout lines just prior to a picture's theatrical premiere is very valuable advertising.

The management of novelization rights begins before the literary rights are negotiated. Some producers manage the whole universe of their pictures, including novelization rights, as part of their negotiations for their picture's story. No matter how strong the novel has been previously, the motion picture likely will become a household name and drive novel sales as no other influence can.

If producers fail to acquire their picture's novelization rights, then they should at least participate in the novelization (or rerelease) publishing profits and should receive publisher commitments relative to the novel's distribution tie-in to the picture's theatrical marketing.

Each picture's novelization should be scheduled with the publisher before principal photography commences, allowing at least five months for the publishing process *after* the novel has been completed.

Product Placements

An effective UPM (unit production manager) will make notes of proprietary items needed for principal photography. These are critical, and depending on a picture's target audiences and how the products or locations may appear in the picture to the audiences, they typically are provided to the production company at no cost.

Motion pictures are the most powerful merchandise vehicles with which other branded merchandise can be associated. More than the typical reach and frequency methods used by advertising agencies to gauge audience exposure, motion pictures can elevate a brand by putting it in the highest sphere of consumer consideration. Even negative use of a product in a motion picture may have substantial positive marketing effects. Because of this, sophisticated brands increasingly participate within and in conjunction with motion picture marketing, which helps propel their products with greater power than they can achieve from alternative promotion and advertising processes.

There is no income amount that should motivate producers to infringe on the integrity of their pictures; however, the best brand relationships have deepened pictures' creativity, increased their profits, and pumped up their marketing campaigns. There are well over a hundred excellent examples of this, such as *Wall Street*. Motorola was one of the only players in the then sluggish cell phone business. It just was not launching at dynamic proportions. When audiences around the world watched Michael Douglas using his cell phone as an indispensable lifestyle device, an entire industry was dramatically launched. Delivery services, clothes, food products and services, cosmetics, hotels, destinations, and automobiles are all major categorical players in this arena, and it is growing.

Producers should carefully review their pictures, even period productions, for opportunities to engage brand relationships that have mutual benefits. Product placement companies will make these arrangements for a modest fee.

Most brands, from private aircraft to bottled water, are very eager to establish these relationships. A call to most corporate headquarters will put a staffer in touch with the company's executive directing product placement.

With a little research on prior pictures, the producer can use comparable brand relationships to assist in negotiations for his or her picture.

All these relationships must be documented, and all documents should be reviewed by the producer's attorney. Items included might be: Who is the insurer in the event of loss or damage to the designer luggage? Is the contract language "a minimum of 5 seconds of brand name recognition" reasonable, and if the picture delivers three seconds, how does this affect the relationship? Is the payment reduced, and if so, by how much and who determines the amount? Working out these details up front seems like a bother at the time and like a dream when problems arise.

Premium Tie-ins

Like product placement, premium tie-ins are related to consumer brands becoming more dominant through their association with a motion picture.

A fast food restaurant chain gives away or sells products related to the motion picture. The public can receive them only through these outlets. They include character figures, special cups, hats, T-shirts, and toy tractors or spaceships. Whatever they are, they must mobilize the picture's target audience to come to a brand outlet primarily through television advertising. As they do this, they also sell the picture.

How much do the producers get paid to participate in such a promotion? Usually not anything directly. They do, though, indirectly—$5 million or $10 million or more—when a television ad campaign is engaged that simultaneously markets the picture. Some of these relationships have more than doubled the amount of advertising that would have been spent launching their motion pictures. In 1998, the strongest opening picture of the year was *Godzilla*. With an amazing number of promotional tie-in partners, the picture grossed over $44 million its opening weekend. Promotional partners with kids, youth, and family target audiences received reciprocal benefits from the producers, whose picture grossed $136 million in the United States and over $210 million in international territories.

Sound Tracks and Music Publishing

The sound track for almost every motion picture will become a substantive income-producing product. For some pictures, including *O Brother, Where Art Thou* and *Moulin Rouge!*, these earnings will rival income from traditional motion picture categories. Knowing this will affect how producers:

- Select the composer and needle drops (use of already released music in the picture).
- Create a separate sound track production and distribution plan.
- Set the sound track duplication and release schedule.
- Handle contract deal points with the composer and other related music contributors.
- Negotiate the sound track distribution and music publishing license(s).

Sound tracks are especially powerful earning and marketing elements of a motion picture when one of the picture's primary target audiences is youth.

Again, the most reliable approach to managing these rights is researching recently released pictures with similar target audiences that have well-managed sound track marketing and licensing. Producers should study the successful deals that have been made, with whom they made them, and how these relationships were managed. From this information the producer should create the model he or she is confident best serves the picture and will be served by it. After consulting with an attorney, the producer should then move forward with the marketing and licensing plan.

Sound track and music publishing normally is licensed to one or two highly skilled and experienced companies. The producer's task is to understand the earnings and promotion power of this license area, evaluate the license, negotiate and manage the license relationship, and set a schedule allowing these rights to be exploited to the maximum earnings and promotion benefit for the picture.

Toys and Merchandising

Even motion pictures that appear unlikely candidates for toys and merchandising should be carefully considered. Often, there are toys or other merchandise items for adult, youth, or children's audiences that seem like an amazing stretch. As producers become more involved in this licensing area, the wide appeal of movie merchandise for extensive global audiences becomes more apparent.

Each picture should be examined exclusively from the perspective of this license category. After a potential product list is made, research ought to be performed using films with comparable target audiences. After the producer prepares a basic merchandise plan, approaches should be made by, through, or after consulting with a producer's representative, who specializes in this licensing area. These licensing companies typically need at least one year prior to the motion picture's theatrical release to prepare.

Retail Game Sales and Electronic Games

For some pictures, this category of products, coming from the motion picture, may have a substantially larger earnings capacity than all other earnings areas of the picture combined. Companies specializing in the game industry understand the power motion pictures have in launching games of all kinds. This category includes paper-based role-playing games, board games, electronic hand-held games, console games, computer games—all sold at retail—as well as arcade games, motion control rides, and the ever-expanding massive, multiuser online games.

Producers and their representatives specializing in this licensing area should analyze a picture's game licensing prospects for the opportunity of representing the picture to this industry. It is best to have each picture reviewed by at least two competing representatives and have an attorney review the representative agreement as well as the licenses.

In-Flight

During preproduction, every picture should be reviewed separately for cover shots needed by its ancillary markets. These add expenses during principal photography but save much more money later. They also increase the picture's ancillary value and allow the producer to deliver a seamless version of the picture to each participating licensee. Cover shots may be needed for international versions, airline audiences (the in-flight version), and the network version that must comply with time and network standards.

There are a handful of excellent and very competitive in-flight distribution companies. Each studio also has an exceptional in-flight department. Producers should meet with competing companies and, with the support of their attorney, enter a distribution relationship.

Planning for this version in development and preproduction allows the producer to budget for cover shots and post-production time, and to deliver a print at the opening of this market, which is during each picture's theatrical release.

Hotels and Motels, Military, Schools, Indian Reservations, Ships at Sea, Prison Systems

It is common for independent producers to use the studio that is theatrically distributing their picture to distribute these rights. Each of these rights areas is a small, five- and six-figure income category, but together they can earn a seven-figure income.

Understanding that these ancillary earnings niches exist allows producers to plan for them, enter relationships with studio or ancillary rights distributors, to exploit these rights, and expand the audience and earnings for their pictures.

Chapter Postscript

The most powerful producers are very involved in planning and managing the ancillary rights release of their pictures. They understand that these are the rights that deliver the largest audiences and profits.

Producers are the parents and ultimate stewards of each picture. They must understand the audience and earnings dynamics of each picture and its full array of ancillary products. They must also measure them, plan them, and enter into relationships with strategic partners to dynamically create, exploit, manage, and ensure the optimal prosperity of these release windows and products.

To succeed in each rights area, the producer must plan early, value each rights area separately, do the research to discover each picture's potential value for each right, use industry specialists, and always include his or her attorney in negotiations and documentation.

Chapter 5

Entertainment Banking

This chapter is a review of the entire process of production funding, including how producers prepare for, borrow, and strengthen their banking relationships for initial and continuing production financing. Beginning with the end in mind is a life practice of many successful people. Production bank financing is the end of the development process and should be part of the development plan from its beginning. Assurance of production financing affects the producer's perception of and ability to develop each motion picture. Development financing most often is raised from private sources. This process is reviewed in Chapters 9 and 10.

With the exception of public offerings, producers should receive most, if not all of their production financing from banks. Knowing that a picture's production financing source is a bank both assures the picture will have solid, leading global territory distribution and that there will be no production financing participant at risk without complete collateral offset.

The Banking Business

Banks are often referred to as institutions. They are certainly governed by more agencies than most other businesses, but banking is a business. Banking decisions are profit motivated and predicated on business principles.

Every time the trade papers carry a story naming a specific bank supplying production funding to an independent producer, that bank's entertainment department receives calls from naive producers. They set up appointments and arrive, armed with a script and budget, ready to pitch the bank as if it were a studio. But banks make their decisions with different criteria than those used by studios.

Knowing someone at a bank, like knowing someone at a studio, is helpful, but it has little effect on the bank's lending decisions. The similarity between banks and studios is that to obtain their support, it is critical to understand their criteria for making decisions and the way in which they operate.

Every bank's inventory is its money. Banks principally earn profits by lending this money at interest. Like most businesses, banks sometimes have shortages or excesses of inventory. Though lending decisions have limited elasticity, when a bank's lending reserves are low, its lending decisions become more restrictive. When lending reserves are high, its lending decisions are more relaxed. It is an important question, and proper form, to ask your loan officer the status of the bank's current lending reserves.

Banks with strong entertainment divisions will always have the capacity to lend, even if they aren't primarily lending bank funds generated from deposits. If the division is making "good" loans, then the loss ratio is low, the loans serviced according to terms are high, and overall profits are high. With a strong loan portfolio, these divisions can perform as the lead bank with other participating banks, as well as engage other outside lending-capital scenarios. When choosing the lead bank that will manage your production borrowing, dealing with one that has a sound, experienced entertainment banking team is very important.

Each bank has loan amount preferences. There are small banks seeking loans in the six- to low-seven-figure amounts, mid-range banks seeking loans in the seven- to low-eight-figure amounts, and more sophisticated banks seeking loans in the mid-eight- to low-nine-figure amounts. It is important to know a bank's loan size criteria.

Basis of Lending Decisions

The ultimate assurance of payment is the borrower's pledged collateral. If the business plan, for whatever reason, is insufficient to pay the borrowed amount according to the terms of the loan, there must be assets pledged to the bank that will repay the remaining balance.

Collateral alone, however, is not sufficient for loan approval. Banks do not want to lend if there is even a modest probability that they will be forced to move on collateral to recover a remaining amount due. The borrower must demonstrate the capacity to service the loan based on existing business operations, or a business plan. Motion picture licenses provide ideal collateral as they are also the natural means of loan repayment.

Producers typically create motion pictures that are made available to international distributors and global licensees, who enter license agreements that provide for an advance payment against the producer's future earnings participation. These payments are due when the pictures become available to the licensees.

The pledged license agreements typically have only one condition before the advance payment is released. This condition is the licensee's receipt of an access letter, making the picture available to the licensee before a specific date. The risk of this delivery, as well as the completion of the picture within its proposed budget, is assumed by the completion guarantee company.

Banks make their lending decisions based on a combination of elements that must be represented clearly and completely in the loan package. For loan approval, this material (the loan package) must demonstrate that the bank has collateral assurance for its return of principal and interest and that the loan can be reasonably debt-serviced through the production company's regular course of doing business. For most production loans, the collateral is made up of license agreements for the yet-to-be-produced motion picture, whose pledged payments repay the loan's entire principal and interest.

Each loan memorandum submitted to a bank should include, and its approval is substantially determined by, the following:

Cover letter. This letter presents what the loan proceeds will be used for, the requested amount, the expected interest rate, the production timing, and the plan and timing for loan processing. The payment plan, collateral, participating distributors, and a brief description of the motion picture should also be presented.

Table of contents. The pages of the bank memorandum should be numbered and there should be a table of contents following the cover letter, which will assist the bank in reviewing the completeness of the package and in locating specific information in the memorandum.

Application. The bank's loan application should be completely filled out, signed, and made a part of the memorandum. Some parts of the application may be referenced by "see page number," if the information is completely set forth in another section of the package.

Activity and cash flow projections. Each of these projections should be month-to-month for the first year and cover at least six months beyond the anticipated active loan period. Each of these projections should have narrative "Notes to Projections," which describe important characteristics about the projections that are not self-evident. The cash flow projection must include the loan proceeds and debt servicing, calculated at the rate represented in the cover letter.

Distribution windows and liquidation breakdown summary. This reveals the picture's planned distribution windows and a conservative version of the liquidation breakdown estimate, including the producer's share of gross receipts.

Collateral. In the initial loan memorandum, this is a descriptive list of the license agreements as they are expected to be provided to the bank. This list should indicate each specific licensee and each estimated license amount.

Conditional documents. The bank will not take any substantial risk. If the license agreements used as collateral specify any conditions not satisfied by the completion bond, these further conditions must also be satisfied. The most common additional condition in these license agreements is that the picture must be released in the United States by one of the 10 major studios. If this is a condition, a copy of the U.S. distribution agreement or a binding commitment letter acceptable to the bank must also be included in the loan package.

Completion bond commitment. In the initial loan memorandum, this may be in the form of a conditional commitment letter that will be replaced with the bond commitment in the final loan documentation.

Loan calculation. To simplify your understanding, a sample calculation is part of this chapter. To further assist producers in preparing these forms, a worksheet is included on the CD-ROM provided with this book. This indicates, in accounting form, the collateral list with individual amounts, the collateral total, the form of the collateral by total and in separate sections (for instance, letters of credit may have a different loan value than bankable contracts), the respective discounts for each form of collateral (letters of credit drawn on major banks, and even bankable contracts from the largest distributors may not have to be discounted in their loan value), the new subtotal, the total loan interest amount, the adjusted new subtotal, the motion picture budget (including a detailed list of the actual production amount, promotion, publicity, sales events, travel, and any other expenses related to the picture, including production company operating expenses), and the remaining amount, shown as a collateral contingency.

The picture's creative information. This section should include the picture's title, a brief story synopsis, a list of the picture's primary talent and their referenced credits, the picture's production dates and locations, and the projected U.S. theatrical release date.

Business history. The production company may be new, a resurrection of a prior company, a merger of other companies, or something else. The bank needs to know about the company's genesis and progress; the roots tell of the branches and the fruit. This section is usually in narrative form.

Organization chart. This is a simple chart that reveals the members of the production company team by their responsibilities and relationships to one another. There is a production company chart in Chapter 9 and a worksheet on the book's CD-ROM.

Principals' biographies and balance sheets. The operators of the business are a key factor in a bank's loan review. The bank looks at the experience of those who manage the business and the experience and balance sheets of those who substantially own the business. The bank may not ask for owners to guarantee the loan, but the owners' financial profiles demonstrate their combined experience and success in asset management. This information typically is presented to the bank through brief, but specific, biographical summaries and recent balance sheets of each individual.

Company financials. These are the production company's current balance sheet and, if applicable, a recent profit-and-loss statement. These should be signed by either an in-house bookkeeper or preferably, reviewed and signed by the company's certified public accountant.

References. This is an important list of references who importantly point to the way in which the producer does business and with whom. This list typically includes the completion guarantor (the firm and the producer's contact); the producer's law firm and primary attorney; the producer's current bank and officer; the producer's accounting firm and primary accountant; substantial trade references and contacts; and clients, studios, distributors, and licensees with whom the producer has dealt, along with each of their contacts.

The Loan Approval Process

Producers usually work with a bank loan officer. This officer helps the producer to:

1. Complete the loan package. The package must be complete before it can be reviewed.
2. Perform a preliminary review. If the loan package underperforms in the loan officer's evaluation, it is rejected. Common reasons for underperformance include insufficient or unstable collateral, an unstable management team, or an unpredictable repayment plan.
3. Present the package to the bank's loan committee. The bank loan committee then reviews the package and approves or declines the loan.
4. Deliver the decision to the producer.
5. Prepare and process the loan documentation.
6. Open the funding facility to the producer.

Production Financing Worksheet

The producer prepares a production financing worksheet that is the basis for the presale plan and the bank financing package.

Throughout the motion picture's development process, global distributor relationships should begin early and intensify with their participation as development proceeds. These relationships should include the U.S. studio, typically providing at least theatrical and video distribution; distributors in the leading international markets; as well as prospective U.S. premium cable and network television licensees. As these relationships advance, it becomes increasingly apparent which of these licensees will enter preproduction licenses.

Except for needing the bank loan collateral, producers would not presell their pictures, as licensees must be motivated with special license considerations to pre-purchase rights. These motivations include acquiring the picture for a lesser license advance than they would negotiate after the picture is completed (typically this discount is up to 20 percent) and taking the picture off the market and away from competing licensees.

Before the producer ever approaches the major international territories for their initial presentation and consideration (see Chapters 1, 3, and 12), the producer will have prepared the first Global Liquidation Analysis for the picture, evaluated the picture in consideration as compared to at least five pictures with similar target audiences and campaign elements, and identified the international distributors with the greatest propensity to garner the highest gross for this picture in their particular territories. These prospective licensees who respond positively to the initial presentation become the representative correspondent distributors for this picture in their particular territories.

If fewer than four distributors in the seven major international territories respond positively and agree to correlate with the producer as the picture continues its development (see the 9 distribution relationship points listed in Chapter 3), then most producers do not commence earnest development. Though there is no license agreement during this time, all the participating distributors will be involved in the development and preproduction of the picture, will represent the picture to the press and the theatrical and ancillary media in their particular territories, and will eventually schedule the picture on their release schedule. The producer will exclusively correspond with and give press, promotion, and advertising materials to these distributors. However, the picture will not be licensed to these distributors until development is close to completion.

At the very first distributor contact, when perhaps the producer has not even acquired the picture's literary rights, these distributors have little motivation to tie up the picture's rights. But as the picture becomes more substantive—with a shooting script, director, cast, locations, production design, film and printed promotion materials, representation at the major markets, firm release dates, and as novelization and other rights mature—each of these distributors becomes increasingly motivated to secure the picture's license for their territory.

The production financing worksheet becomes an extension of the liquidation breakdown and places on paper the various presale scenarios, allowing the producer to select the most advantageous course. This becomes the basis for the presale plan.

Examine the bank financing worksheet in Figure 5.1. This worksheet is for a picture with a production budget of $30 million.

Each loan with its interest will be completely collateralized. The Bank Loan worksheet enables producers to analyze and configure each picture's production funding architecture, early in development, and to adjust the worksheet as the picture matures to the point of production, based on the clarification of each collateral provider. The final worksheet will reflect actual collateral provided and will be part of the Bank Loan Memorandum submitted to the bank for loan approval. This worksheet is configured to deliver the picture $30 million, which is an aggregate of proceeds from the loan, plus cash advances from presold licenses.

The worksheet's first section is entitled "Presale(s) secured with Letter(s) of Credit." This section is a forecast of the total face value of the presale licenses that will be provided to the bank as collateral that are additionally secured with letters of credit. Major licensees do not need to provide this additional security. Typically this collateral category is for mid-range or smaller international territory licensees or North American licensees with limited history or insufficient credit.

This section shows that a total "Observed Value" of these licenses is $15 million. This is not the actual value, as a discount will be applied as an incentive to the licensee to enter this license in advance of the picture's production commencement.

Next, a 5 percent Presale Discount in applied, the net amount of which is the $14.25 million total license amount. The licensee will advance 10 percent of the license

Figure 5.1

Bank Loan Analysis Worksheet

Bank Financing Worksheet
[Picture Title]
[North America Theatrical Distributor's Name]
[Production Company Name(s)]

Assumptions	
Borrowing Period in Months	16
Fully Secured Bank Lending Rate	5.00%
Gap Lending Rate	9.00%
Sale Leaseback Interest Rate	8.00%
Presale Discount Incentive	5.00%
Percent of Sale License Advance	10.00%
Letter of Credit Discount Rate	10.00%
Bankable Contract Discount Rate	10.00%
Unsold Territory Gap Discount Rate	50.00%

Description	Amount	Reference
Presales(s) secured as Letter of Credit		
LC Presales Gross Market Value	$15,000,000	Observed Value of Int'l Territory or N. America Ancillary Licenses
Presale Discount Incentive at 5%	$750,000	Presale Discount Incentive
Gross Transacted License Amount	$14,250,000	Gross Transacted Presale License Amount
License Advance(s)	$1,425,000	10% Cash Advance of the License Amount
Letter(s) of Credit Face Value	$12,825,000	Balance of Presale due upon Delivery
Bank Discount Amount	$1,282,500	10% Risk Discount of Collateral Amount
Net License Amount	$11,542,500	Discounted Collateral before Interest Reserve
Interest Reserve Discount	$726,978	Interest Reserve Discount
Net Loan Value for Production Expenses	$10,815,522	Net Presale Loan Value
Presale(s) secured as Bankable Contracts		
BC Presales Gross Market Value	$8,000,000	Observed Value of Int'l Territory or N. America Ancillary Licenses
Presale Discount Incentive at 5%	$400,000	Presale Discount Incentive
Gross Transacted License Amount	$7,600,000	Gross Transacted Presale License Amount
License Advance(s)	$760,000	10% Cash Advance of the License Amount
Bankable Contract(s) Face Value	$6,840,000	Balance of Presale due upon Delivery
Bank Discount Amount	$684,000	10% Risk Discount of Collateral Amount
Net License Amount	$6,156,000	Discounted Collateral before Interest Reserve
Interest Reserve Discount	$387,722	Interest Reserve Discount
Net Loan Value for Production Expenses	$5,768,278	Net Presale Loan Value
Gap Financing		
Unsold Territories Gross Market Value	$12,000,000	Observed Market Value for Unsold Territory Licenses
Bank Discount Amount	$6,000,000	50% Risk Discount Amount
Gap Financing	$6,000,000	Bank Loan Secured by Unsold Territories*
Gap Interest Reserve	$651,288	Gap Interest
Net Gap Financing for Production Expenses	$5,348,712	Net Gap Loan Value
Tax Shelter & Production Incentives		
Sale Leaseback & Production Incentives	$2,000,000	Gross Value of Sale Leaseback & Production Incentives
Lender Discount Amount	$195,051	8% of Collateral Amount
Net Loan Value for Production Expenses	$1,804,949	Net Loan Amount for S/L & Prod. Incentives
Private Equity		
Private Equity Letter of Credit	$5,000,000	Letter of Credit Provided by Equity Financier's Bank
Bank Discount Amount	$500,000	10% Risk Discount of Collateral Amount
Net Letter of Credit Amount	$4,500,000	Discounted Collateral before Interest Reserve
Interest Reserve Discount	$283,422	Interest Reserve
Net Loan Value for Production Expenses	$4,216,578	Net Loan Value
Production Resources		
Total Net Loan Value for Production Loan	$27,954,040	Total Collateral, Less Discounts and Reserves
Total Loan Interest Expenses Reserved	$2,244,460	Total Amount of Bank Loan Interest Reserved
Cash Collected from License Advances	$2,185,000	10% Cash From License Advances Collected
Total Gross Production Loan and License Proceeds	$30,139,040	Total Available from both the Bank Loan and License Advances
Actual Production Budget (including contingency & interest)	$30,000,000	Physical Production Budget of Picture
Collateral Sufficiency?	Yes	Is There Sufficient Loan Proceeds and License Advances?

amount upon license engagement, in this case, $1,425,000. Most banks in the major international territories have correspondent relationships with the major entertainment bank departments. Though the Letter of Credit language must be "perfected" between the submitting and receiving banks, once this is accomplished, typically the Letter of Credit is applied as collateral at its full face amount, without discount. However, if the issuing bank is small or new (this is rare as most international banks are larger and older than the largest and oldest U.S. banks), then the receiving bank may require a discount on the letter of credit. If so, it is typically .5 to 1 percent, but never more than 10 percent. This example applies a full bank discount. The collateral also must be sufficient to cover the loan's entire interest. This example uses a straight-line interest calculation. The interest reserve used in the final draft of this schedule should come from the calculation from the production budget's cash flow projection/drawdown schedule. After this is applied, this section shows the Net Loan Value of its collateral.

The next collateral section is the same as the first, except that these presales are not secured with letter(s) of credit. Typically these licenses are provided by major international distributors and global networks.

The Gap Financing section sets forth the funds provided by the lending bank collateralized by unsold territories. This amounts to as much as 20 percent of the total production budget, if the production budget is less than $50 million and the unsold territories that collateralize the gap have a forecasted total value of twice the total gap amount. As explained next, as the collateral used for gap financing is not as easily recoupable as the other collateral used; typically these funds are lent at higher rates of interest. In this example, $12 million in expected unsold territory revenues is required to borrow $6 million, with a net loan value of just greater than $5.3 million.

The last two collateral sections provide for scenarios that include sale-leaseback or similar financing and for utilizing financing from private equity sources that use collateral rather than cash. This example uses $2 million in sale-leaseback finance (most often provided through pooling Section 42 and 48 tax legislation-incented sources in the United Kingdom) and $5 million in private equity secured by a letter of credit.

The Production Resources section shows

1. The total net value of the collateral used
2. The total interest reserved within the loan
3. The total liquidity available from the loan proceeds and the license advances that are available to apply against the production budget

In the final analysis at the bottom of the worksheet, the combined license advances and net loan proceeds are sufficient to provide for the $30 million production budget that will include a minimum 10 percent contingency.

Types of Loans

If the production loan is in the form of a line of credit, the producer has access to the entire loan amount but is charged interest only on the loan amount actually drawn. With over $2 million in potential interest, even a 10 percent savings (which is very possible with prudent cash management) will save over $200,000 (the equivalent of a couple of extra visual effect shots during post-production). Draws for a loan of this size may be in minimum increments of six or seven figures each.

Gap Financing

The more sophisticated bank entertainment divisions accommodate gap financing. This financing is based on licenses that are not yet entered. Each bank has a historical international sales matrix that enables them to establish values for unsold territories, predicated on license amounts of the territories already licensed.

Banks customarily will loan up to 20 percent of the production budget, collateralized by all of the remaining unsold territories and rights.

Though the bank loan interest is higher, the producer's advantages to gap financing are primarily that fewer presales are made, allowing higher after-film-completion licenses to be earned from these licensees, and the producer does not have to do the presale work for these territories. Banks participating in gap financing increase their margin of risk. To offset this risk, all remaining international rights to the picture being financed are pledged to the bank as collateral for the loan.

The bank uses two sources to evaluate the unlicensed collateral. The first criterion is at least one (and preferably two but no more than four) presale(s) of the picture from among the seven leading territories. The other is their international sales matrix.

For instance, if the presales totaled $20 million and represented one-third of the presale value for the seven leading territories, the bank could lend against an additional $40 million in collateral value, as $20 million is one-third of $60 million. This additional $40 million is the gap financing collateral.

When to Approach the Bank

Using bank production funding strengthens many aspects of producer operations. The bank relationship and its other related benefits should become very integrated into and affect many aspects of the producer's business.

New producers should meet with their bank of choice even before financing their first development company. Producers should be comfortable with their bank before there is a need for production borrowing. Initial meetings introduce the bank to the producer's business plan, establish the producer's development and production schedule, and clearly show the bank's essential participation in the overall process. Producers should rehearse their commitment to mature participation in the borrowing process, maximizing the ease of loan application and servicing. Unfortunately, this is uncommon, but it is consequently very well received.

Producers should ask the loan officer for permission to use the bank and the officer as a reference to others relative to the producer's intention to use the bank as the production funding source for pictures. Most bank entertainment divisions are willing to allow producers to do this, as long as their representations are in keeping with the relationship. Using the bank as a reference to potential licensees and other sources in connection with the producer's presale plan lends substantial positioning strength, especially for producers introducing new production entities.

Producers should meet with their bank officer about once a month. The bank officer should have the most recent copy of the production company's activity projection (this projection is traditionally for five years, month to month for the first year and annually thereafter).

In addition to production financing and later operating capital funding, bank officers can be well used as business consultants and mentors, contributing excellent business expertise to the production company and opening the way for expanded business relationships.

Chapter Postscript

Banks are vital businesses, eager to expand their customer bases and lending portfolios. Understanding how they operate prepares producers to approach them with confidence and wonderful predictability.

Banks are producers' powerful allies. In addition to production financing and operating capital, they can provide very helpful international and domestic data (useful in many areas, including liquidation breakdowns, international evaluations, international currency, and global industry trends), as well as other information. Producers should engage their bank relationships early and keep them well exercised, as they are vital strategic operating team participants.

Chapter 6

Completion Guarantors

This chapter presents the essential associations producers should have with completion guarantors, and reviews the application process and benefits of an expanded relationship. A completion guarantee sometimes is referred to as a completion bond and is an essential requirement for bank production financing. As is reviewed in Chapter 12, completion guarantors participate fully when engaged by producers during each picture's development, soon after a studio distribution relationship has begun, and after the picture's literary rights have been acquired.

What Completion Guarantees Do

A picture's completion guarantee ensures the lending bank that the bonded picture will be completed on time and within budget constraints. If it isn't, it assures that the guarantor will pay for the related losses. Consequently, the bank does not evaluate the producer's production schedule and budget but relies on the completion guarantor to assure the credibility of these elements.

Completion guarantors are insurers, and the major bonding companies are either owned or backed by large insurance carriers. The completion guarantor, International Film Guarantors, has the largest bonding capacity, bonding pictures with budgets in excess of $100 million. This very professional bonding company is headquartered in Los Angeles, with their guaranty backed by Fireman's Fund insurance carrier. One of the oldest and most well-known insurers is Film Finance. This company is owned by Lloyd's of London, headquartered in London, but its most active office is in Los Angeles. The major guarantors also have sister production insurance organizations owned by their parent insurance company.

Motion picture completion guarantors are highly specialized. To assume the risk of production overruns and completion delays, these companies are classically conservative. They insure a picture whose budget is achievable, incorporate margins for the exceptions that will likely occur, and provide an additional overall contingency.

Producers' Perceived and Real Value of Completion Guarantors

The motion picture industry has a uniquely demanding production process. Producers create new products, one at a time. A producer cannot learn about producing a particular movie (even franchise pictures), and then use this experience to produce the same picture again. Every picture is unique in its production chemistry. Production techniques are sometimes similar from picture to picture, but the above-the-line talent (even if they are the same people), combined with the below-the-line crew and production demands, perform in a substantially different manner each time.

Unit production managers (UPMs) are responsible for planning and quantifying the physical production process in time and costs.

Balanced producers sustain an often painful balance between each of their picture's creative options and its cost. Producers seek production managers who will plan and budget these pictures in a manner that will fulfill the producer's vision. Consequently, the producers also seek and value UPMs who understand and employ economies that allow more production substance to be delivered at less cost. This is a challenging balance to maintain, with many offsets negotiated and often renegotiated for exceptions throughout development and production.

Because of this tightly woven give-and-take planning, negotiating, and budgeting process, some producers resent their relationships with completion guarantors. It isn't that these producers aren't confident in their work. They take meticulous care to achieve a delicate balance between a picture's production quality and its schedule and budget. It is that the producer's sophisticated work is then independently reviewed by the completion guarantor, whose bonding criteria often upset the picture's fragile economy.

Although tradition has it that the only reason a completion guarantor participates in the production process is to facilitate bank financing—and that is the central purpose—guarantors often are and should be invited to contribute more. Each picture's guarantor can be the second set of careful eyes, confirming that the production team, plan, schedule, and budget are sound and achievable. More often than not, the guarantor's observations and suggestions substantially contribute to their picture's overall success.

The guarantor has a fresh evaluation advantage. Guarantors have no political relationships influencing them, so they evaluate from a new, rather than an evolutionary position. Since they often have substantially deeper production review experience than even their most prolific producer clients, they are more current in their references of primary production and performing talent, as well as global costs.

Guarantors should be included in the producer's determination of each picture's director, principal cast, and even department heads. They must keep current on the personal stability and relative performance capacity of all substantial talent. For those about whom they do not possess internal information, they can obtain it from other uniquely expansive and reliable sources. There is no cost for this assistance, and it is exceptionally helpful throughout the planning process. The guarantors will eventually evaluate the bondability of primary talent anyway. It is better to take full advantage of their information when the producer is performing this evaluation—information that can save time and money, and often render these decisions substantially more obvious.

Completion Insurance Relationships

For a business focused on numbers and details, completion guarantors are substantially affected by their producer client attitudes, application approach, and relationship care. It is important for producers to sustain a clear understanding of the operational intent of the completion bond participants.

There are three participating parties: the insurer, the bank, and the producer. These parties participate with a common understanding that, for most pictures—no matter what happens—*the picture will not go into default*. This understanding is the single most influential characteristic of the relationship.

When a picture defaults, the guarantor incurs additional expenses and unwanted production stewardship, and the bank is open not only to potential loan pay-off from sources other than pledged licenses, but also to possible litigation and collection activities. Additionally, the producer must allow the guarantor to assume the governing position in deciding how the picture will be completed and delivered.

Because each participant is substantially motivated to avoid this radical upheaval, completion insurance defaults are rare.

When a picture's schedule or budget or both are threatened, the producers stabilize the problem, if necessary, by revising the collateralized license agreements with new delivery dates, entering and pledging additional presales, if needed, and adjusting the bank loan and completion bond to conform to these changes. This involves sophisticated maneuvering and is made possible by the confidence of all parties in the producer, the picture, and the fairness of their particular participation.

Schedules and budgets that may have appeared to contain egregiously conservative elements prior to production are often embraced as very welcome safety nets during production.

The Completion Bond Package

In qualifying for a bond, the guarantor must become as familiar with the picture and its production as the producer is. The application for a guarantee should reflect the producer's understanding and empathy for this process. The completion bond package should include the following elements:

1. An introductory letter setting forth the picture's title, its total below- and above-the-line budget, its production schedule, the expected guarantee cost,

the anticipated U.S. and leading international territory distributors, the production financing bank and the loan officer's name, and the approximate date the guarantee is needed.

2. A copy of the shooting script (hard copy and disk).
3. A copy of the budget (hard copy and disk).
4. A copy of the script breakdown (hard copy and disk).
5. A copy of the production boards (hard copy and disk).
6. Copies of the major talent deal memos with attachments.
7. References (these are the same as in the bank package discussed in Chapter 5).

To sustain the highest validation integrity, guarantors traditionally prepare their initial planning and budgeting materials exclusively using the shooting script. If their schedules and below-the-line budgets are close to those submitted by the producer, then the producer's budget documentation is reviewed.

If the plans are close, but there are questions, an intermediary meeting with the producer may be set up, or, if it is in keeping with the relationship, with the UPM.

After the review is completed, typically there is a meeting with the producer. At this meeting, the guarantor presents the producer with a provisional acceptance letter. Within or accompanying this letter is a list of items to be resolved to the guarantor's satisfaction before the picture's budget and delivery will be insured. The picture and these provisional items are discussed during this meeting. An acceptance letter is sometimes presented following the guarantor's initial review, but producers should not expect this unless the guarantor has been included in reviewing and responding to questionable issues during the planning and budgeting process.

Some common reasons for provisional letters are:

- Key talent (director or primary cast) are not bondable. Guarantors are necessarily very sensitive to this production aspect. Key talent can cripple a picture. If they are unstable for any reason, they may not be bondable until they restabilize.
- Unstable weather conditions. Most often locations are scouted during a different season than the season of principal photography. In fact, when they are lensed out of natural season, producers can turn the leaves green or amber and crimson, but this problem must be listed in the schedule and budget. Then there are the big items that may occur, like the need to shoot in tropical summer when the picture is scheduled during typhoon season. It is difficult to overcome major weather problems.
- Unstable political or social conditions (insurrection, war, currency problems, and so forth).
- Insufficient time or budget contingencies. Always include a full 10 percent budget contingency.

- Unstable critical talent deal memos or contracts (ability for talent to abandon their commitment for ambiguous reasons, such as benefits or accommodations too sophisticated for the producer's predictable delivery, etc.).

Completion Insurance Cost

Producers typically allow three percent for completion bond expense in their budgets, but usually negotiate less. Producers can suggest bond structures that reduce the insurers' risk and increase their volume, which result in some producers paying close to half of what is commonly budgeted.

Completion insurance is competitive, and although new companies regularly enter the game, just as many bow out. The result is few participants, and they must be acceptable to the lending bank.

Like banks, these insurers specialize in pictures with differing budget ranges. Some insure pictures with six- to mid-seven-figure budgets; others with mid-seven to low-eight figures, and the largest companies insure mid-eight- to low-nine-figure budgeted pictures.

Chapter Postscript

Completion guarantors are essential participants for producers in the production of their pictures. They are sophisticated organizations that reaffirm and often refine a producer's production plan. These organizations are best utilized if invited to participate early, thus facilitating many development and preproduction processes, including talent evaluation, bondability, and banking. When understood and used effectively, completion insurers are welcome production allies who contribute consistently and positively to each picture's production.

Attorneys, Negotiations, and Entertainment Law

This is an introduction to the relationship producers ought to have with their attorneys and associated firms, how producers should participate in negotiating and documenting, the processes that can limit and protect against litigation, and the very valuable extended benefits available to producers from their attorneys and firms.

Attorneys and Their Firms

There are several excellent entertainment law firms, most of which are head-quartered in New York and Los Angeles. Some of these are large, multilocation, multifloored firms; some are full-service, one-location firms; and others are specialized, boutique firms. Large firms are not better than small firms or vice versa. The critical factor is the right attorney, in the right firm, who is well matched to the producer's needs and moral compass.

A producer's attorney should be, and typically is, involved in the producer's creative, business, and legal activities. In other words, the attorney is substantially involved in most aspects of a producer's work.

Seasoned entertainment attorneys bill in the mid-three figures per hour, junior attorneys in the low-three figures. This is not a relationship to be penurious with. A producer's new-contact credibility, capacity to reach every talent and global distributor, and ability to negotiate fair terms and to protect him- or herself are all largely affected by the attorney's industry standing.

It is always best to engage in a relationship with an attorney who has become a well-known presence in the entertainment industry. For the most part, these are also the attorneys who have the experience and understanding that renders them valuable counselors and advisors in all significant business and legal activities. They may also provide exceptional creative counsel. Producers deliver all appropriate matters to their attorney. In turn, their attorney may assign less sophisticated matters to junior attorneys and staff.

Attorneys and the firms they are associated with should be evaluated separately. Simply being represented by a lead entertainment law firm such as Loeb & Loeb (the largest entertainment law firm) has a substantial value. It may not be that the senior level attorney within this firm is the producer's designated attorney, but even a junior attorney will have access to the firm's impressive team of powerful legal icons. Attorneys have access to the full service capacities of their firms, including securities, contract, litigation, and business, as well as creative packaging talent. Additionally, many of these larger firms have offices in global business centers where producers may need them most. Further, producers have an instant sociability (and consequently more direct access) with their firms' substantive clients.

Producers should settle into a relationship with a law firm and an attorney who functions at optimum for their particular needs. There is a balance of benefits that should be obtained. The smaller the firm, the more important the producer's relationship with it. There are several boutique firms with high-profile partners who are powerhouse attorneys to their producer clients. It is not even essential for a producer's firm to be full-service. For instance, if a particular firm does not provide securities work, it may supervise another firm to accomplish this work and fulfill its client's needs in a manner not much different from using another department within a full-service firm.

The following are a producer's most important considerations in evaluating and selecting entertainment law relationships:

1. Does the attorney have a recognizable, positive reputation in the entertainment industry? Does the attorney communicate pleasantly and clearly with the producer? Does the attorney understand the producer's objectives? Is this person committed to supporting the producer in accomplishing these goals?
2. Does the law firm have a recognizable and positive reputation in the entertainment industry? Is it a full-service firm, or are the firm's services able to address the primary needs of the production company?
3. Do the firm's clients have a business sociability that is complementary to the producer's business?

Producers Performing as Attorneys

Producers should never perform the legal aspects of their business without the experience and counsel of their attorney. Having said this, producers should understand that they will be pressed, almost continually, into activities that will demand their knowledge of entertainment law. Further, it is not practical or affordable for producers to have their attorney with them all the time. Consequently, they must obtain a basic understanding of entertainment law to prevent compromising their production company's negotiating power and legal protection. Contract law is the dominant area of law with which producers are most involved. It is no accident that many very powerful producers have either obtained law degrees in preparation for their careers or have hired in-house counsel.

A producer's best legal preparation is a law degree, but even this is not a satisfactory substitute for experience. A producer's first five years should be spent under the tutelage and coaching of his or her attorney. This is expensive only until it is compared with the damages that may occur without the benefit of very involved counsel throughout this time.

Almost everything a producer does has substantial legal consequences. Does this sound paranoid? It isn't. The industry is riddled with stories of overconfident, easygoing producers who were either tossed up like tennis balls and whacked out of the industry, or were severely bludgeoned, both financially and emotionally, before they learned this important lesson: Producers are almost *always* involved in conversations and correspondence about potential relationships. These are contract-related experiences for which producers are particularly held legally accountable. Suits are levied against producers that to them may appear to be ridiculous nuisance suits. These suits eventually come to trial through very congested court systems (especially in New York and Los Angeles), one or two years later. Depositions of verbal conversations overheard by people whom the producer may not even recall were present, along with notes on napkins and casual letters the producer didn't consider or intend to be binding, may be used as evidence.

Producers should ask for and keep copies of everything. When asked if they would like a copy, producers should always answer affirmatively, and then file it.

As with most other responsibilities in life, *experience* in legal affairs increases our power to manage them. However, prior to this experience, if an attorney is not deeply involved in the producer's early-career legal affairs, the producer may make multiple, very expensive, wrong moves.

Contract law is especially slippery and powerful until the language is understood. Verbal representations can be binding, and contract law language definitions do not necessarily correspond with dictionary definitions. What a producer says and writes, hears and receives—whether the producer intends for an item to be binding or not—may be used as contract evidence. Further, it may even mean something quite different from what the producer meant to communicate. Producers must become aware of those communications they engage in that are contract relative.

Producers should:

- Study all phases of entertainment law, particularly contract law (there are several excellent books on entertainment law).
- Have their attorney present during key negotiations.
- Review with and be coached by their attorney for meetings they may attend without their attorney.
- Immediately report everything potentially litigious to their attorney.

- Have their attorney prepare most deal documentation.
- Send all other in-house prepared documentation to their attorney for review before it is used.

Negotiating

The only good agreement is one that is fair to all parties. Getting excited about acquiring something for less than its value is a sure sign of impoverished ethics. Everyone is best served when the deal is balanced to the contributions of all participants.

The all-too-common negotiating scenario is played out by participants who often indelicately demand more for their respective position than is fair. These negotiations are fiery, confrontational, and most often end with all parties feeling shortchanged and, unhappily, distanced from one another.

Fortunately, this does not always occur. There are producers who refuse to engage in negotiations in this fashion, and they find talent, agents, and attorneys willing participants, though initially they may be understandably suspicious.

It is in the best interests of the producer determined to set the pace toward a gentler path to take hold of this alternative negotiating style and use it. In the final analysis, after production and primary distribution of a picture are concluded, this approach consistently ends up being more financially advantageous than the "me first, you whatever" approach to deal making.

There are three vital principles that should be applied to every negotiation and deal-making relationship that a producer enters into. These principles may be thought of as follows.

- The universal approach to deal making
- The negotiations that are on the same side of the desk
- The decision to weigh a deal in proportion to the scope of the picture

The "universal approach" requires simply looking at the deal without preference to a single party, aggressively considering what is fair from all parties' points of view, and then negotiating to secure the best position for each participant. This approach is often easily derailed by one or more party taking the common "car-buying" position—starting at a higher position than is fair, and still expecting the negotiation to end above what they should reasonably receive. The relationship poison associated with the car technique is that even if this party ends up with a greater than fair portion, they still may be discontented that they did not get even more.

"Getting on the same side of the desk" is waiting to negotiate until all parties are working for the good of the picture. Putting the picture first naturally allies the participants, all working together for a common objective. This helps motivate the "universal approach," in which all parties clearly see that from the picture's perspective, the producer is not more important than screenwriter, or the screenwriter than the director, and so on. This puts the negotiators in position to consider the deal elements in light of what is fair and most beneficial for the particular picture.

The process of "weighing the deal to the picture" can be accomplished only by balanced producers. This is especially helpful when negotiating deals with potential profit participants. The producer uses the picture's liquidation breakdown and budget to reassess a lucrative cash-only deal as a percentage of the producer's gross profit less the picture's budget. This process is done typically only for the most substantial contributors to the picture, namely, the writer, director, and principal acting talent. This analysis tends to cast a very constructive deal-making light on the negotiations. It renders an exceptional deal orientation when participants confidentially review and thoroughly understand these numbers and relate them to their own position. For instance, if a picture has a projected, after negative recoupment, producer's gross of $30 million, and the cash-only directors fee is $3 million, this percentage "weight" is 10 percent. The participating point application should not be proportional to the fee amount, as there are risks and time-related-to-point income. With this ratio as a reference, this example could yield the director a $2 million fee plus five points. If the picture achieves its projections, this agreement will provide the director with another $500,000, compared with the fee-only relationship—that, along with long-term earnings from the picture's continuing rights sales. The plus-points terms also deepen the director's relationship with the picture, naturally motivating the director to make the greatest contribution possible in creating the film.

Using this approach to deal making strengthens each individual relationship and establishes a universal integrity among all participants. No one believes another talent cut a better deal because they negotiated more shrewdly. Rather, there is a spirit of fair play and common good. Perhaps the audience won't recognize the source, and this is never the sole reason for a picture's success, but this has a substantial resonant effect on all participants, the work they do, the level of sanity sustained, and consequently, on the picture itself.

How is this achieved? The producer is largely responsible for setting the tone of every relationship. When producers focus first on the picture along with the universal application of the fairness of the deal to all parties, they always influence all other parties associated with the deal. If they haven't dealt with the producer before, agents, attorneys, and business managers initially may be suspicious of this approach. However, it is our experience that engaging these principles has an exceptionally positive effect on establishing solid relationship foundations and arriving at deal parameters that are of high integrity and as close as possible to being unshakable.

Vital Legal Aspects Relating to the Story

A producer's first and continuing stewardship is to discover stories worth telling as motion pictures; then to evaluate, acquire, develop, produce, and liquidate them. Literary rights searches, property reviews, negotiations, acquisitions, and rewrites are a roiling pot of potential litigation!

Literary Releases

Writing is the genius art. Skilled writers may complete five finished screenplay pages a day. For them, a screenplay may represent several weeks of research and five to eight weeks of writing for the first draft, which may be 20 to 50 drafts from being ready to actually submit. If this is a "spec" script, this typically will represent at least three to six months of work and perhaps much more. Such a literary property is potentially worth six or seven figures. The screenplay is the writer's most valuable asset and must be protected.

However, the protection issues relating to stories appear much different from a producer's perspective. A producer's literary department may review an average of 30 property submissions per week. These come in a variety of forms and typically from a variety of sources. A story department may have two very similar stories come through on the same day, from completely unrelated sources. Topical stories may even have several similar submissions during the same month.

The stories most sought after are those that scream to be told and are well written, emotionally-charged page-turners that appeal to at least one major target audience, and contain driving campaign elements for its targets. There are substantial resources available for the acquisition of literary properties with these qualities. Unfortunately, most stories fall into one of the following three categories, from most to least prevalent:

1. Stories that are poorly written and not worth being told.
2. Stories that are well written but not worth being told.
3. Stories worth being told that are not well written.

The third category is the stories most often optioned and put into story development.

Studios and successful production companies are excellent negotiators for literary rights. They are well funded and often prepared to spend more than a fair amount to purchase the all-too-rare great properties. They have every motivation to acquire material from writers—yes, especially first-time writers—employing ethical and respectful business practices. They do not and will not steal stories. In the unfortunate and rare instances when individuals working for these companies are found abusing the creative trust and operating policies of these organizations, they are immediately released.

Most writers find it difficult to empathize with the producer's liability position associated with reviewing such a sea of properties. Indeed, many of these scripts are not read past the fourth or fifth page.

Before submitting their material, writers protect themselves by a variety of means, only to be presented with a literary release letter before studios and producers will accept their material or pitch. These letters substantially limit the writer's legal recourse against the producer and, in their various versions, the writer releases the reviewing producer from legal liability, under certain conditions, and from using "material containing features similar to or identical with those contained in" the material submitted by the writer.

Some writers complain that this gives producers license to steal their material. In fact, these letters substantially limit the legal recourse of the writer. But without literary release letters, producers would be subject to relentless litigation.

A copy of a sample literary release letter is shown in Figure 7.1, as well as on the CD accompanying this book. After a review, it should be abundantly clear why writers may be reluctant to sign. However, considering the high volume of story material reviewed by producers, the similarity between many of these stories and the predominance of rejections, it becomes clear that producers must adhere to this fundamental legal process for their own protection.

Figure 7.1
Sample Literary Release Letter

Submission Release Agreement

Date

(Party Submitting To)
(Their Address)

RE: (Title of property)
Dear Sir/Madam:

I realize that many ideas, programs, slogans, scripts, plans, suggestions, and other literary and/or dramatic and/or musical material (hereinafter, for convenience collectively referred to as "material"), which are submitted to you, are similar to material previously used, previously submitted by others, or already under consideration by you. I further realize that you must protect yourself against any unwarranted claims by refusing to examine any material submitted to you unless you are assured that you shall have the unqualified right to finally determine whether such material or any part thereof is in fact used by you or your successors, assignees, or licensees, and what compensation or consideration, if any, should be paid for such use.

I am submitting certain material to you herewith. In order to induce you to consider this material, I hereby irrevocably waive, release, and relinquish any and all claims that I or any person, firm, or corporation claiming under or though me, may now or hereafter have against you, your successors, assignees, or licensees, and your and their respective officers, employees, and representatives, for any use or alleged use, that you, or your successors, assignees, or licensees may make of any such material. I also expressly agree that your decisions as to whether you, or your successors, assignees, or licensees have used all or any part of such material and as to the compensation or other consideration, if any, which should be paid to me therefore, shall be conclusive and binding upon me and all persons, firms, and corporations claiming under or through me. In the event that I bring any claim in violation of the foregoing sentence, I shall reimburse you for your costs and attorneys' fees in defending such claim, along with any damages you may suffer as the result of such claim.

Figure 7.1 *continued*
Sample Literary Release Letter

I further understand and agree that you are not responsible for the return of any material submitted, and I acknowledge that I have retained a duplicate copy of such material in my possession.

Very truly yours,

(Signature)

(Print name)

(Address)   (Telephone/e-mail)

Relationship to material (i.e., Author, Producer):

Brief story/concept/idea description:

The Step Deal

Writing is a very delicate craft. Consider this scenario. Writer "A" recently won the Best Screenplay Academy Award for a romantic comedy script. A producer has had a promising meeting with this writer to creatively perform a major rewrite of a romantic comedy script optioned by the producer. A relationship is negotiated satisfactory to all parties, is documented, and the writer commences. The producer is enthusiastic to see the script. The writing proceeds on schedule. Two months pass, and the producer receives the first draft. The producer rated the writer's previous Academy Award winning script a 9 out of 10. The producer rates this first draft as a 4 out of 10. The producer and writer have a tense but seemingly productive story meeting. The producer is convinced that the writer now embraces the fire of the story the producer wants to tell.

Three weeks later the new property has been substantially rewritten, but it is no closer than the original draft to what the producer envisions. Two more increasingly tense meetings take place, each without an improved draft. The drafts are different but not any better in the producer's eyes. After three drafts, everyone is testy and uneasy. The writer has worked diligently, probably employing the maximum craft possible on this story. The producer realizes that this writer will never write the story needed. Sadly for the producer, next year, this same writer will author another romantic comedy script that, in the producer's evaluation, will be a 10 out of 10.

I have seen this happen many times. With some stories, exceptional writers may not be able to exercise their considerable craft to the producer's satisfaction. This rarely has to do with the writer's effort and diligence; rather, it is often simply that the writer and story do not connect. Although this may not happen even half the time, it happens enough for producers to approach relationships with writers in a fashion that facilitates the best experience possible.

In the preceding example, the writer and producer entered into their relationship with good intentions, but now a new writer must be engaged, and fees, writing credits, and other deal points must be renegotiated to accommodate the new relationship. This forces the restructuring of the development schedule. Because of the additional development time and writing fees, development and production budgets increase. Further, the original writer renegotiation is typically uncomfortable, and because the writing budget was not configured to accommodate two writers, the new writer negotiation is often entered with less advance cash than the original development plan.

Because of this common phenomenon, producers protect themselves from these time and legal exigencies through entering "step relationships" with writers. Step relationships compartmentalize the writing processes into progressive steps. Each step has a fixed fee value and provides for evaluation and complete pre-agreed-upon exit remedies that allow the producer to be able to terminate the relationship following the review of each initial step.

Following positive creative meetings, perhaps three writers will enter individual step relationships and independently begin writing. It is essential to the integrity of the relationship that the writers know that multiple writers are being used.

The agreement's first step typically calls for the writers to author a synopsis of the story. Whether or not their synopsis is acceptable to the producer, the writers are all paid for their work. If a synopsis is not accepted from one writer, that writer does not proceed. Depending on the terms of the step deal, that writer may not receive any writing credit.

The writers whose synopses are accepted then author a comprehensive treatment of the story. It is possible that all the writers will proceed with this step. Again, the writers are paid for their treatments, regardless of their acceptance. If particular drafts are not acceptable, a writer may not proceed and may not receive any writing credits in the film.

Typically, following the treatment, there is a single writer selected to continue with the final relationship step and write the screenplay. If there are characters, a subordinate story line, dialogue, or other elements the producer wants continued to be developed by one of the other writers for eventual use in the screenplay, there may be a good-faith negotiation with that originating writer to become a cowriter along with the primary writer of the screenplay.

Producers should always do their best to enter step writing deals, even if it is with a single author. This relationship allows for reevaluation at each step and prevents costly renegotiations. This does not imply lack of confidence in the author. It clearly indicates the producer's seasoned understanding of the delicate fundamentals of the writing craft and the preparations necessary to manage this relationship propitiously.

Multiple-author step writing deals always are initially more expensive than single-author relationships. But they may actually cost less in the long run, especially if the original single-author relationship does not succeed.

If there is one place a producer should risk overspending, it is on the story. Producers are best served by a multiple-writer step agreement approach to screenplay development. This prevents the high probability of being pushed off schedule and over budget, and assures that the writers will have crafted the ultimate story.

Literary Greenlight Review

After producers discover literary properties they are interested in, they proceed through a development phase before they are prepared to option or acquire it. This period is called the producer's "internal greenlight" of each project (see Chapters 1 and 12).

Prior to outside participation in the analysis of the story of a proposed picture, producers should receive written permission from the story's author before they refer to the story in any way to anyone outside the producer's organization.

A simple deal memo should be prepared. This letter should express the producer's interest in the property and willingness to invest in a creative and marketing review to discover the viability of the producer's eventual acquisition of the story. The letter should state that the producer is prepared to proceed with this investment pending the writer's approval. In this memo, the producer warrants that the approach to creating a motion picture from the writer's story and its title may be confidentially discussed with a limited number of commercial partners relative to their interest in the eventual distribution of the proposed picture. The producer further warrants that representations will clearly be made that the story rights have not yet been optioned or acquired by the producer, that this is exclusively an evaluation inquiry, and that these meetings will not at all be related to the financing of the picture or the acquisition of the property. The producer acknowledges that this nonexclusive evaluation will not continue longer that a set time (for instance, five months) and may be terminated within 24 hours of the writer's written request to the producer, for any reason.

This deal memo protects the writer and producer from misunderstandings and clearly sets forth the speculative, arm's-length nature of the relationship. It serves as well to warm the writer and agent to the producer's serious interest in the property.

Literary Rights Option/Acquisition

After a picture has obtained the critical in-house greenlight, the first development move is to acquire the rights to the literary property.

If a literary review memo is in force, an initial rapport will already have been established among the producer, the writer, the agent, and/or the attorney.

Mature production companies have internal development funds, allowing them to negotiate and acquire or option properties in a more unregulated fashion than new producers, who may be using development funds from investors for a fixed number of pictures. Whichever is the case, the producer's best approach to deal making is to reveal the production company's position to the writer and/or the agent.

The picture already will have a summarized budget, prepared during the internal greenlight. This budget's story allocation should represent the producer's estimation of a fair acquisition price for the property. This should be affected by how closely the property being acquired resembles the actual shooting script of the picture. The majority of scripts purchased represent little more than a compelling story concept. Many writers are excellent imagineers but not very skilled screenwriters. A separate, detailed story budget, which reflects a conservative and predictable activity and expense schedule for taking the acquired story to a shooting script, should be prepared. These projections should be the centerpiece of the acquisition agreement.

There are two budgets typically at play in this process. The development budget has a fixed elasticity for the option advance. The production budget has a more flexible capacity for the actual acquisition payment(s).

The genesis writer may participate in a step writing arrangement with other writers—the difference being that the genesis writer will have continuing benefits that will not be offered to the other step-deal writers.

Each writer will need payment allocations relative to his or her option/development payments and balance/production payments. The producer has development funding sufficient to pay for option advances and will have substantially more funding through production financing to pay the balance.

The originating writer, together with all other participants, benefits the most upon the picture's successful development. This results, in everyone's principal photography payday, in the picture's successful production, and in everyone's creative satisfaction, fame, and increased value of their craft.

Achieving a successful greenlight is no small feat. Producers should move into the literary rights negotiation with a clear understanding of the creative and global earnings potential of the pictures. They should be further motivated by the fact that their distributors are looking for positive reassurance that their pictures are in active development. Producers want, of course, to realize benefits from the initial development time and money invested. However, first time producers are subject to the check and balance realities of fixed development budgets.

The success of most negotiations are dependent upon these crucial elements:

1. The strength of the story. The stronger the story, the more easily the negotiations go.
2. The flexibility of development and production budgets. If development funds are exceptionally tight, production payouts should more than proportionally increase to offset the front-end shortfall.
3. The strength of the producer and other creative players. Everyone wants to play on a winning team. A strong story, along with a powerful director and/or producer, will have a drawing effect on all other elements.
4. The initial global enthusiasm for the picture. The findings of the in-house greenlight should be shared with all primary participants. The stronger this evidence, the greater will be each player's enthusiasm.

5. The willingness of the negotiating parties to be flexible between the deal points. Everything should equal out. Deal points, for any number of reasons, are rigid. If this creates an unfair position for a participant, then other deal points should be added or increased. If all parties are determined to move the pieces until they are fair and acceptable to each participant, then the deal gets made.

The option agreement includes all the acquisition deal points and all the specifics pertaining to reoptioning the property. This allows the relationship for future good-faith negotiations to proceed without hesitation.

Typically, producers deal with literary agents in the negotiation and acquisition of properties. First-sale screenwriters who are not represented by an agent are especially vulnerable during the deal-making process. Therefore, such relationships are always best served if the producer acts as a protector and tutor and even overcompensates to offset the writer's susceptible position. First-sale screen-writers may have a script similar in creative value to that of a more experienced writer, but since they are new to the bargaining table, they may be paid less for their property. Nevertheless, they should receive a full measure of all the benefits they are due.

Deal Memos, Letter Agreements, and Long Form Contracts

Of the three forms of deal documentation, deal memos are by far the most prevalent form used for most of the producer's relationships. In fact, many relationships never require documentation beyond the original deal memo. Often longer, more formal documents are in the process of being negotiated, but negotiations become protracted, pictures get completed, and finally, it is the deal memo that remains the only document defining the relationship. The notable exceptions are most U.S. distribution and license agreements, which typically are done in the long form.

Deal Memos

Deal memos are the workhorse deal documents of the entertainment industry. These typically come in letter form, originating on the producer's letterhead and containing the following information:

1. Identification of the parties involved in the deal.
2. What each party is specifically contributing to the relationship.
3. What they get for their contributions.
4. Anything else relating to the basic understanding of the parties.
5. Any specific representations from the parties, examples being "I am the sole, original author," or "There are no liens or encumbrances."
6. The county and state of legal jurisdiction.
7. How disputes will be settled.
8. When the deal will be in force.
9. A place for the parties to acknowledge by signature that the deal is acceptable to them, along with a signature date. Although deal memos often

contain some casual letter language, they are very enforceable contracts and are contract-language structured.

Letter Agreements

These agreements are more formalized than deal memos. They are also prepared on the producer's letterhead and are in letter form, but they use more formal contract language, though in a more relaxed format than long-form contracts. These agreements typically use contract titles (Bruce Joel Rubin, herein "Writer"), and contain limited casual letter remarks. The nine contract elements referenced in the previous deal memo are included in the letter agreement, but in more formal contract language.

Long Form Agreements

These agreements are printed on neutral-party blank white paper. They use an agreement title at the beginning and are written to equally express the position of all participants. These documents are in full agreement dress and use formal contract language. They are long, often impressive by their sheer weight, and, frankly, many times the girth is extremely helpful when troubles arise.

The Benefits Associated with the Producer Preparing Deal Documentation

As negotiations come to a close, one of the deal-making parties will take the responsibility to prepare the first-draft deal documentation. Producers should never succumb to the temptation of allowing someone else to prepare this documentation on the basis that it would be one less thing they need to do, or that it may save their legal fees. The document origination benefits far outweigh any other considerations.

Whether prepared by the producer or by the producer's attorney, this allows the producer the opportunity to encounter and deal with deal elements that will reveal themselves in the detail of documenting that were not dealt with between the parties. This enables the producer's deeper understanding of the deal's architecture and allows the producer to establish the deal-making integrity between the parties.

Deal Reviews

One of the best ways for producers to learn contract language and to interpret all forms of deal documentation is for them to review and annotate documents before they meet with their attorneys.

One of the most efficient review techniques is called *line-outs*. This may seem tedious, but the producer should head up a separate sheet of paper or open individual computer files for each participating party and another sheet or file headed *Questions*.

Starting with the first line of the agreement, the producer should check to see if the production company name appears first and is correct. If so, he should draw a line through it. If it says, "herein producer," he should write "producer" at the top of the "us" sheet and then cross the phrase out. If the other party's name is next and it is the same as what he thought it was, he should cross it out and proceed to their "herein" reference. The producer then writes it at the top of their page and then crosses it out on the agreement.

The producer should continue with the entire agreement, heading up new pages or opening new files for each deal point, and then write down each deal point on the sheet that applies to it, with page and paragraph references. Language that has a unique "contract" sense about it (for instance, "not unreasonably withheld," "best efforts," or "favored nations") should, if it is unfamiliar to the producer, be listed on the Questions page with page and paragraph references.

When the producer has completed the entire agreement, he should review all the pages. If there are elements that appear out of harmony with the producer's understanding, notes should be made of these. It is at this point that the producer is ready for the attorney meeting, should ask his questions, review concerns, and direct his attorney to prepare an appropriate response.

This process of line-outs usually goes very quickly and reveals everything important to know about the deals in process. Remember, there are no unimportant phrases or words. Producers should find out what they mean. They may be benefits or pitfalls important to the deal.

The Attorney as Counsel

Some time ago we had a preliminary relationship closed between a producer client and a distributor for an animated feature. The deal was warmly received by both parties, and a precontract closing meeting was arranged. The attorneys substantially took over the meeting, and, within a half day, had all but ruined the good feelings between the parties. At that point, documenting the deal appeared improbable.

One of the attending producers was an amazingly creative writer and animator. He slipped us a sketch. It was a picture of a cow. We were pulling its horns, the distributors pulling at its tail, and the two attorneys were underneath the cow, milking.

This is a bit unfair, as the attorneys for both sides were doing their aggressive best to achieve the finest deal and the greatest protection for their respective clients. However, the picture serves as an excellent reminder that although it important for the actual parties of agreements to allow their attorneys to make their contributions, those parties should continue to sustain control and responsibility for their relationships and transactions.

Attorneys are often the voice of their producer clients. Consequently, it is always appropriate for producers to apologize to other deal participants if their attorneys say something damaging to those with whom they are dealing. Producers should be careful to treat their attorneys with respect, especially in front of others. If producers want to redirect a meeting, it is most appropriate for producers to stop the meeting, take a break with their counsel, and then reconvene, moving in the direction they have decided, in light of their attorney's advice.

Dispute Resolutions

Every form of documentation should declare how disputes should be resolved, if they arise. The primary choices are mediation, arbitration, or litigation.

If the document simply states that it will be governed according to the laws of a certain state, then disputes will be settled by traditional litigation. In major metropolitan areas, because these matters will not be heard for months, this could be very expensive to resolve and the outcome determined by judgments of fact, legal points, and case precedents that may be substantially disassociated with what is a fair resolution by either party's evaluation.

Either of the other two options, arbitration or mediation, referred to by the court systems as ADR (Alternative Dispute Resolution), are preferred by most producers.

The more formalistic of the two ADR methods is arbitration. This process calls for a mutually agreed upon or appointed arbiter (or arbiters) to hear the case, much like a judge who makes a determination that the parties have agreed in advance they will adhere to.

Perhaps the most effective and exercised entertainment industry arbitration organization is The American Film Marketing Association's Arbitration Tribunal, which serves the entire film industry and is serviced mostly by attorneys or retired judges.

For many disputes, the best resolution is mediation. A mediator is like an arbiter, except a mediator explores the issues. There is a resolution only if both sides agree to a suggested proposal. Mediated cases differ most substantially from litigation and arbitration in that there are no winners or losers. Both sides participate in the solution. Both must agree, and the solution often improves the relationship between the parties or at least provides for a future one. Though some become protracted, most mediated issues are settled in one day.

Chapter Postscript

The development, production, and liquidation of motion pictures engages the producer continually in the process of representations, negotiations, and documentation. The producer's attorney should be thoroughly involved in the producer's business. Consequently the selection and use of an attorney and law firm are critical factors in the producer's success and protection. Further, the producer should be deeply involved and increasingly experienced in all manner of legal matters.

Chapter 8

Talent, Agents, and Agencies

This chapter reviews the delicate business aspects associated with producers' relationships with each picture's talent and their representatives. Two effective metaphors for the relationship between a picture's producer and its talent are the relationships that exist between a general contractor of a construction project and the craftspeople, or a symphony's conductor and the orchestra.

Like a general contractor, the best producers are very familiar with, and consequently respectful of, the many talents necessary to create their pictures. The talent will have all, if not more, of the creative juice than these producers originally conceive. Writers, directors, cinematographers, actors, composers, set designers, UPMs, editors, assistant directors (ADs), costumers, make-up, casting directors, TRANSPORTATION (on our computers this always prints in capital letters), special effects, and many other critically important people contribute their measure of brilliance to each picture.

Each of these talents is like a subcontractor in many respects. They maintain independent relationships with the producer—each responsible for performing according to the terms of the relationship—and contribute a crucial service that affects the rest of the picture.

Further, just as a building project would be hurt if the general contractor personally handled the plumbing, electrical, or some other building aspect, so would producers hurt their film project if they didn't delegate their producing responsibilities, such as directing, acting, or editing to others.

The producer/talent relationship is also like an orchestra whose performers must be sensitive to each other in addition to the conductor. At certain moments, the brass section has to sound like one overwhelming instrument, not the trumpet section sounding distinct from the baritones or the French horns from the trombones. Brilliance, if it is out of harmony with other creative elements, fails miserably. A stunning set design that is incongruous with its story's action, costumes, and color, is counterproductive to the picture. The producer, like the conductor, must balance all the many elements of the picture in order to create the finest achievable product. Even during principal photography, though all eyes must be on the director, the director is also a talent who was brought into the picture by the holder of the ultimate baton, the independent producer. As with a symphonic performance, the producer also must have the attention, commitment, and loyalty of all the talent.

Great motion pictures are created by a team of artists who contribute their private interpretation, within the story universe and parameters provided by the producer, and are harmonically tempered by all other immediate craft providers. For a producer to engage such a team of talent may seem improbable. Doing it well consistently, under the inevitable pressure that accompanies every picture's creation, is a clear indication of seasoned genius. Steady-handed veteran producers like Richard Donner, Sydney Pollack, and Ron Howard consistently select, inspire, and negotiate great talent teams for their pictures. These producers commence from a foundation of respecting their cocreators and treating them fairly, which naturally draws the best from them.

Creation in its most celebrated form is both intimate and delicate. Losing oneself in the work and celebrating in the personal and collective triumphs is possible largely because of the temper and tenor of the producer. The producer establishes the universe in which everyone works. When producers are committed, skillful, valiant, wise, grateful, patient, merciful, generous, and capable of being a good friend, then the wrenching, chaotic frenzy that seems to necessarily settle in on the creation of motion pictures can actually be sweet when it is thought back upon.

This chapter focuses on the business aspects of the fragile and crucial task producers undertake to engage talent relationships that stir their enthusiasm for the story, give them the creative freedom to perform, and motivate them both creatively and financially to give the ultimate expression of the story's entertainment fire.

The Relationship Evolution

Since writers were discussed in Chapter 7, this chapter will consider other talent relationships, especially those involving directors and principal actors.

Director and principal cast selection usually commences before the conclusion of the first story read. This search intensifies during the internal greenlight, becoming more informed as studio responses are discussed during the first picture meetings with them. After the literary rights have been acquired, it then becomes a keenly focused, studied experience. At this time, prior pictures of prospective talent are screened and studied in context of the picture in development, and discussions with the producers concerning these referenced pictures become important sources of information.

Directors, then actors, are listed in the order of the producer's preference. This is done prior to global distributor director meetings, and in the next round, distributor actor meetings. It is uncommon for these studios to unanimously agree on the producer's choices of directors or actors. The two primary purposes of these talent-studio meetings are to inform the producer relative to the marketing and relationship advantages that each person being considered could bring to each major territory, and to advance each distributor's commitment through each one's participation in the selection process. During these meetings, the producer's discoveries are presented to the studios—sometimes with video clips—demonstrating the craft and various advantages of each talent.

Following these meetings, the producer reevaluates the talent in the light of the distributors' responses and configures the final producer talent list. This list is confidentially presented to them, detailing the factors that moved the producer to this configuration. Producers should have five or more selections on their acting and directing lists. More often than not, the producer's first choices end up being the top three selections of each of the participating distributors.

Meetings with Talent and Agents

Agents deliver many essential benefits to their talent clients. Among them are negotiating and documenting fair deals and assisting their clients in both the search and evaluation of pictures that will advance their careers.

Creative protectionist producers are classically undercapitalized. One of the consequences of this chronic condition is their aggressive attempts to attach talent to their pictures without the agents' participation, or to represent that talent are attached before the producer, in fact, has a documented relationship. These predeal attachments most often are used to assist these producers in their attempt to obtain production funding for their pictures.

There are many more creative protectionist producers than balanced producers. Consequently, many creative meetings are setups for clients who become entangled in a litany of abuses associated with stories that usually are never made into motion pictures. Agents have, therefore, become fierce guardians of their clients against the several easy abuses associated with this approach. As a consequence, agents save their clients from misrepresentation and having to defend associated legal actions.

Because balanced producers have both development funding and use bank production financing, they have no motivation to set up predeal talent representations. However, they are substantially motivated by other benefits to set up talent creative meetings before deal meetings.

Because each motion picture is a new story, a unique creation and a new business venture, its producers must assemble a new team of cocreators to deliver their independent and harmonic blend of craft and capacity. Therefore, producers need to test each major talent's creative affinity for the picture before negotiating the financial aspects of the relationship. Producers want to know, in strict confidence, whether a particular director or actor has both the vision and passion essential for a critically important creative contribution for the picture in question. So it is during this process that the producer and talent must "fall in love" around a picture. It's comparatively easy to agree on a convenient schedule and monetary amounts, but, if this is the primary basis for the relationship, it yields a thin, incomplete foundation among the picture, the talent, and the producer.

Most producer/talent creative meetings are delicate, especially if they are a first-time alliance. Fortunately these meetings are often accomplished with the cooperation and blessing of their respective agents. If not, producers should be prepared for a well-deserved, testy agent response.

If, for any reason, there is a meeting with talent before an agent is called to participate, the producer should immediately assure the talent and agent in writing that:

1. No representation will be made to anyone outside the production company that the talent has been contacted regarding the picture, or that any relationship exists between the talent and the picture, the producer, or the production company.
2. The producer will not talk with the talent about money or other deal points without their agent's participation.
3. Should there be future discussions about the picture, these will be accomplished with the agent's participation.

If such a meeting takes place, most agents will not be placated by this letter or any form of repentance on the part of the producer. It is always best to take creative meetings prior to business meetings with the knowledge and participation of the talent's agent.

The purpose of the creative meeting is to obtain the most essential element in the producer's evaluation: how the talent feels about and envisions the story. Beyond reviewing their preceding pictures and discussions with prior producers, it is in these creative meetings that producers can receive a clear revelation of a picture's director and lead cast.

Once these creative meetings are finished, the producer then prepares to negotiate the deal.

Attorneys as Agents

Talent with brand-significant names may use their attorneys in negotiations along with their agents. Other major talent may use only their agents, and still others only their attorneys. Just as agents become very expert in the legal aspects of deal making, so do some attorneys develop an affinity for the creative aspects of these negotiations. And, for some talent, their attorney may be their agent.

Planning the Deal

When planning the proposed talent deal structure, it is best for producers to create the production deal first, then the development deal. The producer first discovers what may be a fair fee for the performer's services, keeping in mind the talent's current quote (usually what they were last paid), in context with the picture's projected gross, its budget, and the services demanded of the talent. The talent's fee, then, should be within the bounds of the production budget, or that talent should not have been considered in the first place.

Development Negotiation

It is essential that the production deal is agreed upon first, including the schedule, the payment amount (including points), the talent's credits, and all other associated benefits. Once the production deal is agreed upon, the stage is set for development negotiations. The production relationship will not commence until after the motion picture has been completely developed.

The deal's development period typically will last somewhere between 6 and 12 months. Producers should add a contingency period to the actual development schedule to provide for unforeseen scheduling and other unexpected issues. These typically are associated with script problems or talent schedule conflicts.

The development negotiation is really a deal within a deal, since the basis of this agreement rests on the production deal points. These deal points include how long the development period will be; if there are to be renewals (and if there are, how long and how much these will be); if this is an exclusive or nonexclusive deal, which, if it is exclusive, actually will bind the talent to a specific performing schedule.

If the deal is nonexclusive and has an unspecified start date, then it will have a significantly lower development fee value, since it does not interfere with other talent relationships. Nonexclusive development deals are much easier to negotiate and have lower up-front fees; however, they can be very challenging in terms of schedule coordination as the development of the picture matures.

If the producer binds the talent to a set performance schedule, the producer should assume that during the picture's development, the talent will turn down other offers that conflict with the agreed-upon schedule. Consequently, the producer should include a fair "pay-or-play" payment guarantee, which ensures that the talent will be paid, regardless of whether or not the talent actually performs the production services.

Advance fees cover two general categories: the expenses incurred by the talent and representatives to investigate and negotiate the deal, and talent compensation for the value the producer receives in attaching the talent to the picture.

Development fees typically begin at one percent of the production performance fee and are often much higher than this. For example, if a director's production fee is $3 million, the corresponding development fee would be at least $30,000. Most directors and writers also provide services in a picture's continuing development and should be paid fees commensurate with their services.

Mature production companies typically have generous financial elasticity to match the demands of their deals. In contrast, newer production companies may be limited to rigid development budgets. In every case, though, talent should receive fair value for their participation. Even producers with budgetary restraints have the option to entice their talent with additional profit participation. The critical producer objective in these negotiations is not to end up with the maximum points or dollars, but to attach the ultimate team who feel appreciated, well treated, and confident in their relationships.

Points Participation

It is an advantage to the picture to have the director and principal cast participate in the profits of the picture. Nothing can take the place of the talent commitment and enthusiasm that comes with being a central participant in the telling of a great story. However, it always makes a difference, sometimes substantially so, when a producer adds the relationship-deepening qualities of profits participation in the form of points in a picture. This is no clever ploy, just good business.

Because points are most often represented by percentage, the producer should calculate the projected value of these points in dollars by applying the points percentage to the liquidation breakdown of the producer's gross profit. This renders a critical point of reference for the producer, especially when evaluating a talent's offer. If this valuation is represented to others, it should always be given with the explanation that these are projected figures and cannot be guaranteed.

Definitions of long-form contract participation are typically several pages long. The sophisticated nature of these definitions renders some net participations greater than gross participations. The fairest point definition producers should make with their talent is for the talent to participate in the producer's actual gross profits. This is all the money that the producer earns from a particular picture before any of the producer's overhead is deducted. This is the amount that should be participated in by talent who have points in the picture.

Producers may finance in-house individuals or organizations who will directly license some of their pictures' rights. If they would have used a distributor to license these rights, that distributor would have deducted a distribution fee. It is therefore fair for the producer to apply such distribution fees and actual out-of-pocket direct distribution expenses before the talent profit participation. Regardless of the producer's sales ability, this fee should be the lowest commonly applied by industry-independent distributors. The fairest deal is the one in which all the parties participate at the same level.

Preparation of a Fair Deal

Like the genius strategist Napoleon, who is known for "winning his battles in his tent," the industry's most prosperous producers owe much of their success in every area to studied tent work. Before talent and their representatives are approached, producers should become thoroughly familiar with all of the important aspects of each of the players under consideration. They should clearly measure the deal points and ensure they're in balance with the unique contributions of the talent, the demands of the picture, and its budget.

All the producers' research, analysis, and presentation preparation combine to assure them of the ultimate creative team attachment. In addition, it serves to reassure the talent and their representatives that they are appreciated, appropriately valued by the producer, are receiving a fair deal, and are beginning a relationship that is well planned and as unshakable as motion picture production and distribution can be. The beginning of this relationship should be reaffirmed in the producer's documentation and deal performance.

Agents as Creative Resources

For producers, agents and talent attorneys can be exceptional creative resources for talent, both inside and outside their agencies and firms. In seeking to make allies of these important resources, producers will find their studied approach will yield them easier negotiations, fairer deals, and pictures with talent who are more content to deliver their maximum creative capacities. This approach will also avoid difficult negotiating deadlocks and development delays.

Talent Reserve

Producers should begin their first-choice talent negotiations having their secondary talent offers completely prepared and ready to go. Having done this, producers create at least two advantages for themselves: they won't be negatively influenced in the negotiations because they rely exclusively on a single talent; and if the need arises, the producers are prepared to segue into a secondary talent approach without loss of time. It often seems like the secondary choice would be a distant second. But this is not necessarily so, particularly when you look at the long list of distant seconds—more than a dozen of whom have been, in retrospect the past three years, absolute genius selections—in comparison to the producer's first choice.

The Participation of the Producer's Attorney

Following the preparation of a talent proposal, producers should present a written summary of the deal proposal to their attorneys for review and comments. For even the most experienced producers, these reviews are often very beneficial.

Further, new or obscure producers often benefit by allowing their attorneys to make the initial talent/agent contact. First impressions are important, and the substantive point-of-reference of the attorney and law firm is often more beneficial in the establishment of the relationship.

Chapter Postscript

Although there are personal objectives involved, the strongest tie that binds producers and talent is the fact that great stories may become wonderfully entertaining motion pictures. The most effective beginning for the producer/talent relationship is in initial meetings, in which each party is allowed to test the other's creative affinity for a particular picture, followed by deal-making meetings that have the blessing and participation of the talent's agent and/or attorney.

Research, planning, and preparation will help render talent attachment a predictable and pleasant experience.

Chapter 9

Development, Production, and Producing Company Structures

This chapter presents the basic business structures of and the relationships between the companies used by producers to operate their motion picture development and production operations.

The Power of Company Structure

The purpose of each company's structure is to:

- Provide the business entity with a legal identity recognized by governmental bodies (city, county, state, and federal governments), tax authorities, and other businesses and individuals
- Establish an independent, tangible, tradable business presence with the capacity to increase in value
- Deliver company owners increased business/trading capacities, legal protection, and expanded taxation options

An actor, owning three screenplays and functioning as an individual from a fully operational home office, is treated substantially different from this same actor, with the same assets, who forms an independent production company around these assets. However, that individual's capacity to communicate does not automatically increase, nor, unfortunately, do the screenplays become better; but the individual's deal-making power and the responsiveness from other businesses may be more immediate and serious than to the actor as an individual.

If a talent wants to coproduce a picture with a production company, a talent/company deal naturally transpires. If a production company wants to coproduce with another production company, a company-to-company coproduction deal transpires. The deal point array and relative benefits of the company-to-company transaction are much more extensive and potentially more beneficial to the talent than the talent/company transaction.

The Companies

Producers achieve maximum structure benefits through using three levels of companies. Each level has separate companies. The advantage of having multiple companies is that they deliver to the producer operating clarity, clear accounting separation for all profit participants, and critical picture-to-picture legal protection.

As represented in the chart in Figure 9.1, these three levels are the production company, the development companies, and the producing companies.

Figure 9.1

Business Structure and Revenue Flow

Production Company

The production company is a holding company for the producer's interests in all the development and producing entities. The production company is the producer's brand presence. Mandalay Entertainment, Caravan Pictures, and Castle Rock Entertainment are examples of these production companies.

The production company is the business entity for its owners, administrative team, permanent creative team, distribution group (unless operated as a separate entity), story department, producer's support team, and accounting operations. Producers develop and produce their motion pictures through their development and producing companies.

The production company is the producer's command central. Through this entity, the executive team defines, develops, and manages the producer's objectives. This company retains continuing relationships with all studios, talent, banks, completion guarantors, and other entertainment organizations. It also reviews all literary properties, receives all pitches, and receives all the advertising and public relations for the companies.

The production company is most often a corporation or limited liability company (LLC), which provides the producer with the most historically safe legal protection.

Development Companies

Development companies fulfill all the creative and business development of the pictures that are selected by the producers. The producers are typically the senior development directors of each development company, supported by other members of the production company's staff.

Each development company is established to develop a fixed number of pictures, usually at least three and less than ten. The development company referenced in the company diagram is organized to develop three pictures.

If the producer uses private investors, the development company is the entity in which these investors are invited to participate. If there are investors in the development companies, these companies are normally a limited partnership or a LLC, delivering the investors the greatest protection and the producer the greatest operating power.

Limiting the number of pictures developed by each of these companies yields specific earnings potential for these companies and further, segments liability.

Producing Companies

Because in many ways, each picture is substantially a separate business, it is highly beneficial for accounting and legal reasons to incorporate each picture as a separate business entity. This is the only picture this company will ever produce. The single company status isolates both the picture's accounting and its liability from the producers' other pictures. Each producing company is wholly owned by the production company and typically set up as a corporation or LLC.

Company Interrelationships

The permanent office location for each of the producers' companies is most often in the production company office.

As the producers' holding company, the production company usually owns all of each producing company and either all, or the producers' share of, each development company (if the development companies have investor partners).

Development Company Financing

Development is that creative gestation precursor essential to motion picture production. Each new development company is launched around a very specific plan, prepared by the producer, to develop and produce a specific number of pictures over several months. This plan is set forth in a month-by-month activity projection. The capital need for this company is discovered through the preparation of a cash flow projection that corresponds with the company's activity projection. These projections are presented in Chapter 10.

Seasoned production companies partially finance development from their own profits. Studios and coproduction relationships are also common resources for development financing. If balanced producers use private financing for their pictures, it is allocated for the picture's development. There are financial advantages unique to motion picture development financing for both production companies and investors.

Investors evaluate investment offerings primarily by each offering's risk, term until potential investment recoupment, investment amount, and earnings potential. Consider these qualities in the following risk evaluation comparing investing in motion picture development and motion picture production.

Motion Picture Development vs. Production Investment Risk Evaluation

Description	Development	Production
Risk	Development only	Development, production, and distribution
Term until recoupment	18–24 months	36 months
Investment amount	$1–$2 million per picture	$15–$50 million per picture
Earnings potential	300% gross yield over 5 years	(assuming achieves U.S. theatrical distribution) Break even to 200% gross yield over 7–9 years

This analysis clearly exhibits where private investors should invest, and why production investments should reside with global distributors who have the capacity to protect their participation within their respective territories and markets.

Production companies seeking private investors for their development companies typically offer them 50/50 ownership in the partnership, 80 to 100 percent of the first proceeds received paid to the investors until they have recouped 100 to

120 percent of their original investment, and thereafter, an equal sharing (50 percent/ 50 percent) of the partnership's earnings.

Earnings flow into the development partnership from its sale of all rights, title, and interest from each fully developed picture to one of the production company's producing companies. The amount of each of these sales is preset as part of the development company offering. Typically this amount is equal to or greater than the amount necessary to return all the investors' capital with the sale of the first two developed pictures if the company is configured for developing three pictures.

For example, if the development company's total capitalization is $2 million, and the investors receive 100 percent of all income until they recoup 120 percent of their investment, then the sale of each developed property could be $1.2 million, plus a partnership participation in the continuing profits of each picture. This relationship is structured to recoup the investors' investment, plus a 20 percent return, from the sale of the first two pictures ($2.4 million). This leaves the investors additional earnings from the sale of the third picture to another producing company owned by the production company. Additionally, the development company and its investors participate in the profits of the completed pictures.

Another highly appealing quality of this investment structure is that the investors' potential continuing earnings come from assets worth substantially more than the developed stories. The three pictures in this example have a combined developed value of about $2 million. With production budgets of $25 to $40 million each, the three pictures have a combined production value of $75 to $120 million. This is impressive leverage of approximately 37/1 to 60/1.

Securities

Investment offerings of all kinds must conform to state and federal securities laws. These laws and regulations are highly sophisticated, and producers should have the offerings prepared by their legal and accounting advisors. The planning and preparation of a development investment memorandum is discussed in Chapter 10.

Forms of Companies

There are several forms of company structures, each having several advantages. Producers are best served meeting with their legal counsel, who will lead them through a series of questions, the answers to which should reveal the best company structures for their use.

If there is just one person involved, a production company may be commenced as a sole proprietorship. Often, these organizations may commence their legal life as simply as filing a fictitious name with the county clerk in the county where the producer's office address is listed, and then publishing this name in a newspaper, according to the directions given by the county clerk. This gives the producer the documentation needed to open a bank account and officially use the name recorded in the county of residence. This is quick and inexpensive but does not give the producer legal protection that comes with more sophisticated company structures.

Once a production company is ready to commence earnest business, most attorneys will suggest they incorporate. This delivers the owners (shareholders) personal legal protection from actions that may be taken against their corporation. When the corporation is still limited in its shareholders and earnings, it can receive special tax status that will allow the tax liabilities to be passed through to the shareholders, so they are not burdened with an additional corporate tax.

Similar owner protection can be received from the more popular limited liability company (LLC) structure, which has single taxation rather than double. In most states, the cost of filing an LLC is the same as that for filing as a corporation.

Chapter Postscript

There is a business entity pattern common among balanced producers that provides them with the greatest operating power, structural stability, flexibility, investor benefits, and personal and picture protection. Producers who model their operations after this pattern will receive these proven benefits.

Development Financing

This chapter discusses the purposes of development financing and the methods and resources from which to secure this financing.

The Essential Power of Funded Development _____

Producers often share a common understanding about the schedule and resources it takes for the average motion picture to fulfill production; however, the schedule and resources for a motion picture to complete development often garner more questions than answers. For example, does a picture's development time include, and should related overhead expenses be charged to, each "go" project for reading scripts and listening to pitches that lead to the discovery of that project's story? And are not most of a motion picture's final development activities and expenses also part of its preproduction, and should therefore eventually be allocated to its production budget? The answer to these questions is certainly yes.

Producers should plan, finance, and manage their pictures' entire development process to enable them to move through development at a steady, confident pace that will continue through production and distribution.

Every picture has its unique development and production schedule. The following is an example of a typical picture's schedule.

This model demonstrates that in a well-planned and sufficiently funded independent production entity environment, 14 (almost 60 percent) of the 24 months of a typical picture's complete development and production process is spent in development. As producers invest the majority of their time developing pictures, this should be, as is done in the best operated production organizations, a finely orchestrated process, performed according to schedules, budgets, and accountability in keeping with the integrity of the picture's production processes.

Motion Picture Development and Production Schedule

Description	Approximate months	Cumulative months
Development prestory acquisition (reading, researching, internal greenlight, first studio greenlights)	5	5
Story acquisition	1	6
Development [shooting script evolution of original drafts, rewrites, and polishes; talent attachments; global rights delineation and liquidation plan; development marketing material origination and subsequent versions; global distributor meetings and collaborative relationship engagements; physical production prep (all elements including location considerations/site visits/relationship explorations, production boards, budgets, schedules, etc., exploration and determination of production design, visual and sound effects, and other production elements unique to the picture that demand development planning and articulation); presale/completion, bond/production banking prep and fulfillment; commence trade/consumer PR; engage U.S. studio distribution agreement; publisher and other ancillary product relationship establishment, etc.]	8	14
Preproduction	3	17
Principal photography	3	20
Post-production	4	24

Most producers have multiple pictures in development and production at the same time. Multiple pictures sustain a continuous flow of projects and allow their production company to amortize (distribute) fixed development overhead costs over several pictures. Even with amortization, development overhead typically averages $400,000 per picture—not including story rights, writers' fees, and talent attachment expenses. In addition to these expenses, the accomplishment of the 21 development steps (as listed earlier) typically takes the development team 18 months, and often longer.

Producers should understand that development is the foundation of each picture. A strong foundation allows producers to produce their pictures with predictable confidence. A weak development foundation is the number one reason pictures don't get made, dissemble during production, or have lackluster earning power.

Understanding this, producers ought to ensure that each aspect of their picture's development is just as intricately organized, budgeted, and sufficiently funded as its principal photography.

Development Funding Sources

The most common sources of development funding are from:

- The production company
- A studio
- Private investors
- Coproduction relationships
- Government agencies

Production Company Financing

Most mature production companies fund at least some of their development expenses from cash flow or bank credit facilities. For many of these companies, this funding is only interim and is repaid to the production company when either a separately funded development company is set up or the picture is acquired by its producing company.

Studio Financing

In the main, studio development financing for independent production companies comes through the studios' production departments. Young production companies are most likely to take advantage of these accommodations, which often include offices on the studio lot and more traditional development financing that includes story acquisition and talent attachment. These expenses are accrued by the studio and charged against the producer's pictures that go into production.

Use of studio development financing usually relegates the producer to a close production and distribution relationship with the studio, referred to as the studio producer relationship discussed in Chapter 2. The primary studio motivation in these relationships is the ownership and distribution of significant pictures.

Investor Financing

Balanced producers often engage in relationships with a limited number of sophisticated private investors who provide development financing for their pictures.

Mature balanced production companies sustain cash flows from earnings and maintain bank credit facilities substantially greater than are needed to finance all their development expenses without engaging investment capital. Many of these companies still elect to use development private-investor partners. The primary motivation for this is that development investor partners:

- Promote a more focused management for each picture's development progress
- Provide tighter control of development expenses (which, for many production companies, may easily slip out of control)
- Balance the producer's risk
- Expand capital availability

In Chapter 9, the terms and company structure that best accommodate development investors are presented. Producers should prepare such offerings with the assistance and under the direction of an experienced securities attorney.

The discovery of private investors who have the funds and inclination to invest is not sufficient reason for a producer to approach and engage in a development relationship with them. There are state and federal securities and exchange commissions (SECs) that have established regulations to which all investment offerings and relationships must conform. These regulations both protect investors and provide a structure that governs and identifies investment offerings.

Development offerings are most often prepared for the exclusive review and participation in an SEC investor category called *sophisticated* or *accredited investors*. This SEC category varies from state to state but basically refers to investors who are experienced in investments similar in amount and risk to the one being offered and possess a specific minimum net worth that demonstrates even greater sophistication and the investor's ability to risk the investment's failure.

The advantages of using this offering category are that first of all, the producer has an exclusive relationship with investors who are durable and experienced, thus allowing for less fear of investor impact if the development company, for any reason, fails to achieve its objectives. It also makes for smoother presentations to experienced, business-savvy potential participants. Another important advantage of sophisticated/accredited investor offerings is that they are simpler, less expensive, and less time-consuming to prepare than nonrestricted public offerings. Sophisticated investor offerings are restricted in their content, presentation, and number of participants. Among other minimum requirements, sophisticated investor offerings must conform to SEC regulation language. This language gives investors and their representatives reference to each offering in relation to the laws governing it. It also includes complete and clear declarations of the risks related to the investment.

Sophisticated investor offerings are restricted in the number of potential investors to whom they may be offered and also by the number of investors who may participate. Consequently, the offerings are numbered, and a log is kept of each investor who has been presented an offering copy, those retrieved, and certainly, the number of investment interests actually purchased. Depending on each state's SEC regulations, the number of participating investors may be limited to as few as 10. This restriction keeps the investor group to a manageable size, but it may result in a high per-investment amount (one-tenth for example), which may further restrict the number of potential investors.

For many sophisticated investors, managing their investment portfolio is their primary business. Most of these investors diversify their investments into a portfolio balanced with a mix of secure investments (treasury bills, municipal bonds, mortgages, etc.) and risk investments (stocks, business investments, etc.). As these investments mature, the returning funds must be reinvested to maximize earnings and restrict tax exposure. This return and reinvestment phenomenon sustains a continuing participation among potential investors in reviewing and investing in new projects.

A producer's first development offering is often the most challenging to prepare and fund. However, following the initial offering, subsequent offerings are simpler to author and fund. Typically, some of the original investors want to reinvest in one or more of the producer's future development entities, and new investors are now substantially easier to engage, using the first development company as a powerful point of reference. Recently, a Los Angeles-based independent producer, whose accountant keeps a list of investors who would like to participate in this producer's future development partnerships, reported that their current list exceeds 1,000 investors. This is unusual for several reasons, including the fact that most producers or their representatives will not add an investor's name to a list that exceeds more than 50 or 100. However, this points to the availability of investors for development company investments. To temper the previous statement, most producers will find it challenging to obtain their initial development financing. But sophisticated investors are just that. They are skilled investors, looking for exceptional investment opportunities. They wisely tend to shy away from untried management teams and industries in which they are inexperienced.

Coproduction Company Financing

Production companies can receive development financing for their projects from other production companies that have development funding and, consequently, are seeking the strongest stories.

The two most desperate development positions for producers to be in are to have one or more sterling stories that have passed their internal greenlight but they do not have sufficient capital to develop them, and to have development capital and either only weak stories to choose from or no story that has passed their greenlight.

Both these conditions are common among producers, but the second is the most urgent and most common—common enough, in fact, to motivate the development and consequent production of too many motion pictures each year that are sufficiently strong for greenlight, but fail to ignite the producer's creative fire. These pictures are made because if producers wait too long for a project, they may run short of allocated development funds for the number of pictures the money was raised for. If this is the case, either new funding must be infused or fewer pictures are developed. In either case, the eventual development expenses may become too high to be reasonably applied to the completed pictures.

Most producers have several pictures in their development pool. Because there are typically more development funds than there are truly great stories, producers are generally very receptive to story pitches from other producers seeking funding through coproduction relationships. Codevelopment/production relationships are most often set up for a single picture. One production company provides the story and the development progress related to it; the other company provides the development capital. They both share in the development and production of the picture. Equity is divided according to the value of each party's contributions.

Government Agency Financing

Most countries have an Economic Development department. The common mandate of these departments is to grow their countries' productivity and enliven their industries. Many of these countries provide a broad variety of support, including tax incentives, rebates, loans, and outright grants. Some of these are exclusive to entities headquartered in or at least residing in these countries; others may be participated in by those globally, if the production entity complies with the specific program's criteria. Countries may be further bolstered by additional jurisdictional government bodies (states, provinces, and territories) with similar incentive programs. Some programs are offered by a collaboration of multiple countries, such as the European Union.

Although information on these programs is readily available (much of which is an astounding bundle of difficult-to-navigate documents) from the agencies that regulate them, as these programs come and go with the government bodies that oversee them, it is most beneficial, safe, and sane to use a legal or accounting group that specializes in the specific program(s) that may apply, allow them to evaluate, recommend the strategy, apply and manage the relationship. Whereas some countries do not provide any development funding, other countries provide much of it, for those who qualify.

The Process of Securing Development Financing

There are seven basic steps to obtaining development financing, described as follows.

1. Develop a Plan

This is the cornerstone to success in obtaining the necessary funding. With a plan, there is order and hope. Producers should evaluate their resources (operating team, stories, cash flow) and recommit to or redefine their mission statement (why they are in business, the kind of pictures they want to make, the way they want to make them, style of doing business internally and with others, etc.). They should also make decisions about the basic development planning possibilities, including the number of pictures to be developed within the new development company, the stories (if any) that the producer has, and the most logical sources from which to receive development funding.

2. Prepare the Activity Projection

This is a list of the primary activities performed for the company's pictures during their development. These activities are presented in a month-by-month spreadsheet format, showing in a single projection each separate activity for all the pictures developed.

The activity projection shown in Figure 10.1 has been set up for the development of three pictures. This basic form is currently being used by several production companies for planning and managing their development companies.

This example is predicated on a particular producer's resources. The activities and format are universal. The layout may be very helpful to producers in planning their individual development entities. The timing represented is just an example—producers should not expect their plan to be timed like those in the example.

There are two activity projections on the CD-ROM supplied with this book. One is set up in the projection's format, but ready to be filled in. The other provides the projection with its live sample. This sample can assist users with points of reference until they become familiar with the planning process.

The far-left column is labeled *Activity*. Below this heading is a list of the major development activities, generally in the order of motion picture development progress. The rest of the columns to the right of the activity column list the succeeding months from 1 to 24, except for the last three columns, which present dates beyond those months listed.

Various points about how the producer accomplishes the activities referenced in this projection have been presented in previous chapters, are chronicled in Chapter 12, or are presented later.

The initial activities are labeled *Start-up*. Some categories are for new producers who have not previously engaged an attorney, publicist, or entertainment bank, or who have not started trade press releases for their production company.

UPM (Unit Production Manager) Retention will be a new concept to some producers and many UPMs. If a producer does not have an in-house person who performs production budgeting work, it would be helpful to retain a *development UPM* who provides various aspects of this work during the development process for each picture. Retention increases both the consistency and integrity of the work. Just as breakdowns, boards, schedules, and budgets from a UPM are usually more thorough and better planned than if done by a UPM not attached to a picture, so is the work of a UPM who is retained to do all the UPM-related development work for a slate of pictures.

The *Development Creative* section primarily charts the producer's story discovery plan. This plan includes developing stories that are already internally greenlit, as well as soliciting and reading scripts (as part of the search for new properties). Subsequently, the producer goes through the process of garnering the U.S. and international distributor greenlights.

In large measure, this process writes the picture's definition. It is each picture's as-detailed-as-possible creative and business definition. Substantially and naturally, it comes from preparing each picture's liquidation breakdown, audience research, and campaign development, as well as traditional creative preparation.

For most pictures, *attaching the director,* which includes researching, creative meetings, and negotiating, precedes attaching lead talent and most other development functions. A director is fundamental to each picture's creative life. It is essential that the director be brought in early and allowed to participate in all other facets of a picture's development and production.

The first five activities on the projection's second page are a continuation of *Development Creative* and are part of the picture's preproduction.

Development Production charts the development of the production blueprints and schedules that match and are created from the script. These detailed production category breakdowns are combined with the overall production approach provided by the production team, and culminate into schedules, locations, special production unit relationships, and a production budget that is coordinated and eventually signed-off by the picture's completion guarantor.

Figure 10.1
Sample Pictures, Ltd. Activity Projection

Activity Projection
Sample Pictures Development, LP

Prep Date: January 2, 2005

A C T I V I T Y	05							06						
	1	2	3	4	5	6	7	8	9	10	11	12	13	14
	Jun	Jul	Aug	Sep	Oct	Nov	Dec	Jan	Feb	Mar	Apr	May	Jun	Jul
Start - Up	GenCon			L'Vegas	AFM			Toy Fair			Lic'ing Fair	Cannes	GenCon	
UPM Retain	-													
Entertainment Atty Retain	-													
Publicist Retain	-													
Write/Release Opening P.R.	-													
Entertainment Bank Open	-													
Prep & Release Distributor Anncmt.	-													
Pay General Partner Pre-Dev. Fee	-													
Development Creative														
Read Screenplays & Lit Properties		-	-	-	-	-	-	-	-					
Internal Greenlight (Motion Picture Valuation, Budget Smry)			-	-	-	-	-	-	-					
First Distributors Greenlight			-	-	-	-	-	-						
Option Screenplay / Lit Rights					1				2				3	
Write Picture Definition					1				2				3	
Story scope and superobjective; Budget; Target audiences; Production schedule; Domestic theatrical and other major distribution street dates; Comparables; Earnings Projections.														
Distributor Creative Correlation							1		1,2	1,2	1,2	1,2	1,2,3	1,2,3
List Director Considerations									2	2	2		3	3
Meetings						1	1		2	2	2		3	3
Select, Negotiate, Document					1									
List Primary Acting Talent					1				2				3	
Meet, Select, Negotiate, Document						1	1	1	1		2	2	3	
Story Meetings & Breakdown						1	1	1	2	2	2	2	3	3
Additional Screenplay Drafts						1	1	1		2	2	2	3	3
Shooting Script							1		1		2	2	2	
List Key Production Talent														
Cinematographer								1						
UPM, Music, Art Dir, Costuming, Spcl FX								1	1	1	1	2	2	2
Meet, Select, Negotiate, Document								1	1	1	1	2	2	2
Spot Promotion							1print		1	1	2	2	2	2
Prep Picture Logo and Printing											2print			
Storyboard								1	1	1		2	2	2
Development Production					AFM							Cannes		
1st Pass Production Budget														
Shooting Draft Breakdown and Production Boards													2	2
Production Budget										1				2
Production Schedule										1				2
Completion Bond Set										1				2

ACTIVITY	1 Jun 05	2 Jul	3 Aug	4 Sep	5 Oct	6 Nov	7 Dec	8 Jan 06	9 Feb	10 Mar	11 Apr	12 May	13 Jun	14 Jul
(Events)	GenCon			L'Vegas	AFM			Toy Fair			Lic'ing Fair	Cannes / E3	GenCon	
Picture Marketing, Prdctn Funding														
Establish Presale Financing Plan					1									
Presale Negotiations						1			2	1,2	1,2	1,2	1,2	1,2,3
Document Presales										1	1	1	1	2
Create and Present Bank Memorandum									1					
Trade Releases						1	1	1	1,2	1,2	1,2	1,2	1,2,3	1,2,3
Consumer PR								1	1	1	1	1	1,2	1,2
Picture Introductory Meetings with Studios					1				2				3	
Enter Domestic Theatrical Agrmnt											1			
Publisher Novelization Negotiations							1		1	2	2	2	2	
Engage Bank Production Funding											1			
Ancillary Rights Development														
Ancillary Events	GenCon			L'Vegas				Toy Fair			Lic'ing Fair	E3	GenCon	
Establish Rights Liquidation Plan					1				2				3	
Prepare Video Game Demo						1				2				3
Video Game Programmer Negotiations								1				2		
Begin Video Game Programming										1				2
Meet, Select, Negotiate Stock Artist														
Begin Stock Artwork Production						1,2								
Prepare Prelim Card & Toy Art Stills							1,2							
Meet, Select, Negotiate Game & Toy Partners														
Begin Toy & Game Artwork Production											1			
Prepare Prelim RPG Artwork														
Meet, Select, Negotiate RPG Partner													1	
Begin RPG Artwork and Game Dev.														
Sell Picture to Producing Company														
Pre-production												1		
Principal Photography													1	1
Post-production														
Theatrical Trailer														
Release Dates and After Market														
Sell Foreign Rights					1				1,2	1,2	1,2	1,2	1,2,3	1,2,3
Paperback Release														
Ancillary Releases														
Domestic Theatrical Release														
Domestic Video Release														
Premium Cable TV Release														
Network Television														

Figure 10.1 *continued*
Sample Pictures, Ltd. Activity Projection

Activity Projection
Sample Pictures Development, LP

Prep Date: January 2, 2005

ACTIVITY	15 Aug	16 Sep	17 Oct	18 Nov	19 Dec	20 Jan (07)	21 Feb	22 Mar	23 Apr	24 May	As #'d	As #'d	As #'d	As #'d
Startup		L'Vegas	AFM			Toy Fair			Lic'ng Fair	Cannes				
UPM Retain														
Entertainment Atty Retain														
Publicist Retain														
Write/Release Opening P.R.														
Entertainment Bank Open														
Prep & Release Distributor Anncmnt.														
Pay General Partner Predev. Fee														
Development Creative														
Read Screenplays & Lit Properties														
Internal Greenlight (Motion Picture Valuation, Budget Smry)														
First Distributors Greenlight														
Option Screenplay / Lit Rights														
Write Picture Definition														
Story scope and superobjective; Budget; Target audiences; Production schedule; Domestic theatrical and other major distribution street dates; Comparables; Earnings Projections.														
Distributor Creative Correlation	1,2,3	1,2,3	1,2,3	1,2,3	1,2,3	1,2,3	1,2,3	1,2,3	1,2,3	1,2,3				
List Director Considerations														
Meetings	3													
Select, Negotiate, Document	3													
List Primary Acting Talent														
Meet, Select, Negotiate, Document	3	3	3											
Story Meetings & Breakdown	3	3												
Additional Screenplay Drafts	3	3												
Shooting Script			3											
List Key Production Talent	3													
Cinematographer		3												
UPM, Music, Art Dir, Costuming, Spcl FX	2	3	3	3	3									
Meet, Select, Negotiate, Document	2	3	3	3	3									
Spot Promotion	3	3	3	3										
Prep Picture Logo and Printing	3print													
Storyboard		3	3	3										
Development Production			AFM							Cannes				
1st Pass Production Budget			3											
Shooting Draft Breakdown and Production Boards				3										
Production Budget				3										
Production Schedule				3										
Completion Bond Set	2				3									

ACTIVITY				AFM						Cannes	As #'d	
	15 Aug	16 Sep	17 Oct	18 Nov	19 Dec	20 Jan 07	21 Feb	22 Mar	23 Apr	24 May		
Picture Marketing, Prdctn Funding												
Establish Presale Financing Plan												
Presale Negotiations	1,2,3	1,2,3	1,2,3	1,2,3	1,2,3	1,2,3	1,2,3	1,2,3	1,2,3	1,2,3		
Document Presales	2	2	2	3	3	3						
Create and Present Bank Memorandum			3									
Trade Releases	1,2,3	1,2,3	1,2,3	1,2,3	1,2,3	1,2,3	1,2,3	1,2,3	1,2,3	1,2,3		
Consumer PR	1,2	1,2	1,2,3	1,2,3	1,2,3	1,2,3	1,2,3	1,2,3	1,2,3	1,2,3		
Picture Introductory Meetings with Studios	2			3	3							
Enter Domestic Theatrical Agrmnt		3	3									
Publisher Novelization Negotiations	3	3	3									
Engage Bank Production Funding	2				3							
Ancillary Rights Development												
Ancillary Events		L'Vegas				Toy Fair			Licing Fair	E3		
Establish Rights Liquidation Plan												
Prepare Video Game Demo		3										
Video Game Programmer Negotiations												
Begin Video Game Programming				3								
Meet, Select, Negotiate Stock Artist	1,2,3											
Begin Stock Artwork Production			1,2,3	3								
Prepare Prelim Card & Toy Art Stills												
Meet, Select, Negotiate Game & Toy Partners						3						
Begin Toy & Game Artwork Production					2				3			
Prepare Prelim RPG Artwork					3				3			
Meet, Select, Negotiate RPG Partner			2		2							
Begin RPG Artwork and Game Dev.							3		3			
Sell Picture to Producing Company												
Pre-production		2	2	2	2	3	3	3	3	3		
Principal Photography	1	1	1	1	1	1	1	2	3	3	2:Apr/07-Jul/07	3:Apr/07-Jul/07
Post-production							1	1	2	2	2:Aug/07-Nov/07	3:Aug/07-Nov/07
Theatrical Trailer											2:Jun/07	3:Oct/07
Release Dates and After Market												
Sell Foreign Rights	1,2,3	1,2,3	1,2,3	1,2,3	1,2,3	1,2,3	1,2,3	1,2,3	1,2,3	1,2,3		
Paperback Release								1			2:Jul/07	3:Nov/07
Ancillary Releases									1		2:Aug/07	3:Dec/07
Domestic Theatrical Release									1		2:Aug/07	3:Dec/07
Domestic Video Release										1:Oct/07	2:Feb/08	3:Jun/08
Premium Cable TV Release										1:Apr/08	2:Aug/08	3:Dec/08
Network Television										1:Apr/09	2:Aug/09	3:Dec/09
A C T I V I T Y	15 Aug	16 Sep	17 Oct	18 Nov	19 Dec	20 Jan 07	21 Feb	22 Mar	23 Apr	24 May	As #'d	As #'d

Picture Marketing, (Production) Funding are just as they appear. These processes are presented substantially in Chapters 2 through 6.

Ancillary Rights Development charts the typical ancillary rights events for an ancillary rights-expansive picture. The liquidation of these rights is closely correlated with the picture's creative development. Many ancillary rights licensees additionally require time for manufacture, and ideally these ancillary rights' consumer products should be on retail shelves just before the picture's release date or as a day-and-date release (see Chapter 4).

Sell Picture to Producing Company refers to the formal activity of selling all rights, title, and interest of each developed picture to a separate producer-owned producing company, as presented in Chapter 9.

Unless the producer has identified the picture to be developed, the Production and Distribution dates are estimates. Once the U.S. theatrical date is projected, the other distribution dates are laid in according to traditional distribution window timing, as presented in Chapter 1.

3. Prepare the Cash Flow Projection

After the producer has projected specifically how development of a series of pictures will be accomplished, then a cash flow projection may be prepared. This projection applies expense amounts to the achievements chronicled in the activity projection, plus the related overhead, such as rent, phones, salaries, and taxes. Some of the production company's expenses are passed through to the development company. For instance, the producer typically is one of the development directors, so a portion of this salary, office space, and equipment will be paid by the development company during the picture's development.

A cash flow projection sample is presented in Figure 10.2. Like the activity projection, this is only a sample. Producers should prepare their projections with the assistance of their accountant and/or business manager and apply expense amounts appropriate for their organizations.

There are two cash flow projections on the CD-ROM supplied with this book. One is in the sample projection's format but without amounts, and ready to be filled in. The other has the sample projection's amounts filled in. This projection may assist users with points of reference until they become familiar with these expenses.

Extending for five years, this projection indicates expenses incurred monthly for the first 24 months and annually thereafter. Many production companies prepare internal cash flow projections monthly for the first 36 months, and annually thereafter for greater planning and analysis clarity.

The top of this projection lists the sales events attended by the producer, as well as the most significant activity benchmarks from the activity projection. These are not mandatory but are a very helpful reference.

Below the activity references are *Cash Receipts,* a listing of all the development company's income by projected receipt date. Each category should be referenced here, including, but not limited to, investments from the producer, private investors, and loans, as well as income generated from the sale of the developed pictures to the subsidiary-producing companies. If this sale includes a development company profits participation in the pictures, the income from this participation should also be shown. The investment amounts are usually left blank until the expenses are completed and totaled. Once the expenses are identified, the producer will know how much is needed to fund the picture's development.

Following cash receipts is a listing of the (development) *Expenses.* The first items listed are options and retainers for literary rights and production/performing talent. Following these expenses are professional fees, then overhead items, followed by the investors' (in this example, Limited Partners) participation. (This is usually left blank until expenses are completed.) Payroll is listed, then a contingency, followed by the total expenses for that month.

Below Total Expenses is the *Monthly Balance,* which is the month's total income less the month's total expenses. On the next line is *Cumulative Cash Flow,* which lists the monthly balance plus the cash remaining from the prior month.

After all expenses are filled in, the preparer can examine the total cumulative cash flow for the month following the first picture's theatrical release date and have a starting point in estimating the amount of development financing necessary to develop the proposed picture. Depending on development duration, it may be necessary to calculate the cash flow projection monthly for the first 24 months in order to determine how much the development company will need until it is self-sufficient.

Typically, development companies are set up for a fixed number of pictures, and the most expensive categories terminate after the pictures have sold to the producer's producing companies. After this time, the remaining expense categories substantially diminish.

Following the first expense pass, the producer often will reassess the basic elements of the plan. This includes looking at the number of pictures to be developed, the activity projection timing, and the major category expenses. There must be a balance between a sane development/production schedule, income and expenses, and producer/investor motivations. Several revisions typically are made to these two projections before a balance can be obtained with which the producer is content.

4. Select the Development Team and Advisors

The development company will be operated by a team, including the development director(s), an operations person, and development assistants. There will also be outside professionals, including an attorney, banker, completion bond company, physical production specialist (retained UPM), and a publicist.

The dynamics of the development team are projected into the pictures that they produce. Additionally, many investors look first to the development team when evaluating the development offering. The development team is reviewed in Chapter 11.

5. Formulate the Investment

Even if the investment is completely internal, separate development entities should be formed and financed. As this occurs, terms of the investment or loan must be

Figure 10.2

Sample Pictures, Ltd. Cash Flow Projection

Cash Flow Projection
Sample Pictures Development, LP

Prepared: January 3, 2005   M o n t h s

Description	1 Jun	2 Jul	3 Aug	4 Sep	5 Oct	6 Nov	7 Dec	8 Jan	9 Feb	10 Mar	11 Apr	12 May	1st Year Totals	13 Jun	14 Jul
Events	GenCon				Scrmply 1				Scrmply 2					Scrmply 3	
							Director 1				Director 2				
				Las Vegas	AFM			Toy Fair			Licensing Fair	E3, Cannes		GenCon	
												Sell Pic 1			
U.S. Theatrical Release															
Cash Receipts															
Investment Funds	6,500,000	-	-	-	-	-	-	-	-	-	-	-	6,500,000	-	-
Production Sale	-	-	-	-	-	-	-	-	-	-	-	5,200,000	5,200,000	-	-
Picture Participations	-	-	-	-	-	-	-	-	-	-	212,500	-	212,500	-	-
Total Cash Receipts	6,500,000	-	-	-	-	-	-	-	-	-	212,500	5,200,000	11,912,500	-	-
Expenses															
Brokerage Fees	650,000	-	-	-	-	-	-	-	-	-	-	-	650,000	-	-
Literary Rights Acquisition Advance	-	-	-	-	100,000	-	-	-	100,000	-	-	-	200,000	100,000	-
Writers' Fees	-	75,000	-	-	-	-	140,000	140,000	-	140,000	140,000	140,000	850,000	-	140,000
Director Retainer	-	-	-	-	-	-	300,000	-	-	-	300,000	-	600,000	-	-
Talent Retainers	-	-	-	-	-	-	-	-	-	-	-	-	-	-	-
Unit Production Manager	5,000	-	5,000	5,000	5,000	5,000	5,000	5,000	5,000	5,000	5,000	5,000	55,000	5,000	5,000
Publicist	5,000	5,000	5,000	5,000	9,000	5,000	5,000	5,000	7,000	7,000	5,000	7,000	70,000	7,000	5,000
Attorney, Entertainment	17,000	5,000	5,000	10,000	10,000	10,000	10,000	10,000	10,000	10,000	10,000	10,000	117,000	10,000	10,000
Producer's Representative	10,000	10,000	10,000	10,000	10,000	10,000	10,000	10,000	10,000	10,000	10,000	10,000	120,000	10,000	10,000
Foreign Sales Representative	-	-	-	5,000	5,000	5,000	5,000	5,000	5,000	5,000	5,000	5,000	45,000	5,000	5,000
Accounting	500	500	500	500	500	500	500	500	500	500	500	3,000	8,500	500	500
Picture Artwork	15,000	-	-	-	20,000	14,000	6,000	-	20,000	14,000	6,000	-	95,000	-	20,000
Picture Promo Production	30,000	30,000	30,000	30,000	20,000	10,000	10,000	-	20,000	10,000	10,000	-	200,000	-	20,000
Rent & Parking	8,000	4,000	4,000	4,000	4,000	4,000	4,000	4,000	4,000	4,000	4,000	4,000	52,000	4,000	4,000
Telephone	7,000	3,500	3,500	3,500	3,500	3,500	3,500	3,500	3,500	3,500	3,500	3,500	45,500	3,500	3,500
ISP, Web Hosting/Maintenance	1,000	500	500	500	500	500	500	500	500	500	500	500	6,500	500	500
Office Equipment	30,000	400	400	400	400	400	400	400	400	400	400	400	34,400	400	400
Printing	20,000	500	500	500	500	500	500	20,000	20,000	30,000	500	500	113,500	20,000	500

	1	2	3	4	5	6	7	8	9	10	11	12	**Total**	13	14
Supplies, Misc. Office	1,500	750	750	750	750	750	750	750	750	750	750	750	**9,750**	750	750
Pstg / Dlvry Service	1,500	750	750	750	750	750	750	750	750	750	750	750	**9,750**	750	750
Media Research	2,000	2,000	2,000	2,000	2,000	2,000	2,000	2,000	2,000	2,000	2,000	2,000	**24,000**	2,000	2,000
Motion Picture Sftwr	5,000	3,000	1,000	-	-	-	-	-	-	-	-	-	**9,000**	3,000	-
Advertising, Trade	30,000	4,000	4,000	4,000	20,000	4,000	25,000	4,000	45,000	20,000	4,000	4,000	**168,000**	20,000	4,000
Picture Web Site Development	-	5,000	5,000	5,000	5,000	-	5,000	-	5,000	5,000	5,000	-	**30,000**	5,000	5,000
Travel & Ent. / Markets	10,000	10,000	10,000	30,000	10,000	10,000	10,000	10,000	10,000	10,000	10,000	20,000	**150,000**	20,000	10,000
Ancillary Rights Manager	-	-	-	5,000	5,000	5,000	5,000	5,000	5,000	5,000	5,000	-	**40,000**	5,000	5,000
Video Game Demo	-	-	50,000	-	-	-	-	-	50,000	-	-	-	**100,000**	-	50,000
Ancillary Stock Artwork	-	-	-	20,000	20,000	20,000	20,000	20,000	-	-	-	-	**100,000**	-	-
Card Game, Toy, & RPG Artwork	-	-	-	-	-	-	-	-	-	-	-	-	**5,000**	-	5,000
Ancillary Event Promotion	-	-	-	-	-	100,000	-	50,000	57,500	-	-	-	**207,500**	7,500	7,500
Ancillary Event Publicity	-	-	-	-	-	-	-	-	5,000	5,000	5,000	-	**15,000**	-	5,000
Ancillary Event Travel & Ent.	-	-	-	-	-	-	-	5,000	5,000	5,000	5,000	-	**20,000**	-	5,000
Insurance (E&O, GL & Office Contents)	2,083	2,083	2,083	2,083	2,083	2,083	2,083	2,083	2,083	2,083	2,083	2,083	**25,000**	2,083	2,083
Fees															
Producers/Mngng Dev. Dir.	10,000	10,000	10,000	10,000	10,000	10,000	10,000	10,000	10,000	10,000	10,000	10,000	**120,000**	10,000	10,000
Development Directors (2)	12,000	12,000	12,000	12,000	12,000	12,000	12,000	12,000	12,000	12,000	12,000	12,000	**144,000**	12,000	12,000
Development Assts. (3)	9,000	9,000	9,000	9,000	9,000	9,000	9,000	9,000	9,000	9,000	9,000	9,000	**108,000**	9,000	9,000
Receptionist/Office Manager	2,500	2,500	2,500	2,500	2,500	2,500	2,500	2,500	2,500	2,500	2,500	2,500	**30,000**	2,500	2,500
Payroll Taxes @ 18%	6,030	6,030	6,030	6,030	6,030	6,030	6,030	6,030	6,030	6,030	6,030	6,030	**72,360**	6,030	6,030
Benefits	1,800	1,800	1,800	1,800	1,800	1,800	1,800	1,800	1,800	1,800	1,800	1,800	**21,600**	1,800	1,800
Readers	2,000	2,000	2,000	2,000	2,000	2,000	2,000	2,000	2,000	2,000	2,000	2,000	**24,000**	2,000	2,000
Contingency @ 3%	29,067	6,009	3,849	4,119	10,104	6,339	20,799	16,884	17,619	18,414	17,649	14,004	**164,861**	14,409	16,944
Operating Reserve															
Total Expenses	997,981	206,323	132,163	141,433	346,918	217,653	714,113	579,698	604,933	632,228	605,963	480,818	**5,660,221**	494,723	581,758
Partnership Participations															
Total Limited Partner Participation	-	-	-	-	-	-	-	-	-	-	148,750	3,640,000	**3,788,750**	-	-
Total General Partner Participation	-	-	-	-	-	-	-	-	-	-	-	-	-	-	-
Monthly Balance (expense)	5,502,019	(206,323)	(132,163)	(141,433)	(346,918)	(217,653)	(714,113)	(579,698)	(604,933)	(632,228)	(542,213)	1,079,182	**2,463,529**	(494,723)	(581,758)
Cumulative Cash Flow	5,502,019	5,295,697	5,163,534	5,022,101	4,675,183	4,457,531	3,743,418	3,163,720	2,558,787	1,926,560	1,384,347	2,463,529	**2,463,529**	1,968,806	1,387,049

Figure 10.2 continued
Sample Pictures, Ltd. Cash Flow Projection

Cash Flow Projection
Sample Pictures Development, LP

Prepared: January 3, 2005

Description	15 Aug	16 Sep	17 Oct	18 Nov	19 Dec	20 Jan	21 Feb	22 Mar	23 Apr	24 May	Year 2	Year 3	Year 4	Year 5
Events	Director 3	Las Vegas	AFM			Toy Fair			Licensing Fair	E3, Cannes				
		Sell Pic 2				Sell Pic 3								
U.S. Theatrical Release									Release 1		1:4/07	2:8/07, 3:12/07		
Cash Receipts														
Investment Funds	-	-	-	-	-	-	-	-	-	-	-	-	-	-
Production Sale	-	5,200,000	-	-	-	5,200,000	-	-	-	-	10,400,000	-	-	-
Picture Participations	212,500	-	-	-	212,500	141,667	-	1,730,600	396,667	141,667	2,835,600	28,615,862	13,301,159	223,125
Total Cash Receipts	212,500	5,200,000	-	-	212,500	5,341,667	-	1,730,600	396,667	141,667	13,235,600	28,615,862	13,301,159	223,125
Expenses														
Brokerage Fees	-	-	-	-	-	-	-	-	-	-	-	-	-	-
Literary Rights Acquisition Advance	-	-	-	-	-	-	-	-	-	-	100,000	-	-	-
Writers' Fees	140,000	140,000	-	-	-	-	-	-	-	-	420,000	-	-	-
Director Retainer	300,000	-	-	-	-	-	-	-	-	-	300,000	-	-	-
Talent Retainers	-	200,000	200,000	200,000	-	-	-	-	-	-	1,000,000	-	-	-
Unit Production Manager	5,000	5,000	5,000	5,000	5,000	5,000	5,000	5,000	5,000	5,000	60,000	-	-	-
Publicist	5,000	5,000	7,000	5,000	5,000	5,000	1,000	1,000	1,000	1,000	48,000	5,000	5,000	5,000
Attorney, Entertainment	10,000	10,000	10,000	10,000	10,000	10,000	10,000	10,000	10,000	10,000	120,000	-	-	-
Producer's Representative	10,000	10,000	10,000	10,000	10,000	10,000	10,000	10,000	10,000	10,000	120,000	-	-	-
Foreign Sales Representative	5,000	5,000	5,000	5,000	5,000	5,000	5,000	5,000	5,000	5,000	60,000	-	-	-
Accounting	500	500	500	500	500	500	500	500	500	3,000	8,500	4,100	1,500	1,500
Picture Artwork	14,000	6,000	-	-	417	417	417	417	417	417	42,500	5,000	5,000	5,000
Picture Promo Production	10,000	10,000	-	-	417	417	417	417	417	417	42,500	5,000	5,000	5,000
Rent & Parking	4,000	4,000	4,000	4,000	4,000	4,000	2,000	2,000	2,000	2,000	40,000	12,000	800	320
Telephone	3,500	3,500	3,500	3,500	3,500	3,500	1,750	1,750	1,750	1,750	35,000	2,000	2,000	2,000
ISP Web Hosting/Maintenance	500	500	500	500	500	500	250	250	250	250	5,000	600	600	600
Office Equipment	400	400	400	400	400	400	-	-	-	-	3,200	-	-	-
Printing	30,000	500	500	500	500	20,000	500	20,000	500	500	94,000	15,000	5,000	5,000

Line Item											Total			
Supplies, Misc. Office	750	750	750	750	750	750	750	750	750	750	**9,000**	400	400	400
Pstg / Dlvry Service	750	750	750	750	750	750	375	375	375	375	**7,500**	750	750	750
Media Research	2,000	2,000	2,000	2,000	2,000	2,000	-	-	-	-	**16,000**	1,000	-	-
Motion Picture Sftwr	-	-	-	-	-	-	-	-	-	-	**3,000**	-	-	-
Advertising, Trade	50,000	4,000	4,000	4,000	4,000	40,000	4,000	30,000	4,000	4,000	**172,000**	15,000	15,000	15,000
Picture Web Site Development	5,000	-	-	-	-	-	-	-	-	-	**15,000**	-	-	-
Travel & Ent. / Markets	10,000	10,000	30,000	10,000	10,000	10,000	10,000	10,000	10,000	20,000	**150,000**	-	-	-
Ancillary Rights Manager	5,000	5,000	5,000	5,000	5,000	5,000	5,000	5,000	5,000	5,000	**60,000**	-	-	-
Video Game Demo	-	-	-	-	-	-	-	-	-	-	**50,000**	-	-	-
Ancillary Stock Artwork	-	40,000	40,000	40,000	40,000	40,000	40,000	-	-	-	**200,000**	-	-	-
Card Game, Toy, & RPG Artwork	20,000	30,000	-	5,000	5,000	25,000	-	-	-	-	**55,000**	22,500	-	-
Ancillary Event Promotion	-	7,500	-	50,000	50,000	-	32,500	-	-	-	**130,000**	30,000	-	-
Ancillary Event Publicity	-	-	5,000	-	-	5,000	5,000	5,000	5,000	-	**25,000**	10,000	-	-
Ancillary Event Travel & Ent.	-	-	10,000	-	-	10,000	10,000	5,000	5,000	-	**35,000**	15,000	-	-
Insurance (E&O, GL & Office Contents)	2,083	2,083	2,083	2,083	2,083	2,083	2,083	2,083	2,083	2,083	**25,000**	500	500	500
Fees														
Producers/Mngng Dev. Dir.	10,000	10,000	10,000	10,000	10,000	10,000	5,000	5,000	5,000	5,000	**100,000**	-	-	-
Development Directors (2)	12,000	12,000	12,000	12,000	12,000	12,000	6,000	6,000	6,000	6,000	**120,000**	-	-	-
Development Assts. (3)	9,000	9,000	9,000	9,000	9,000	9,000	4,500	4,500	4,500	4,500	**90,000**	-	-	-
Receptionist/Office Manager	2,500	2,500	2,500	2,500	2,500	2,500	1,250	1,250	1,250	1,250	**25,000**	-	-	-
Payroll Taxes @ 18%	6,030	6,030	6,030	6,030	6,030	6,030	3,015	3,015	3,015	3,015	**60,300**	-	-	-
Benefits	1,800	1,800	1,800	1,800	1,800	1,800	900	900	900	900	**18,000**	-	-	-
Readers	2,000	-	-	-	-	-	-	-	-	-	**6,000**	-	-	-
Contingency @ 3%	20,304	13,989	12,294	10,959	6,184	6,949	5,016	4,056	2,691	2,766	**116,565**	4,766	1,247	1,232
Operating Reserve	-	-	-	-	-	-	-	-	25,000	25,000	-	-	-	-
Total Expenses	697,118	480,303	422,108	376,273	212,332	238,596	172,223	139,263	92,398	119,973	**4,027,066**	163,616	42,797	42,302
Partnership Participations														
Total Limited Partner Participation	148,750	3,640,000	-	-	148,750	73,750	-	-	-	3,791,013	**7,802,263**	14,226,123	6,629,181	90,411
Total General Partner Participation	-	-	-	-	-	78,788	-	-	-	3,791,013	**3,869,801**	14,226,123	6,629,181	90,411
Monthly Balance (expense)	(633,368)	1,079,697	(422,108)	(376,273)	(148,582)	4,950,532	(172,223)	1,591,337	304,269	(7,560,331)	**(2,463,529)**	-	-	(0)
Cumulative Cash Flow	753,681	1,833,378	1,411,271	1,034,998	886,416	5,836,948	5,664,725	7,256,063	7,560,331	-	-	-	-	(0)

prepared between the companies. The pictures, production company, and investors should receive the greatest amount of protection, along with the most efficient tax consequences possible. If there are private investors, they will need reasonable incentives and protection also. This step typically is accomplished by the producer's accountant and attorney, who assist in the deal formulation, tax considerations, and securities issues. Many of the basic considerations relating to this step are reviewed in Chapter 9.

6. Prepare the Investment's Documentation

Even if the production company is the sole investment source, documentation must be prepared and entered into with legal, producer income, and tax consequences that facilitate the plan's formal engagement.

The producer's attorney usually prepares this documentation. If funds are raised from private investors, a securities attorney should be involved. No securities documentation should be distributed until it has passed an attorney's review.

7. Make the Presentations and Fund the Development Company

Regardless of which of the four sources of development financing the producer receives, an offering will be made, and, after acceptance, the documentation will be completed and the funding obtained.

If the funding is to come from private investors, and this is the producer's first private offering, it is often constructive to make a list of potential investors, another list of people of influence who may recommend sophisticated investors to consider the offering, and another list of brokers, investment counselors, and securities dealers. The sources in each category should be prioritized and a plan prepared as to how to approach each source.

Raising private capital is especially challenging for the first development company owned by a new production entity. For these producers, a strong team (presented in Chapter 11), with exceptional stories under consideration, with at least one picture's internal greenlight analysis completed that indicates a producer's share of earnings that is twice the picture's production cost, making a professional presentation, and offering a motivating investment are critical to success in receiving the necessary development capital.

Chapter Postscript

Like production, development should be thoroughly planned, completely financed, and precisely executed to ensure a picture's success. Also, like production, development should be helmed by a skilled team to ensure a smooth transition into funded production and then into the hands of the various global territory licensees that are prepared to receive and exploit each picture.

c h a p t e r 1 1

The Team

This chapter reviews the internal and external players who are the operating and advisory teams of the production and development companies. It also presents the considerations related to planning the team, as well as evaluating, employing or retaining, and setting compensation and fees for all the players.

The Complete Team

No producer would attempt principal photography without a whole production team, yet some producers operate their businesses without a complete operating team.

Producers must have a person handling each of the stewardships demanded by their business. Most production companies begin with a sparse in-house team, supported with outside professionals that may include an attorney, accountant, producer's sales representative, foreign sales organization, PR firm, or an advertising agency. These may provide critical services at a more reasonable cost than comparable full-time in-house executives. Regardless of the source, producers should be able to perform all the functions necessary to their business in a coordinated, seamless fashion.

The organization charts in Figures 11.1 and 11.2 present the basic positions that are necessary to operate an independent production company and its development companies. Keep in mind that many development companies have a fully staffed and operating life of two to five years, depending on the number of pictures they are designed to develop. Thereafter, they may exist for 20 to 25 years,

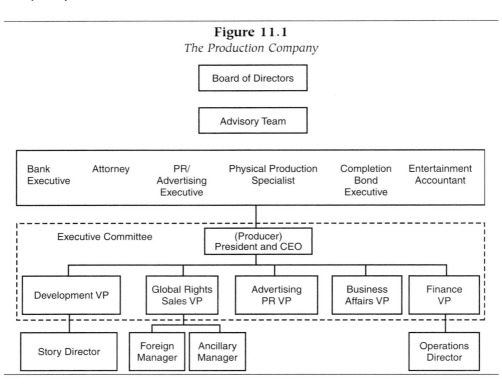

Figure 11.1

The Production Company

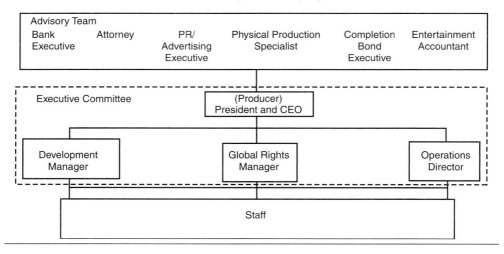

Figure 11.2

The Development Company

depending on their charter, but their primary activity is to accept and disburse income. The production company, on the other hand, has a continuing life and supplies most of the development and producing companies' operating and advisory team.

Company Structure

The production organization and producing entity structures are recommended to be single taxation, subchapter S corporations, limited liability companies (LLCs), or limited partnerships (LPs), to provide optimal legal protection for the principals and to facilitate growth, mergers, acquisitions, and so on. The development companies are most often LPs or LLCs. Because of their deeper legal precedent with tax law and general litigation, we especially recommend using subchapter S corporation structures.

Corporations are owned by their shareholders. The shareholders create a board of directors who are responsible not only for establishing the corporation's constitution, policies, and procedures, but also for appointing corporate officers, who are responsible for operating the organization.

In corporations, the shareholders wield the ultimate power. In their majority, shareholders can remove and replace members of the board of directors and override any other governing power within the organization.

On the production company chart in Figure 11.1, the board of directors is shown in a separate box, since it is rarely involved in the day-to-day operations of the corporation. Its members usually just meet annually, when they review annual reports and projections and participate in the review of matters related to mergers, acquisitions, substantial capital restructuring, or changes in corporate policy and procedures.

The Production Company's Team

The production company's chart shows three tiers of the team. The first tier is composed of a six-member advisory team; the second tier, an operating team with six key players who are the production company's executive committee; and the final tier, the executive committee's staff.

The Advisory Team

Every production organization is substantially benefited by its advisory team. The members of this team are entertainment industry professionals who are rarely available or affordable for executive positions within a production company. They are seasoned industry icons, and their advice, counsel, the relationships they have with other powerful people, and their deal influence amplify the production company's industry position, broaden its reach, and sharpen its business and creative focus. This team is especially important for newer production entities.

The most common members of production company advisory teams are:

- An entertainment bank executive
- An entertainment attorney
- A brand-making professional who is most often an executive in a public relations firm or advertising agency
- A physical production specialist who is usually a line producer or UPM
- A completion bond executive
- An entertainment accountant

Some of the advisory team members may serve on the production company's board of directors, but their primary function is to serve the company individually as mentors in addition to providing more customary professional services.

Most potential advisory team members have no natural business motivation to serve as a member of a production company's advisory team except that they are mature in their professional duties in the industry and may be persuaded to guide organizations that need their help. The keys for newer production companies to win the support of these powerful people are the ethics and achievement commitment of the producer, the kind of pictures the producer is committed to create, and the approach the producer is taking to produce and distribute these pictures. Producers who are organized, focused, and determined to produce important, but not necessarily big or broadly commercial pictures are often the ones who are well received by these potential team members.

The production company may actually also retain the attorney, brand executive, physical production specialist, and accountant in an industry customary fashion. Typically, in these relationships, the team member is engaged in the company's exceptional situations, while someone else on their staff fulfills the more traditional needs. The remaining team members are the bank and completion bond executives, who are paid fees for the services that are extraordinary to their organizations with which they provide the production company. For instance, a bank executive may assist the producer in obtaining a credit facility from a foreign bank, a competing domestic bank, or a commercial organization.

The services provided by and the process of selecting and engaging a relationship with a bank are reviewed in Chapter 5, completion bond executives are covered in Chapter 6, and entertainment attorneys in Chapter 7. Though certain loans may be too large or small for the bank with which the advisor is associated, usually legal and bonding services are provided through the organizations with whom the producer's advisors are associated.

The services provided by a physical production specialist are presented in Chapter 10. This person usually is selected by research and reputation. Producers most often become familiar with line producers and UPMs by the pictures they have worked on. Like most industry talent, these professionals are very busy but quite approachable. Producers should meet with the three to five strongest candidates, present their company's purpose, and explain the relationship desired. Often the selection is obvious, but if not, producers should review their notes and discuss their options with their advisory and/or operating teams, and then make their decision. After the selection is made, producers should contact the other candidates in writing, thanking them for their time and consideration, as well as writing the selected person, reviewing immediate plans, and expressing enthusiasm for their advisory team participation.

The Executive Committee

The executive committee consists of the producer and the department heads. These are the people responsible for ensuring that the company's objectives are fulfilled, its mission statement brought into continually finer focus, and its achievement-dynamic amplified. Responsible for all earnings and accountable for all operating expenses, this committee typically meets once a week, where it reviews company progress and revises projections.

The producer's corporate title is usually chief executive officer, president, or both, and the department heads are vice presidents. The producer is the team leader responsible for the ultimate creative and business bottom line of the company. The producer's duties are presented more fully in Chapter 12. The producer may have a subordinate officer who is primarily responsible for directing the department heads. This person may also serve as the chairman of the executive committee and have the corporate title of executive or senior vice president.

The primary stewardships of the development vice president are in soliciting and discovering stories. After they are greenlit, the vice president manages their development in the development company, under the direction of the producer, who is typically the development company's development director.

The *global rights sales vice president* is responsible for preparing the initial liquidation breakdown for each picture that comes under the scrutiny of an internal greenlight and the continuing revaluing, sales strategy, presales, and all initial and continuing rights liquidation of the company's pictures. This vice president may direct the activities of a staff, including a foreign sales manager and an ancillary sales manager, as well as the vice president's assistants.

The *advertising and public relations vice president* is responsible for establishing and sustaining the production company's brand to the entertainment global trade and global consumers, and for establishing each motion picture's initial brand with the global entertainment trade and global consumers. This person also manages the continuing brand in conjunction with the various global distributors, reviews and manages the producer's position relative to the media plans and media buys prior to and during the theatrical and videocassette releases, and audits media and public relations' expenses fulfilled by distributors on behalf of the producer. This vice president also may direct the activities of a staff of one or two assistants, plus the activities performed by promotions/public relations firms, advertising agencies, and other related vendors.

The *business affairs vice president* typically has a law degree and directs the deal documentation preparation for development and production-related issues, along with sophisticated rights sales and distribution. These vice presidents closely correlate their work with the company's attorney, direct an assistant, and usually participate in development and production negotiations.

The *finance vice president* manages the company's cash flow, accounting, tax management, government agency reporting, management reports, and the company's information systems. This VP also manages the relationship with the company's entertainment accountant and manages the efforts of the operations director and department assistants, if there are any.

The Development Company's Team

The development company is a completely separate business entity from the production company. It has its own accounting records, government agency reporting, income, and expenses. However, it is most commonly at least half-owned by the production company. The two entities have several common elements. Usually the development company physically resides in the production company office and uses the same receptionist, and most of its team are also members of the production company team.

Like the production company, the development company's team has three tiers. The development company's executive committee typically has four members. These are the development director (usually the producer), the development manager (commonly the development VP from the production company), the global rights manager (who is the production company's global rights sales VP), and the operations director (who is an employee unique to the development company).

A producer easily presses full-time attention into development director duties, after a development company's first picture has completed its internal greenlight successfully. The development company usually pays the producer for serving as its development director, while it is paid proportionally by the production company for fulfilling duties there. The same is true for each other member of the development company's advisory team, with the exception of the operations director. This person is usually exclusively fulfilling duties for the development company. The operations director serves under the direction of the production company's finance VP, and may continue in the production company's "family," moving to the production company's succeeding development companies.

The *development manager* is responsible for story search, evaluation, recommendation, and all aspects of each motion picture's creative development and preparation, in every respect, for physical production. This person uses the development VP's production company staff and physical production specialist on an expense-paid basis.

The *global rights manager* is responsible for establishing each picture-in-development's global value, by territory and right, and for preparing promotional, publicity, and marketing materials, meeting with global media and studios, negotiating and preselling some of these rights, and preparing all other rights for future sales. This person also manages all global film market activities. Some of the most critical liquidation relationships—for instance, those with U.S. studios—may be carried out by the producer. But even for these, the global rights manager is responsible for ensuring that they are accomplished.

The *operations director* is responsible for keeping the development company on task and holding the entire team accountable in order to sustain balance between the timing allocated for developing its motion pictures and the budget the team has to achieve this task. This person also fulfills all day-to-day accounting functions, through the delivery of trial balances to the finance VP for the purpose of adjusting entries and preparing interim, monthly, and quarterly reports.

Optimizing the Teams

There are as many production companies whose operating temperament is chaos separated by moments of sanity as there are companies whose operating temperament is steady, progressive achievement. The difference is rarely the amount of work being done, but rather the approach the teams take to accomplish the work.

Operating temperament is set more by the producer than by all the rest of the combined team. It is crucial that each producer accept this responsibility. Producers set the pace. They establish the operating style. They determine the stability of the relationship government within the team and with all the others with whom the producer's team relates.

Among the highest achieving and happiest production company teams there is one management principle observed more consistently than any other. This is the observance by the producer, and subsequently by the rest of the executive team (and so, the staff), of including these three phases in most things they do:

1. They plan through study and evaluation.
2. They do what is planned.
3. They evaluate what was done.

These phases are deeply interrelated, and employing all of them optimizes the producer's capacity to accomplish every desired task and sets the standard for the team to approach their stewardships in a similarly constructive style.

Planning our work creates the greatest assurance that the work we do will accomplish our short- and long-term objectives. *Working* moves us forward to the achievement of our objectives. *Evaluating* our work motivates, makes enlightened planning possible, and inspires more confident and focused work. Sacrifice any one of these three critical phases, and predictable achievement is crippled.

Applying this principle is especially helpful when selecting new teams or organizing or reshaping existing production or development teams.

Planning has been emphasized throughout this text. Just as discovering a picture we want to produce is only the beginning of planning how we are going to develop, produce, and distribute it, so is preparing a mission statement that sets forth why we are in business only the beginning of planning how we will achieve our objectives. Part of each producer's plan should be identifying the talents and capacities needed and desired in the individuals who will be their advisory, operating, and staff teams. The team members should embrace the production company's mission statement, contribute to its clarity, and share the producer's approach to doing business.

Discovering, Negotiating, and Compensating

Producers are best served by team members who are not just good at what they do, but also have the attributes, character, and operating styles complementary to the producer and the rest of the team.

Discovering

For existing teams that have vacancies, the best approach to filling them is to write a description of the person sought, their stewardship, and compensation. This description should be circulated among the executive and advisory teams. Additionally, industry personnel agencies and advertising in the trade papers should be used to allow fresh, vibrant talent to have the opportunity to join the team. Set a time for the decision. Include those in the decision-making process who may share stewardships or parallel positions with the open post. Attempt to adhere to the time, but never select someone less than the stewardship demands. Team orientation and releasing someone are emotionally and financially expensive. It is always better to wait for someone who appears sure.

For new production teams, start with the advisory tier. These members are easy to spot, evaluate, and approach. Once they are in place, then use them as resources for the production executive committee. After the executive committee is set, use them and the advisory members to recommend staff.

Negotiating and Compensation

Before negotiating, research what the industry's fair compensation for a particular position's services is, then temper this amount according to the company's projected budget. Negotiate the best relationship possible with the person, and after the negotiation has concluded, agree to start them at a little more than they expect. Good will motivates a positive attitude and usually increases industry.

Production companies are naturally rigorous environments. Participating in a winning production team demands everyone's personal excellence. Driving successful pictures is emotionally—and should also be financially—rewarding. It is very good business for producers to set a percentage of pretax profits aside (perhaps 10 percent) for all employees to annually participate in. Some producers require new team members to vest (mature) in their relationship for 6 to 12 months before they qualify to participate. Sharing profits builds team spirit and loyalty, which fosters a happier and more profitable environment.

Chapter Postscript

New and existing producers are well compensated if they understand all the business and creative functions that must be accomplished to do the work required by their production and development companies. These functions should be defined in terms of the advisory, operating, and staff tiers of the team. Producers should have complete teams to ensure their capacity to accomplish the company's goals.

The producer sets the operating style of the team. The producer should demonstrate a style that promotes the team's sure, successive achievement.

There is an abundance of very talented prospective team members. A good plan to discover them, patiently executed, using team resources, will draw them in. Both regular team evaluations and allowing team members to participate in the company's rewards promote solidarity and mutual success.

Chapter 12

Production Company Operation

This chapter presents the operations of production companies and their related development and producing organizations. The prior chapters have presented the independent fundamental operating principles of these companies. This chapter demonstrates both how they work together and the business elements that join them.

The operations of these companies in their complete forms are also revealed in this chapter. For those who have experience with the operating performance of the most successful production companies, the operations presented in this chapter may seem more cumbersome or thorough than necessary. Consider the performance of a new driver compared with the performance of an experienced one. Seasoned drivers may speed through yellow lights, may turn without using their signals if they don't see any oncoming traffic, and may consistently drive a few miles over the speed limit on the freeway. These are not recommended operating styles but may become entrenched habits of experienced drivers.

As dexterity increases, so does confidence. As this occurs, one has a natural tendency, especially under pressure (and producers operate under extreme conditions), to cut operating corners and to increase operating speed. Abbreviating, or especially missing any development or production steps, places the creative and earnings life of a picture at risk. As with experienced drivers, accomplished producers often press pictures through the production process with amazing agility and success. However, like the best race car drivers, fine producers occasionally trash pictures that would otherwise have been successful and performed well in the marketplace, simply because those producers slighted certain steps or passed them altogether.

Because this natural tendency exists, it is necessary to establish a development and production checking system through which each picture passes. This chapter presents this system.

It falls upon the development vice president to ensure that each picture accomplishes all the steps. No one likes to be told they are going too fast or don't have their seat belt on, especially the producer who is most often the company chief and who stands to lose the greatest amount from a picture's failure. But it must be done. By establishing this process, a production company can successfully maximize operating integrity, as well as each picture's creative and financial success. And to present the most comprehensive operating profile, the example in this chapter is of a new production company.

Defining and Establishing the Production Company

As presented in Chapter 10, producers should write a mission statement that sets forth their purpose for creating their company, along with the manner in which they intend to conduct their business. This statement is often several pages long in its expanded reference format for the executive committee and pared down to less than a page for use by others.

There are several advantages for two or more principals rather than one to create a production company. Multiple principals typically deliver a better system of checks and balances for the company—each principal reviews and, from a similar position of power, holds the other accountable for performance. If each principal shares the mission of the organization, but delivers different experience and capacities, the company's overall strength and operating ballast are increased. There are several excellent examples of this, including Ron Howard and Brian Grazer with their Imagine Entertainment empire, and Mel Gibson and Bruce Davies in their Icon Pictures powerhouse. With each of these teams, both are producers, but one is more deeply creative and the other has a stronger business background, thus delivering an excellent balance to their respective organizations.

If the organization has more than one principal, these individuals should agree on the company's mission, their respective stewardships, contributions, equity, operating control, earnings, and profit participations. They should also enter a written agreement or separate management contracts, reflecting these deal elements and others natural to such agreements. (They should be certain to include buy/sell terms and the method of dispute resolution.)

It is always best to have the producer's entertainment attorney or some other lawyer involved in both negotiating and preparing the principals' documentation. The attorney should also prepare and file the company's formation documents with the state and direct the initial organizing meeting.

The Story Search

Most mission statements share one critical common goal—that the production company find and acquire the kinds of stories it is formed to produce and distribute. The search for these stories will be a preeminent activity throughout the life of the production company. This should be the first focus of newly formed companies.

Although there is an abundance of scripts, only a few are worth producing. The search should start immediately and continue in an organized fashion. Chapter 7 provides information about the legal aspects of story review and the need for literary release forms.

In contrast to the stunning volume of stories presented to producers from traditional trade sources is the smaller but just as vital proportion of stories discovered from nonindustry sources. Usually producers have their private treasure house of folks who may be willing to champion their story cause, including family, friends from childhood, teachers, and others. This group can become a pipeline of continuing story discovery. Most of these connections, when asked, will recommend stories they believe will make great motion pictures, thus maximizing the benefits from this source.

Producers should make a list of everyone who may be willing to participate as story resources and compose a letter that can easily be customized for each person, telling them they now have their own motion picture production company and are looking for stories that may make great motion pictures. Specifically, they should enclose two self-addressed and stamped postcards, asking the group to take a moment right then to list at least one story from a book or other source that they could recommend. Then ask them to keep the other card in a conspicuous place for the purpose of making future recommendations. Producers should include their fifth-grade teacher who was a story wizard, their Peace Corps companion who read a book a week, and so forth. They may be tough to track down, so the new producer should try the Internet or give the list to an assistant to do the detective work. This has proven to be a stunningly fine source of story discovery by some of the industry's most notable producers. Great stories from unpublished journals, out-of-print books, and those known only to storytellers and have never been written down are also some of the most remarkable finds. It is essential that producers commence and continue the story search and review process throughout the predevelopment company preparation.

Stories of interest to the producer should be represented to investors only as such, unless they have been greenlit by a U.S. studio and distributors in the six major international territories. It should be emphasized to prospective partners that, in large measure, their confidence in the new production company stems from the fact that it will develop and produce only pictures that are closely coordinated with global distributors.

However, potential investors will ask if producers have stories they are interested in and will want to hear them pitched. This is dangerous, because tastes in stories differ widely, and in an even more critical consideration, although producers may be excellent in their craft, they may be weak in their capacity to pitch an investor on a particular story. Producers should expect story queries and be prepared by having multiple stories ready and their pitches well-rehearsed.

For investors, more important than story point of reference should be the producer's representation that they have several stories with development and production potential ready for the internal greenlight process.

Development Company Emphasis

As story discovery and development come before production and distribution, and these activities originate in the producer's development companies, the first order of business is the planning and financing of the first development company. The need for this process and its thorough analysis is presented in Chapter 10.

Many production companies are launched with only their development company financing and teams (these are presented in Chapter 11), because developing their first pictures is typically their entire initial business.

If this is their position, these producers begin by preparing the first activity projection of the development company. A sample of this projection and its review are presented in Chapter 10. Following the preparation of the activity projection is the preparation of the cash flow projection, also presented in Chapter 10, which expresses the costs of the development company's activities.

Most development companies will be financed privately, according to the methods referenced in Chapter 10. If this is the case, producers will analyze the cash flow projection in relation to the total operating cash needed and the potential income earned by the development company. The private investor's participation is then applied to the cash flow projection and reviewed for its impact on the producer and its appeal to the investor. This process determines the basic deal points offered to the private investor. Often several operating models are analyzed by passing their criteria through the projections until the producer settles on the ultimate balance among the number of pictures to be developed, the development pace, the total investment amount, and the appeal to potential investors.

Preparing the Investment Offering

With the activity and the cash flow projections prepared and the investment offering plan configured, the producer is ready to commence authorship of the confidential investment memorandum, with the assistance of the producer's attorney and business consultant or accountant.

The business consultant or accountant prepares:

- The activity and cash flow projections as they will appear in the offering
- The notes to these projections
- The offering's use of proceeds
- The more detailed source and use of funds analysis
- The tax consequences

The producer prepares the introductory letter, the partnership business section (a representation of the production company's mission statement as it applies to the development company, including the kinds of pictures and properties the development company is seeking), and the development team summary biographies.

The attorney authors the memorandum, including the final draft of the business planning materials prepared by the business consultant or accountant and the producer.

Assembling the Team

An important part of the offering memorandum includes information about the producer's team, insofar as it is assembled at the time the offering is published. Who will be managing the partnership's business is crucial to prospective investors. They learn early that a great plan is only as impressive as the team assembled to carry it out.

The producer should have most of the advisory team assembled and represented at the time of the offering, as this team represents much of the assurance that the producer will be able to accomplish the development company's plan.

As the attorney prepares the first draft of the development company's investment memorandum, the producer will be setting appointments, meeting, and selecting advisory team members. Chapter 11 comprehensively presents the producer's advisory team categories and how to approach them.

Producing the Investment Memorandum

After the team is selected, the producer completes the biographical summaries for the advisory team members and others who are identified in the proposal, the final draft of the introductory letter, and the business section of the memorandum.

The producer reviews the materials prepared by the business consultant or accountant and delivers all these materials to the attorney, after which the attorney prepares a final draft of the memorandum for the producer's review. The attorney makes final content polishes, and hard and computer disk copies are given to the producer.

The attorney should have offering samples that the producer can review for ideas on the look of the published draft. Having prepared many of these over the years, our suggestion is to focus on the content. Keep it clean and simple in presentation. Investors may be impressed with the glitz of an ornate-looking offering for a moment, but their decision will be based on the deal, the plan, and the people. In the final analysis, glitz has little effect on a positive decision.

Some producers use designers to prepare the offering's look. Whatever the cosmetic, the master is prepared and copies made and numbered for presentation to prospective investor-partners.

Raising the Development Financing

Though producers who are funding their first development partnership may make presentations to several people, and the offering is structured to accommodate 10 or more investors, it is common for there to be fewer than five investors who actually participate. Typically, one investor will be enamored with the offering's merits and will influence one or more investor associates to join in the relationship.

As to the most effective approach, each investor should be considered individually. Some investors prefer to be in a group presentation, whereas others prefer a private meeting. Each investor should be approached with their most effective method and setting in mind.

It is well to remember that the person to meet with is the actual investor. Sophisticated investors often have assistants who afford professional courtesy to the myriad offers that barrage these sources. Producers should begin this process by amassing lists of investors, brokers, finders, and people of influence they know who might invest or open the direct doors to them of others who have the means to invest.

Most investors' knowledge of entertainment investments is limited to the deep well of dreadful stories associated with investing in the production of independent pictures. Most investors have never had the opportunity to invest in independent motion picture development.

When you meet with the investor:

1. Make the entire presentation brief (under an hour). Let them know before the meeting how long it will take.
2. At the beginning of the meeting, let them know that first they will receive an overview of how the most successful independent producers do business, then hear how the production company is poised to operate. Following that, there will be a review of this particular offering, allowing the investors to consider the relationship in whatever manner they may be interested in.
3. After this has been told to them, proceed with the presentation of the three areas referenced earlier. For most investors, this is a new and fascinating business playing field. They often have questions and comments.

Most investors place their confidence in the person rather than the documentation. The offering is expensive, and the information it contains is critically important. Investors will want to be entirely convinced that the producer understands the industry, this particular plan, and that this venture has a high probability to succeed. A producer needs solid confidence that comes from experience, team integrity, a deep understanding of the plan, and a commitment to the plan's success. Many investors have an uncanny sense for this. If they believe the producer has these qualities, they are more likely to consider the offering seriously. If not, then they will pass. The presenters need to be prepared. They will have accumulated a substantial investment in this venture to this point. The professional production values of the memorandum and even the impressive deal points will not overcome a producer's weak profile. It is important to meet potential financial partners when the producer is at his peak potential in these four areas.

Prior to these meetings producers should meet with their attorney and banker. Their attorney will review with them the appropriate legal approach to these highly regulated relationships. Their banker will assist in opening an escrow account for the receipt of investment income from the sale of the development company's interests.

Investment Partner Communications

Once a producer has received the investment capital, there is often no immediate motivation to communicate with the private investors, who, before this time, were sought after with the producer's passion, sincerity, and rapt attention.

Though the partnership agreement may not require communication with partners more than annually, it is good form and builds relationship integrity to prepare and send a letter, at least quarterly, informing them of development, production, and distribution progress.

Producers build confidence in their investors through beginning this relationship with a letter of appreciation and encouragement to them. Then they should set triggers in their schedule for similar letters to continue. This will be challenging to do after development commences, but should be done, even if the letters are prepared by an assistant.

Working the Development Plan

The development activity projection used in the investment offering is the producer's representation to the investors of what will be done and when it will be accomplished. The activities in this projection are the investors' benchmark expectations and also should be used by the operating team to gauge the company's progress.

Each activity in the projections should be accomplished as if it is crucial to the initial and continuing success of the production company and its pictures. Each item should be finely planned, collaborated upon as a team, and accomplished at its zenith.

The producer's activities in order of priority are described in the next sections.

Story

Producers should work on story *every day*. This should be well-rounded work, including reading and reviewing fresh coverage and analysis reports. In addition, they should send more letter and postcard requests (referred to earlier), research story leads, and, where appropriate, write, as well as direct writers.

Advisory Member Meetings

Producers should meet with each member of their advisory committee immediately after funding has occurred. Copies of the current development activity projection should be given to and reviewed with each member. Suggestions relative to the plan, story suggestions, and team candidate recommendations should be elicited. Meeting with the advisory members as a group is often most effective, but because of tight schedules, it's not often possible.

The banker will transfer the entire invested funds from the escrow account to the development company's working and savings accounts. Retainers will be advanced to the attorney, the UPM, and possibly the publicist.

Finding and Securing the Team

The advisory team is an excellent resource for recommendations for executive team members. Stewardship definitions and remuneration parameters should be given to the advisory team members, and their help in finding excellent candidates should be requested.

A clear advertisement should be placed in one or more of the daily entertainment trade papers with a request for faxed, e-mailed, or carrier-mailed resumes. One or more industry personnel agencies may be another excellent resource for candidates. Of these three resources, the executive team, followed by the agencies and finally the trade papers, is most likely to recommend the best people to the producer.

From these responses, the producer first will interview, perhaps reinterview, and then consider the finalists with the counsel of the appropriate advisory committee members. Next, the producer negotiates with the lead candidates and then prepares and enters a management agreement with the finalist. Entering these agreements with each new member of the executive committee is essential.

Once the executive team is assembled, the first meeting should be held. Each member should attend this meeting prepared with a written stewardship definition that includes the people for whom they have immediate higher and lesser accountability. These definitions should be reviewed, harmonized, and adopted by the entire committee. Doing this allows the team to begin with a clear mutual understanding of each person's responsibilities and accountabilities. This has a wonderful effect on the team's efficiency, peace, and stability.

Often the executive team members will make their own staff recommendations. If these are not sufficient to fill the entire staff, recommendations should be sought from other executive team members and the three sources referenced earlier. As each staff member is attached to the team, they should also prepare, submit, and have harmonized their stewardship definitions, as referenced earlier. These definitions should be available to every team member. Executive team meetings usually occur weekly at a regular time and place, as determined by the members.

U.S. and Major International Territory Distributor Announcements

The first creation of new production companies should be their at-least printed introductory announcement to every major global distributor. Because there are so few balanced producers, the most important aspect of this announcement is the definition of the relationship the producer seeks to have with these distributors.

There are multiple distributors in each of the U.S. and major international territories, and every one of them should receive a personal letter with their announcement. As reviewed in Chapters 2 and 3, all distributors have their unique liquidation values and characteristics for specific pictures, and consequently, every distributor is important to the producer.

The quality of this announcement should demonstrate that the production company operates in the same manner as the finest production entities in the industry. In other words, it should look "major studio."

The announcement introduces the new motion picture production entity and its first fully funded development company. The announcement incorporates the spirit of the production company's mission statement, and, moreover, presents the company's operating profile as one that develops and produces those motion pictures that these distributors want to distribute.

The producer will introduce the company in a personal letter to the distribution chief of each studio and major international territory distributor. The number of pictures on the production company's first development slate should be listed, along with the producer's intent to make a picture-specific pitch to the distributor for their initial distribution interest consideration, in the future. Stated clearly in this letter is the producer's position that the production company will develop and produce only motion pictures that first receive distributor interest. The producer should assert that the company will continue a close relationship with the distributor throughout development and production to ensure each picture's strongest production values, to achieve its maximum audience performance in their territory, and to assure the distributor of the greatest support of marketing and public relations materials to help prepare each picture's audiences.

These letters, with their collateral materials, should be sent to these individuals and their organizations before press or trade ads, demonstrating how the production company will proceed with press announcements relating to each picture.

The producer should break trade press releases and publish trade paid advertising three to five days following the distributor's receipt of their packages. The process, overall appearance, and quality of the ads and press releases should continue to appear as if they come from a studio or major independent producer

Story Selection and Initial Greenlights

All submitted stories are reviewed by the development manager. Stories that the development manager recommends to the producer (who must approve them) are then passed on to the production company's executive committee for their approval for investment in the story's internal greenlight. This investment is typically 120 to 150 work hours plus research and comparative media acquisition costs. There are now excellent sources (see the information sources listed in Chapter 14) to support this work produced in-house. If accomplished by an outside greenlight source this may cost $10,000 to $50,000. This may appear time consuming or expensive, but the results will reveal several critical business aspects of the picture that will inform and enable the producer to succeed in the development of the picture, or abandon the project until it has a reasonable possibility to succeed.

Among an extensive list of enabling information, the internal greenlight will:

- Largely determine a picture's economic feasibility
- Reveal its target audiences by weight (the percentage of each major target audience within the picture's unique audience universe)
- Point to the studio with the highest success profile in releasing pictures with similar audiences, campaigns, and above-the-line elements
- Indicate the most likely production funding structure and even its optimal season to theatrically release

Stories that receive the committee's approval then pass through the internal greenlight process under the direction of the development manager. This process largely consists of the following steps.

1. **Script Campaign Breakdown**. Like a budget breakdown, the script is reviewed and all the elements that lend themselves to the picture's 30-second television commercial that will be used as the primary driver for its U.S. theatrical release are culled from the entire script into the Script Campaign Breakdown form, similar to the one shown here. A version of this form is on the enclosed CD.

Script Campaign Breakdown

Production Company: Over-the-Top Pictures

Picture Title: Spare Parts

Date Prep: 4/22/04   Analyst: MCS, ZM

Page #	Setup	A streamlined spaceship streaks TOWARD CAMERA. The beautiful red and green planet in the distance suffers a series of brilliant, violent explosions high in its atmosphere.
1		
Page #	Setup	The controls and machinery glow and spark ominously. The instruments still working all read in the red danger zones.
1		
Page #	Setup	THREE MEN man the controls, struggling to keep the ship moving.
1	Line	COMMANDER: Damn shields are gone! We're gonna fry if we don't blow up first.

---

2. **Campaign Creative**. A professional copywriter, deeply exercised in writing the copy for theatrical release television campaigns for the leading campaign creation entities (see Chapter 14) creates the voice-over "spine" for the commercial and a final 30-second television commercial script is created (see the following). This script is the critical foundation to the greenlight. Using sources deeply exercised in this process is critical. to delivering valid results.

SAMPLE SCRIPT
MAJOR ENTERTAINMENT
"LOVE UNDER PRESSURE"
:30 SCRIPT

Internal Greenlight Draft

		Cumulative
Video	Time	Audio
		(Wild sounds throughout spot)
Charlie in his BMW takes the MLK Blvd exit off the Fwy. (96)		(S.O.) Two drum sticks smack together counting a steady single rhythm about 50% greater than a resting heartbeat. More music cues
	:02	VO: IN EVERY CITY

Rachel rides with her father through Beverly Hills in the rainy night, police car following them. (45)	:04	VO: THERE ARE PLACES …
Rachel sits with a few girls at a multiracial table, Charlie smiles at her, she hesitates, then smiles back. (7)	:06	VO: WE FEAR TO GO

3. **Campaign Beat Analysis.** The number of emotional beats in each of the 11 major categories are counted in the 30-second television commercial script (see the following). The results are tallied and the emotional beats of the proposed picture's campaign are analyzed. The percentage allocations of the emotional beats are the pictures "campaign signature," and will allow the picture to be defined by its target audiences and their percentage of dominance.

Campaign Beat Analysis

Data Entry Worksheet

Production Company: Picture Title:

Campaign: Date Prepared: Analyst:

Emotions					Sci-fi/ Fantasy		Cultures			
Romance	Drama	Comedy	Action	Risque	Supernatural	Horror	Men	Women	Youth	Kids

Directions:

Each beat scores one point.

Drama beats are every visual, VO, or sound that reveals the story.

Culture beats are those that speak directly to that particular target. If a child is in the scene, this is not necessarily a kids beat. Culture beats have an extreme perspective of that culture. Each beat may not be a particular culture beat.

4. **Campaign Signature.** As referenced in the following example, by applying the Campaign Signature quotients to a studio or an alternative source's audience analysis matrix (see Chapter 14), the picture's target audiences by dominance are computed automatically as the picture's beats are recorded. This report reveals the proposed picture's beats and target audiences as percentages, ranks audience dominance, and reveals studio picture profiles such as Romantic Comedy, Date Picture, Buddy Picture, and so on, as well as major blended audience.

Great Producer

Amazing Script

Date Prepared: 7/20/2004
Analyst: SP

Traditional Audience Profiles	Target Audiences Beat Score Translation	Campaign Appeal As a %	Rank
Women 18+	34.0	29%	1
Men 18+	32.0	27%	2
Youth 12–17	30.0	25%	3
Kids 5–11	23.0	19%	4
Total	119.0	100%	

Major Blended Audiences	Score	As a %	R
Youth/Young Adults 16–25	33.0	28%	2
Older Women 25–49	33.0	28%	2

Emotional Category	Campaign Score # of Beats	As % of Total Beats	Rank
Romance	5	12%	4
Drama	10	24%	2
Comedy	13	31%	1
Action	6	14%	3
Risqué	2	5%	
Sci-Fi/Fantasy	0	0%	
Horror	0	0%	
Men Culture	2	5%	
Women Culture	3	7%	
Youth Culture	1	2%	
Kids Culture	0	0%	
Total	42	100%	

5. **Preliminary and Then Final Comparative Pictures Gathered and Analyzed**. Pictures released in the past five years that appear to potentially have similar target audience, campaign signatures, and above-the-line elements to the proposed picture are identified. Typically this is a sampling of 30 to 70 pictures. The primary 30-second commercial used in the U.S. theatrical campaign, prior to each of these picture's theatrical premiere undergo a Campaign Beat Analysis, then passed through the Audience Analysis Matrix, compared with the greenlight picture. Those very close in target audiences, campaign signature, and above-the-line elements are compiled into a report (typically four to eight pictures) showing their composite average earnings, release dates, releasing studios, directors rated, lead cast rated, tag lines, and other information helpful to identify the market and business characteristics of the picture being analyzed.

6. **Global Liquidation Breakdown**. This is a global gross and net earnings forecast of the proposed picture. This also indicates the final producer's share of profits in relationship to the picture's all-in costs.

7. **Comparative Campaign Spending Breakdown**. Reviews the media buy for each of the comparative pictures including total advertising dollars spent and release pattern of the comparable picture, supplying the producer with vital information for evaluating and influencing the U.S. theatrical release pattern, media buy, brand alliances, promotion, and other related campaign aspects.

This information becomes the producer's vital business bulwark for understanding each picture's business and marketing qualities as well as the producer understands its creative aspects. Screening the similar pictures' campaigns is worthy of intense study and is very informing relative to the most effective marketing approaches as well as those who created and employed them. Other reports often very informing to this process include:

1. Brand Tie-in Ad Spending. Identifies the total ad dollars spent by brand tie-in partnerships. Identification of likely brand tie-in categories as well as partners.

2. Proposed Director and Actor Rankings. A list of proposed directors and actors and their rankings in the major territories.

3. Distribution Executive Tracking. Identifies the distribution teams that have exhibited the greatest release success for pictures most market-like the proposed picture and the studio in which they currently reside.

When producers discover a picture that passes an internal greenlight, they also then have the information they need to proceed in engaging their U.S. and international strategic distribution relationships. If the rights have not yet been acquired, then the producer should approach the rights holders or their representatives and enter a nonexclusive relationship that allows the producers the right to continue the final steps of development discovery.

The next step is approaching a U.S. studio for both a validation that the forecasted earnings rendered from the greenlight analysis are valid, and to engage the studio in a confidential, arms-length, best-efforts, no-obligation, exclusive first-look, development collaboration.

In preparation for these meetings, the studio presentation materials must be prepared. The most critical discovery the studio must determine is the high and low earnings capacity of the picture and how easy or difficult the marketing of it will be. The single element that will answer these questions for them is the picture's 30-second television commercial.

A campaign production entity is selected, after competitive pitches, that has demonstrated its abilities unique to the picture and that regularly delivers the campaigns that are used, to the picture's first-choice studios. Though the picture is only in script form, the campaign entity polishes the campaign scripts, records voice talent, may produce some original visuals, creates titles, creates and captures storyboards, may discover and use some existing footage, identifies music and sound effects, and creates a 30-second commercial that clearly demonstrates the picture's marketing and earnings power.

After the materials are prepared, the studio presentations are made, as referenced in Chapters 1 and 2. If the studio concurs that with a director and cast of the dimension and chemistry represented are attached, they believe the picture could earn similarly to the pictures you give as references, and they are willing to give the development collaboration requested, then the international territory meetings are set, as reviewed in Chapter 3. Should no U.S. studio relationship be engaged, then the producer moves on to another project. This may seem brutal. However, it is nothing compared with spending extensive time and funding on projects that do not have sufficient business feasibility to warrant distribution.

The U.S. studio relationship is comfortably engaged, through the producer sending a confirming letter to the studio, referencing the gentle nine-point relationship commencement referenced in Chapter 3.

As also presented in Chapter 3, after establishing the U.S. studio relationship, the producer then prepares to meet with the picture's potentially strongest distributor in each of the seven major international territories, as outlined in the plan prepared by the development manager. Usually most of the materials prepared for the U.S. studio are applicable to their international territory counterparts. If a major market is about to occur, the international territory meetings usually are set around the schedules for that event.

After relationships have been commenced with the international territory distributors, confirmation letters are prepared and presented to each of these, with a new letter to the U.S. distributor, stating that the project has commenced fully financed development and will be announced in the industry trade papers on a date that you specify in the letter.

These negotiations proceed as presented in Chapters 7 and 8, and should include the agreement with the author for a joint press release announcing the right's purchase. The conditions of this release should allow the producer first to notify in writing each of the U.S. and international distributors of the acquisition, then follow this notification with press releases and paid trade announcement regarding the picture's development commencement. As has been reviewed in Chapters 1, 2, and 3, this process of distributor participation and trade culture escalates each picture's value. It also raises the level of anticipation among the participating distributors.

Predirector Picture Development

Once the story's rights are acquired, the picture's game is afoot and will not wane until almost a year following its theatrical release.

This process commences with a special executive committee meeting. In this meeting the picture's basic development, production, and marketing plans and schedules are set, and development and marketing assignments are accepted by all the team members. The story's predirector development is reviewed and decided upon. Also, this is the time that director, acting talent, and production department heads are considered.

The picture's initial trade-brand presence is created at this time, including what will be shown and said in the immediate paid trade announcement, in the future sales conferences, and on the marketing materials sent to the participating distributors. Although the name may later change, as perhaps will the original look, this presence is crucial to the picture's initial and continuing marketplace positioning.

Work now begins on the story's predirector development substantially under the direction of the producer and development manager.

Director Attachment

Once the director is attached, this person will substantially drive the physical development and production of the motion picture. The earlier the director is attached, the greater the creative cohesion and harmony of every aspect of the picture. Producers who are also directors by craft but who will use another director for the picture are especially well served by the earliest possible director attachment, so that every creative element is a collaboration.

Differences in producer/director creative vision have weakened many pictures and literally destroyed others. Early director attachment naturally establishes a strong producer/director collaborative creative foundation.

The producer presents a written list of director recommendations, distilled from the executive committee's recommendations, to each advisory team member for that person's notes and suggestions. Some of the producer's executive and advisory team will have multiple experiences with the directors on this list and will render exceptional counsel relative to the consideration, approach, and eventual relationship with the director.

After checking each director's availability, the producer next prepares a final priority list of directors, considering advisory team input, additional creative research, and discussions with other producers who have experience with these directors.

Then the producer prepares correspondence for the U.S. studio and each international territory greenlit distributor, confidentially revealing the directors being considered, in their order of priority, and requesting each distributor's preferences and comments. Typically this letter is presented in person to the U.S. studio, and, if it is close to a film sales conference, also to the international distributors. If appropriate, a demonstration reel is prepared that accompanies each distributor's letter.

Tempered by distributor responses, the producer creates a final priority list of directors. It is rare that the producer's decision will match every distributors' first choice. This being so, the producer's letter to each participating distributor usually includes an explanation of why the final three director candidates were selected in the particular order they were. This letter also states that the producer is now proceeding to attach the picture's director.

As reviewed in Chapter 8, producers must meet about the story with the director before talking about compensation. Most directors comfortably accommodate these initial creative meetings, since they may have their own production companies, and businesswise, are negotiating their own agreements and using their attorneys and agents primarily for documentation and counsel.

It is during the initial creative meetings with the three leading directors that it often becomes apparent who should direct the picture, because of the director's affinity for the story and the director and producer's natural ability to communicate and respect each others' position, relative to developing and producing the picture.

After the producer reviews the creative meetings' events with the advisory and executive teams, a director decision is made and offering parameters are approved. A negotiation meeting is then set with the director and the director's entourage. If the director's attorney has been asked to participate in the negotiation, the producer's attorney should also participate.

As presented in Chapters 7 and 8, the director's relationship should be negotiated and documented. Part of this negotiation should include this relationship's press announcement.

The U.S. studio and international distributors are then notified of the successful attachment of the director, followed closely by a jointly coordinated press release and paid trade announcement in the entertainment trades.

The Producer/Director Relationship

The producer is the ultimate parent of the picture. The producer discovers the story, holds the initial vision of it as a motion picture, provides the environment and resources for the picture to be developed and produced, and even selects the director. However, the producer has simultaneous multiple-picture responsibilities. The final preparation and actual production of the picture is so intense that one person must be exclusively focused on each picture: the director.

The producer sustains the ultimate authority and power throughout the process. It is important that the producer exercise this authority only with the director. The department heads and all other production participants are accountable to the director, not the producer. When the producer works directly with any of the team reporting to the director, it is done only as an adjunct to the director, not as an authority superior to the director. The director must sustain position integrity with the production team as its ultimate voice. It is standard operating procedure, and everyone knows the director works for the producer. All should also understand that the director has complete power to produce the picture on behalf of the producer.

Most producers are *very* involved in each picture's development and production. Particularly when it comes to script development, talent attachment, storyboard creation, location selection, and the final post-production and sweetening. Even after the producer reviews the dailies, the director may receive a call requesting reshoots, rewrites, and other major alterations. But this is between the director and the producer.

It is always in the best interest of the picture that the producer and director sustain this relationship integrity. To all who work on the picture, the producer creates an aura of respect for the director as the development and production chief of the picture. The director listens and responds to the producer who is, after all, the picture's creator and ultimate authority.

This is a fairly easy concept in discussion, but typically, it can be challenging for both directors and producers to sustain during the intense heat of time and financial pressures that almost always attend development and, especially, production. As producers and directors often remind each other, it isn't the first development or production challenge and its accompanying burdens that test and tax the relationship, it is the tenth or twentieth. It is at the time that neither party can recognize the picture's original schedule or the budget targets.

The truth of this working relationship is that most producers cannot direct every picture they produce. They must use directors. If the picture is going to be infused with the life it needs, the director must feel the creative freedom and the leadership control over all aspects of the picture. Directors must respect that the ultimate creative and financial ownership and responsibility belongs to the producer. The director is allowed the opportunity to create the picture, because the producer has put it in the director's hands. The producer is ultimately responsible for the picture's creative and financial success. Consequently, regardless of the extensive genius and energy directors pour into their pictures, the director should respect the producer's position and respond to requests even if they seem unreasonable.

Steven Spielberg produced and Richard Donner directed *Goonies*. These two powerful, gifted creators labored together under increasingly intense pressures as the picture progressed. Each respected the other's position. Challenging demands and decisions were made by both of them in their respective stewardships. Peace was maintained, and an excellent picture was delivered. More recently, James Cameron created the landmark achievement picture, *Titanic*. Tom Sherek at Twentieth Century Fox made suggestions. Cameron listened, considered, and responded. Each was under intense creative, time, and financial pressure. Cameron later credited Sherek with the suggestion for what Cameron said was a better ending for the picture. In the final analysis, it isn't who has the greatest power, but rather how well the creative team works together to deliver the most creative and financially successful picture.

Shooting Script

The core development team now is composed of three members, the director in the primary position, along with the producer and the development manager. The producer still has the ultimate control, but the director is rightly the head of this core team, as the director is the only member of the team who is exclusively associated with this single picture.

The first focus of the core team is the story. The picture must have a first-draft shooting script prior to the intricate and intense planning and budgeting that are essential for its creation. The story will go through further rewrites as other key collaborators are attached, but the basic story will be recommended by the director and finally decided upon by the core team, tempered by executive team review and comment. This review is a key contribution to the picture's success.

Often the director is a writer and may participate in the writing of the drafts leading to the shooting script. Even if this is so, it is best to enter a multiwriter step deal, as presented in Chapter 7. This will ensure the greatest probability for the script's predictable on-schedule completion and the creation of the strongest shooting script.

Typically the director and producer will insist on having the first-draft shooting script before they approach the potential lead cast talent.

Lead Cast Attachment

The producer and development director will have drawn up a proposed list for the lead cast before the director is set. The director and producer will use this list and the director's considerations to prepare a collaborative list that is presented to the advisory team. This committee's recommendations, then, and the collaborative list will be presented to the executive committee. With the director, this team will prepare the final list of lead actors under consideration.

Following much the same process as the director selection, the U.S. and international distributors are contacted, their responses are weighed (considering the TVQs and marketing values of each performer in the various markets), and a final actors priority list is prepared.

The actors are approached, as presented in Chapter 8, and negotiation and documentation occurs. After all that, distributor notifications are sent out prior to press releases and paid trade announcements.

Preparing for Physical Production

Once the first draft of the shooting script is completed, physical production preparation commences in earnest. This includes attaching the picture's UPM, or line producer. The UPM now becomes the central participant in the physical production process. This person will create the original and the many permutations of the picture's production breakdowns, schedules, and budgets. Various portions of these materials, along with the shooting script, will be studied and used by department heads and others in their individual planning and performance.

Production department heads will be recommended by the director and reviewed by the producer, and a final review and acceptance are made by the advisory and executive teams. The key department heads will be approached through creative discussions that will expand into negotiations and then attachment to the picture.

Creative collaboration from the newly added genius pool of the department heads will deepen the color and dimension of the picture, further perfecting the script and bringing the picture into clearer focus.

Development of physical production now begins in earnest, with locations being determined, departments making staff arrangements, the balance of the cast being attached, and, of course, the continual enhancement of the script in response to the reality of these elements.

Maturing Marketing Materials

As talent is attached to the picture, so are their representative reels, including those from the director, actors, cinematographer, production designer, and composer. Through many of the excellent film commissions, reels are even provided on the picture's locations. The compilation of these elements, together with print elements, combines for a rich resource to create the picture's print, film, and video presentations for the major markets. When these are presented to participating distributors, they use them to promote the picture within their respective territories.

Preparing the Production Bank Financing Facility

Since the completion bond advisor's company usually bonds all of the production company's pictures, and the bank advisor's bank finances most of the pictures, each of their companies are regularly brought up to speed on the picture's progress. In addition to the referenced advisory meetings, at least two additional meetings with documented picture plans should be set up prior to placing bonding and lending requests with these institutions.

Typically five to nine months pass between the story acquisition and the placement of the production loan request with the bank. During this time, the most aggressive distributors for the picture become apparent. (All distributors should be aggressive, but some are more than others.) Also, conditions within these territories change from the time of the first greenlight. Mergers, acquisitions, and changes in the economy are largely responsible for these shifts.

Because of these phenomena, the global rights manager should revise the picture's liquidation breakdown at least monthly, and again just prior to preparing the picture's presale plan and bank loan analysis. The presentation of how to prepare the plan and analysis is in Chapters 3 and 5.

The UPM then prepares a fresh budget for use with the preparation of this documentation.

Once the bank loan analysis is prepared, it is presented, along with the presale plan, to the executive committee for approval. Following its approval, the bank loan memorandum, as described in Chapter 5, and the completion bond memorandum, as described in Chapter 6, are prepared by the production company's finance vice president. The bond memorandum is prepared and presented first, since the completion bond company's intent will accompany the bank memorandum.

Each of these memoranda is mature intent documents. Their purpose is to receive a contingent commitment from each participant, so that when the producer provides the imminent elements declared in the memoranda, each respective entity will participate in the picture's production funding. The production company must be bondable to engage the production bank loan, and the bank loan facility must be available to draw the picture's presales into it.

The producer meets with the bonding organization and receives the completion bond contingent commitment first, then meets with and receives the bank's contingent commitment.

The U.S. Studio Distribution Agreement

As thoroughly reviewed in Chapter 2, this agreement affects all other rights, relationships and earnings and is central to the picture's global success. This is the time when producers should obtain their picture's U.S. theatrical distribution.

As suggested previously, the studios are excellent marketers as well as negotiators. They understand the value of a picture, and, as they have global liquidation power, they prefer to acquire all global rights.

Fortunately, there are 10 competitive U.S. studios. These studios have become very open to a broad spectrum of distribution relationship configurations. Each wants the valuable inventory, the product with substantial earnings power.

As reviewed in Chapter 2, U.S. theatrical distribution rights are usually more of a liability than an asset. Typically the producer plans a studio distribution relationship that is a combination of U.S. theatrical (the right with the least earnings potential) and U.S. video (the right with the greatest earnings potential). Each is an excellent offset to the other. Also, the timing of these two distribution windows is very close, with video earnings primarily driven by the picture's theatrical campaign.

Though the U.S. theatrical and video distribution rights bundle is the most common studio relationship approach, as the picture matures through development, the U.S. studio may become much more aggressive in negotiating for specific or all international rights, as well as for specific or all ancillary rights. Many of these distribution proposals are extremely competitive with those the producer has developed throughout the picture's development and preproduction. The producer should analyze the studio proposal and compare its gross potential, distribution fees, and costs, as well as the producer's internal costs, against these factors in the existing relationships. Then, with the counsel of the advisory and executive teams, the producer must decide the best financial course of action. The studio offer would need to perform substantially greater before it should be considered over the existing distribution relationships.

To clearly compare the offers, producers must also recalculate the picture's bank financing worksheet. The studios do not provide a bank letter of credit, so their contract will receive a larger bank discount than the international presale collateral, as reviewed in Chapter 5.

The Presales

The presales (refer to Chapter 3) are entered into with those licensees discovered during the presale analysis, and they usually include at least one major international territory (often two or three), and frequently U.S. premium cable or network television. The international license strategy and approach is presented in Chapter 3 and the premium and network television rights in Chapter 4.

When motion picture development becomes this mature, the picture is a familiar name among trade participants in the major territories and in the United States, and more often than not, consumer press has begun.

By this time the producer has been approached by other international distributors who compete with the participating greenlight distributors. The producer maintains the integrity of the participating distributor relationships; however, the competing distributors will become increasingly interested in engaging license rights for the picture.

The producer prepares and presents a preferential license opportunity to the proposed presale licensees. In the licensee presentation meeting, the producer first reveals the name of the bank providing the picture's production funding and the completion guarantor providing its bond. Next, the producer presents the plan for this particular distributor to obtain the rights to the picture for its territory by entering a presale license agreement. This license calls for a traditional license advance, paid against the producer's share of a revenue-sharing relationship with the licensee. The differences in this license are (1) that the advance amount is discounted by approximately 20 percent compared to what they would be expected to advance after the picture is completed (most often this is only 5 to 12 months away); and (2) that only 10 percent of the license advance is due at the license signing; the balance is not due until the licensee has access to the picture and its associated elements.

The producer makes this offer only to the distributors that are part of the presale plan. The offer is made at the time when these producers should be especially motivated to secure the picture's rights, and to receive the financial advantage associated with the license advance discount. This is good business for both the distributor and the producer.

The appeal for this relationship is heightened by the licensee's advance amount typically being no more than the lowest amount the licensee may earn from the rights being purchased.

If there are U.S. ancillary presales, these are offered in much the same manner, with similar discounts, as discussed in Chapters 1, 4, and 5.

Engaging the Completion Bond

The completion bond (refer to Chapter 6) is necessary for the bank loan and is formally requested immediately following the securitization of the presale documentation.

The request for the completion bond is made in writing with the most recent shooting script, production budget, and supporting documentation. The completion guarantor's legal counsel will structure the lending bank, the producer, presale distributors, and the guarantor itself into an interparty agreement. This agreement, when closed, will call the engagement of production funding. Producers should allow at least eight weeks for the completion bond to close; this includes concurrent documentation between the completion guarantor and the bank, where presale documentation that details the technical delivery of the picture has been perfected.

Engaging the Production Bank Loan

The collateral and completion bond are presented to the bank to engage the production loan (refer to Chapter 5). Processing the loan includes conforming the letter(s) of credit language to language that is acceptable to the bank. This process may take five to ten working days.

At this time, the producer forms the picture's producing company as a corporation or LLC. As presented in Chapter 9, this organization is a wholly owned subsidiary of the production company and will produce and own the picture. After the production line of credit is open, the production company begins making the several advances to the producing company as it will continue to do throughout the completion of the picture.

The first expense of the producing company is the purchase of all rights, title, and interest of the picture from the development company, according to the production company's purchase agreement with the development company.

Final Preproduction

During final preproduction the producer:

- Closely participates with and supports the director. As frenetically paced as this time is, this is the last sane time the producer can participate with the director until principal photography wraps. The creative look of the picture is substantially established during this period. The script receives special producer scrutiny for the apparent creative reasons, as well as special needs that include writing, panning, and budgeting for international territory and ancillary media cover shots.

- Sets the picture's novelization relationship with a publisher, even if the story has been or currently is in release, as explained in Chapters 1 and 4.

- Pursues potential premium tie-in and product placement relationships. To accomplish this, the global rights and advertising VPs combine their efforts in preparing the presentations, setting the meetings, and negotiating the relationships, as reviewed in Chapter 4.

- Prepares, in cooperation with the U.S. and international distributors, the picture's ramp-up consumer PR and advertising; the print, TV commercial, and trailer title, look, teaser, and long-form element list; layouts; boards; title research and treatment; along with related activities. Some of this is for release soon after principal photography begins, and the rest is for the several releases that will escalate as the picture approaches the global marketplace.

Principal Photography

As principal photography commences, primary location accommodations are made for special production guests, including development company partners, U.S. studio representatives, prebuy participants, international territory greenlight participants, and trade and consumer press. Appropriate invitations are sent to these guests, and as they respond, their individual arrangements are made.

The producer reviews all the picture's dailies, consulting with the director relative to the picture's creative progress, and informing the director about the picture's distribution and marketing. The producer will be on location from time to time, as well as with the picture's post-production team, which most often begins assembling the picture within two weeks from the beginning of principal photography.

The initial consumer press releases are staged and rolled into the U.S. and global territories. Trade press and paid announcements are released.

As the picture is produced, the marketing reel expands; the teaser trailer is assembled and released to the theatrical distributors; the primary trailer(s) start and continue to assemble; and promotional coverage is captured, assembled, polished, and released, according to the marketing plan. Copies of all press releases and promotional materials are sent to the major distribution participants.

The picture's up-to-the-minute promotional reel is exclusively exhibited in the appropriate global markets.

Post-Production

The director is usually the post-production supervisor. As this process begins, soon after principal photography commences, assemblies are sent to the director for review. The digital post-production process, Web use, and digital phone transfer have been extremely useful in *fixing it in principal photography,* which is most often much better and less expensive than the traditional fixing it in post.

In addition to more traditional post-production duties, the producer supervises in-house produced trailers and ad spots. The producer also reviews the preparation and audience testing of distributor and trade specialist produced trailers in two or three versions, and television commercials in four or five versions. If the picture's title is in question (this process is often excruciating), it will also be market and audience tested before it is eventually decided.

As post-production is completed, international sales substantially heat up, and the U.S. and major international distributors deepen their marketing preparation.

The Picture's U.S. Branding

The picture's total U.S. audience size and earnings are substantially determined by the effectiveness of the picture's branding during its theatrical release. The picture's total earnings are not determined so much by the picture's theatrical gross, as they are by the power of the picture's campaign, the reach and frequency of its media buy to its target audiences, and the word-on-the-street among the picture's targets. Box office grosses can also be negatively affected as much as one-third by marketplace anomalies including picture release glut, weather, spectacular national news, or sports events.

The producer is never busier than during a picture's post-production and pre-theatrical release. In fact, it is not enough to make an outrageously fine motion picture. Audience reactions to a picture's early trailers are excellent indications of the content and texture that should be used in the picture's strongest television commercials, as well as its trailers that will be shown closer to the picture's release and the clips shown during celebrity show visits.

At the time the television campaign begins (about three weeks prior to the first theatrical street date), the picture's novels should be flooding check-out stands with the picture's one-sheet on their covers. The publisher will want to correlate the timing of the paperback release with the timing of the television campaign.

If the premium brand tie-in(s) were entered into six to nine months previously, these brand-partner commercials will begin airing immediately before and then into the picture's theatrical release.

The week the picture opens, the PR and advertising departments at the studio are at full throttle. Theatrical premieres and entertainment, morning, news, and other television shows are sporting celebrity and picture highlight segments; entertainment and other publications have eye-grabbing photos and articles about the picture, and literally every other promotional and purchasable device is employed to establish and turn up the heat on making the picture a living legend.

The Global Territories and Ancillary Markets

Once the picture is completed, lab access letters are delivered to prebuy distributors and special screenings are set for the other international greenlight distributors, as discussed in Chapter 3, and for major ancillary rights media, as presented in Chapter 4. This is the completion of the primary cycle of discovering, producing, and bringing a picture into the market. A checklist of the entire motion picture development and production cycle follows.

Story search
Begin development company's design and deal preparation
Assemble or tune the team
Produce the development company investment offering
Subscribe the development company partners
Begin and continue partner communications
Work the development plan
Story review and selection
Greenlight evaluation to determine business feasibility
Predirector picture development
Director search and attach
Cause the first draft shooting script to be created
Attach the lead cast
Physical production preparation
Prepare and mature the picture's marketing materials
Prepare the bank financing facility
Enter the U.S. studio agreement
Design and enter the picture's presales
Engage the completion bond
Engage the bank loan

Complete the final preproduction
Principal photography producer's duties
Post-production producer's duties
The picture's U.S. branding
Selling the open global ancillary markets and international territories

Chapter Postscript

Before the production company begins the process of developing, producing, and liquidating its motion pictures, the operating plan and the team that will run it should already be prepared and in place.

This team and their organizations establish and finance the development companies; discover, qualify, and develop the stories; commence and manage the marketing of the pictures; fund the production of the pictures; produce the pictures; mature their marketing; and manage the global distribution of the pictures. These are seven individually critical processes of assuring that the production team produces the pictures it wants, and that each picture individually has the greatest opportunity for artistic and financial success.

Producers must understand how all the pieces fit together and how the team accomplishes the work and sustains the critical checks and balances during the process. Thoroughly understanding the whole process and preparing for its successful operation are essential to achieving the team objectives of producing consistently profitable pictures that please their audiences and fulfill the producer's creative passion.

Chapter 13

The Producer's Business

This chapter presents the producer's role in the process of multiple picture production, the establishment of the production company brand presence with the global entertainment trade and consumers; the balancing act between business, artistic, and personal objectives; the management of library pictures; and the advancement of team vitality and allegiance.

Multiple Picture Management

As demonstrated in the previous chapter, shepherding a single picture through the complete cycle, from discovery, internal greenlighting, and development through production and distribution, is a wonderfully complex process. When producers plan multiple pictures, their activity projection reveals the hyper-challenge of simultaneously managing a picture in post-production, starting another's principal photography, moving another picture through predevelopment evaluation, and reviewing new stories.

The single picture activity and cash flow planning that is reviewed in Chapter 12 must be done for each picture proposed in the producer's multiple picture development plan. Each picture must be considered separately, yet with the full consideration of both the distractions, as well as the beneficial amortization of time and expenses that each picture in the plan has on the others.

The capacity to manage multiple pictures is directly related to how well the producer understands the entire development/production/distribution process. It also depends on the planning and work ethic of the individual. Juggling is a useful analogy to this process. Each juggling rotation has its unique arc and rhythm. A good juggler sustains the integrity of each individual rotation, while focusing on the balance between the three rotations. Similarly, producers must sustain the individual creative and business integrity of each picture, while they focus on the creative and business balance among all the pictures.

Seasoned producers adhere to the most successful processes of multiple picture development and production by thoroughly planning for the needs and timing of each picture, and focusing on the pictures as a group, in such a fashion that each picture actually benefits the other creatively, financially, and perhaps most especially in their galvanizing effect upon global strategic partner relationships.

Time and Budget Economies

Investors are not the only parties pressing the producer to be engaged in multiple pictures. Most of the producer's primary relationships—such as licensees, agents, bankers, and sales teams—are more dedicated, supportive, and reliant when the producer has several pictures in process.

Studio Relationships

Licensees are motivated in their relationships with producers who both deliver pictures that perform strongly and provide a regular high volume of pictures. It is a combination of these two qualities that determines a producer's value to each licensee.

During a meeting with studio licensees, a producer may pitch a new picture for studio greenlight, review cast considerations for another picture, and deliver marketing elements for another. The greater the number of significant pictures delivered by a producer, the stronger the producer's relationship is with licensees.

Agents

As presented in Chapter 8, most agencies have packaging agents, who combine internal story and performing elements with other creative elements represented outside their agencies in order to motivate the making of pictures that substantially include their clients.

The most organized production companies are those that are the most sought after by agency packagers. These agencies are pleased to meet and assist such producers on their pictures, as well as use the opportunity to approach them with agency packages. And multiple picture production necessitates regular agency meetings. This keeps the producer's operating style and integrity fresh and vital with these firms.

Banks and Completion Guarantors

Some pictures will develop and produce in a smoother fashion and achieve greater income performance than others. Bankers and insurers tend to have a greater sense of balance and stability with those producer clients who are driving multiple pictures. Further, a slate of pictures allows the producer to offer offsetting guarantees among these pictures to banks and bonding companies. Such cross-collateralized relationships must be entered into within the bounds of the agreements set forth with the several profit participants associated with each picture. This often establishes a substantially deeper deal stability and relationship confidence with insurers and banks that is unique to multiple-picture production.

Sales Events

Though independent producers' pictures normally are represented by domestic studios at U.S. theatrical and video events, the producers or their representatives usually represent their pictures with the six major territory greenlit distributors and at foreign territory sales conferences. Similar to the U.S. studio relationship, having multiple pictures strengthens foreign territory relationships. Additionally, multiple pictures allow the producer to amortize these significant expenses over several pictures.

Establishing the Production Company Brand Presence _____

Production companies, especially new ones, must establish and then advance the heat of their company's global trade and consumer brand presence. As has been emphasized throughout this book, strategic relationships with studios, global distributors, banks, completion guarantors, attorneys, agents, and a broad array of other major industry category participants are mandatory. The stronger these relationships, the greater the operating benefits. For key close relationships this is best developed through consistent, confidential communiqués outside the press that are confirmed in the press. For relationships in general, a well-thought-of reputation, appropriately, is almost entirely established and sustained by the performance of the producer's pictures in the global marketplace. In fact, the *trade* brand respect for a production company is chiefly a mirror for the global *audience* respect for the producer's pictures.

Who we are always speaks louder than who we say we are. Likewise, a production company is substantially known by its pictures rather than its mission statement. Understanding this basic reality, producers who want to establish their production company brand with its audiences will be benefited by correlating their picture selections with their mission statements. If a producer becomes committed to produce a picture that is outside the scope of the company's creative charter, but wants to sustain the company's brand presence, then perhaps the producer should create another production entity for that picture.

Because each motion picture's campaign is necessarily intense and focused on that picture, typically little campaign emphasis is given to the production company or the studio. Further, it is almost unheard of for production companies or studios to launch a campaign exclusively on themselves, or even a campaign where they are the dominant focus. This is the prevailing notion in the current culture of the motion picture industry. Like many cultures, this practice is not necessarily the most effective way to drive audiences to pictures delivered by the production company and the studio. It may be a profitable exercise for producers and studios to consider if there may be motion picture marketing advantages associated with a production company's name becoming an icon to audiences.

There are lessons to be learned by other global consumer brands and the way in which they are marketed. Nike, IBM, Microsoft, and many other brands have specific product commercials, as well as primarily brand commercials that, in turn, drive consumer response to their individual products. If the new product release (which every nonfranchise motion picture is) is driven by a brand name that has consumer confidence, the new product's reception and success are substantially more predictable. For their target consumers, Nike's new basketball shoe, BMW's new roadster, and McDonald's new kid's meal are all "must-have" purchases. Their target consumers are all substantially motivated to buy because of their perception of the brand.

From an audience perspective, Disney is currently the only studio/production company with a brand reputation for delivering a specific kind of motion picture entertainment. The U.S. studios have a general reputation for delivering high quality entertainment, but not necessarily delivering a certain style of entertainment. Associated with their style, U.S. studios are not known for skewing to any particular target audiences.

Consider the similarities of the motion picture industry to the fashion industry. Just as there are high-, medium-, and low-profile department stores, there are flagship, medium- and low-profile multiplex theaters. Just as high-end department stores offer greater perceived quality and more sought-after brands and other department stores commonly offer lesser or unknown brands, so do the finest multiplexes offer the strongest pictures at their earliest release, whereas the other theaters deliver lighter or more eclectic fare, and/or pictures at later release dates.

Most brands are known by their style rather than their product categories. For instance, Marc Jacobs provides a range of consumer products, but each product has this brand's quality and style associated with it, and consumers know that brands such as Marc Jacobs are offered in higher profile retail stores. The brand is sold in large measure because of product integrity, and specific new products are successfully launched, substantially benefited by the strength of the brand presence with its targeted consumers. It is a well-exercised retail concept, but one little used in the motion picture industry.

Pictures by Steven Spielberg, Adam Sandler, and George Lucas have a consumer-brand presence. They owe this primarily to audience satisfaction with their prior pictures, but also because of their respective companies' continual and highly effective promotion and public relations output. But what of Imagine, Castlerock, and even DreamWorks? These companies are well-known names within the trade, but they are largely without product definition to audiences.

Production companies who create a strong consumer brand presence will deliver a powerful marketing advantage for their pictures. This important marketing edge will render their pictures easier to sell and, consequently, more valuable to global licensees.

Production companies committed to becoming audience icons will refocus their companies' motion logo, include new brand marketing language in their distribution agreements, and increase their company brand strength in their pictures' advertising and promotion campaign.

Sustaining Business, Artistic, and Personal Objective Balance

As independent producers review their responsibilities, and more pointedly, as they perform them, it becomes inescapably apparent that unless managed well, a producer's life can easily be consumed entirely with motion picture activities.

Producing well is an exceptional accomplishment and immensely satisfying. But for most of us, it is essentially important to participate in the lives of our family members. Further, to be whole, balanced, and prepared, it is beneficial for us to study ancient and New Age thought, to meditate, and to discover ourselves and life anew through such acts as caring for a child. We need to advance our understanding of new technologies, to participate in and be nourished by the arts, to keep and occasionally review a personal journal. Additionally, we can balance ourselves by caring for those less able than us, and perhaps even by planting and caring for a garden.

Work is the lubricant of life. When we cease to be productive, we tend to lose our purpose and place. But it shouldn't consume us. We must plan for *seasonings* of our life, or ours will be bland, lacking full symmetry and fulfillment. Family, contemplation, study, the arts—these are the desserts of life. Without them, we will wake up one day and find ourselves separated from our central motivators.

In the words of historian Will Durant, "To seize the value and perspective of passing things, we want to know that the little things are little and the big things big, before it is too late. We want to see things now as they will seem forever, in the light of eternity." To strike balance in our lives between the big and small, but important things, is not as impossible as it might seem. It is largely a matter of perspective, planning, and performance.

The most effective and productive leaders we know in the entertainment industry have written their short- and long-term life objectives, which they frequently revise. Doing so allows them to temper their passionate, classically well-planned filmmaking commitments. They use their written objectives to develop a detailed written plan in which they pencil in specific appointments for their daily, weekly, monthly, and annual schedules. Yes, they actually schedule personal time with family, along with times for service, reading, study, and even (perhaps especially) play.

The power of scheduling these activities provides for balance in their lives and even gives them occasion to respond, "I'm sorry, I am booked then, but we can get together…." By keeping as faithful to their schedules as possible, these people prosper in their family relationships, thrive as teachers and learners, and experience the truly good things of life, each of which keeps them happier, more productive, and by their admission, more creative.

In the main, producers love their work and immerse themselves in it. This is essential to achieve their finest pictures. But if this is done to the exclusion of other rich aspects of life, they may become personally weak, even in motion picture production.

Managing Library Pictures

As reviewed in earlier chapters, motion pictures premiere in each major distribution window. Then they become library pictures, continuing their audience and earnings life primarily in global television syndication.

A wonderful phenomenon of this industry is continual audience evolution. Some television syndicators constructively measure audience evolution in seven-year cycles. Whatever the year of the picture's television premiere, in seven years, newborns will be seven years old and are a new kids audience. Seven-year-olds grow to be 14 and become a new youth audience; 14-year-olds become 21 and thus a new young-adult audience. By the time 21-year-olds become 28 and are beginning to start families, they view entertainment from a substantially new lifestyle perspective.

Because of audience evolution, pictures should be reanalyzed by their target audiences every five years. Some pictures will warrant a more aggressive rerelease strategy than others. A picture's reanalysis will assist the producer in an accurate valuation for new television syndication licenses. Other pictures may justify rerelease strategies that include release through higher distribution windows, creating new advertising and public relations campaigns, negotiating campaign tie-ins with other consumer brands, and novelization rerelease, among others. Motion pictures, which are the producer's inventory, should be regularly and thoroughly evaluated, kept fresh and valuable to prior audiences, and marketed to new target audiences with reasonable aggression.

Theatrical Rerelease

Most motion pictures play very well on in-home media, especially as television screens enlarge, increase in clarity, and have sound advances that bring them close to theater grade. But most motion pictures are produced to be experienced on a large theater screen, with pristine, powerful sound. No lights, no phones, no commercials—just pure, undiluted audience-story absorption.

Newly evolved audiences may prefer to experience rereleases of some of the highest impact pictures in the theater. Rereleases of Disney animation classics, *Star Wars*, and *Gone with the Wind* all have demonstrated this, especially for epic and niche pictures. It appears that there may also be new audiences and income for many other audience-proven pictures. A ridiculously short list of these examples include *Ferris Bueller's Day Off*, *Superman*, *Rocky*, *Robin Hood: Prince of Thieves*, *A Room with a View*, *Dances with Wolves*, *On Golden Pond*, *Toy Story*, *Ghost*, *Home Alone*, and The *Karate Kid*.

It should be considered, as reviewed in Chapter 2, that each picture's campaign and media buy almost exclusively determines the success of its opening week. If the distributor is not committed to an aggressive rerelease, the picture will most likely fail. Market data and original-picture release data combine to make a strong argument in favor of the likelihood that several major motion pictures will potentially perform well if rereleased, either in theaters, on video, on premium cable, or on network television.

Currently, Buena Vista is the only studio that boldly exploits their pictures in this way, and only those pictures that primarily exploit the kids (5 to 11) audience. And they do it well. A review of the theatrical grosses of these rereleases provides a clear confirmation of the power of rereleased pictures with new-evolution audiences. *101 Dalmatians* was rereleased theatrically during the 1985 Christmas holidays, earning $31 million, and again, almost six years later in the summer of 1991, earning almost $61 million. *Snow White and the Seven Dwarfs* was rereleased in the summer of 1987, earning $46.6 million, and in the summer of 1995 this picture earned $41.6 million.

Advancing Team Vitality and Allegiance

The production and development company team is best served by the producer who analyzes and directs from the perspective that the process they are engaged in is a whole and living entity. The team is responsive to everything that affects it, thereby increasing or decreasing in its health, vitality, and productivity. Producers who understand this regularly evaluate and revitalize the team.

Much like a fruit tree, healthy teams produce appealing, good fruit, in the form of pictures and related products. And like that fruit, both products and people leave the company in their seasons, and this is a healthy sign of productivity. Some team members progress beyond the capacity of the production team; others may not be able to sustain the team's performance integrity. For either of these reasons, it is best for them to go.

Also, just as trees become burdened with unproductive growth that needs to be trimmed, so production teams may have members who are more like anchors than sails. Though this process is most often uncomfortable, pruning provides for the best growth, both for these individuals and the team. Between these two extremes exists the necessity of caring for the team. This can be sufficiently accomplished only when team members are individually and regularly reviewed (twice per year is optimal).

Producers strengthen their team members when they seek for opportunities to help expand their experience, education, and stewardship. This can be done effectively through providing team members with both the means (such as expenses for classes in Web design, digital special effects, and foreign languages) and motivation (promotion, prizes, perks, bonuses, and/or pay increases for successful achievements). Providing team members with the means and the motivation results in a team that is continually expanding its performance capacities and deepening team commitment and solidarity.

Sustaining business, artistic, and personal objective balance applies to all members of the team, not just the producer. Producers can provide a broad range of benefits to their teams, which, in return, can create the greatest success attainable. These benefits begin with each team member understanding and performing in harmony with the company's mission statement, and encompass spouse and family travel accommodations and office environment perks, including exercise rooms, nursery care, a well-stocked kitchen, and a library.

Chapter Postscript

Dream expansively, plan comprehensively, work valiantly, and live completely.

Reports, Data, and Producer's Principles

This chapter presents and analyzes industry data particularly useful to independent producers, presents information sources enabling producers to keep current on this data, and brings together in a list, the cornerstone principles presented in this book that form the independent producer's most predictable foundation for success.

Entertainment Industry Statistics and Reports

Accessing, updating, and using regularly published entertainment data, the reports derived from this data and associated data matrices can powerfully enable producers to perceive and forecast their pictures' target audiences, global earnings, ancillary products, optimal marketing strategies and potential brand partners, among other highly beneficial information.

Barry Reardon retired as Warner Bros. distribution president March 19, 1999, after serving the studio in this position for 17 years. Reardon exercised his excellent natural audience sense and deep distribution experience in the release of scores of successful pictures. This sustained Warner Bros. for 16 years as one of the leading three studios—eight of those years in first position, and five of those years in second position. In his 31-year career, he participated in and, more often, was the lead innovator in the way motion pictures were distributed.

Reardon amplified his natural marketing savvy by using a powerful studio distribution database that tracked all major releases, not just those of Warner Bros. This database was substantially developed by Reardon and continues to assist the studio in making the most predictable decisions regarding high-impact, motion picture distribution.

Every picture, regardless of its earnings, provides a lesson for its producers and distributors. There are so many elements that affect a picture's earnings, including:

- The creative heat of the picture's campaign to drive its target audience, especially the television commercials and theatrical trailer, but also radio, print, outdoor and PR
- The overall target audience saturation density of the media purchased—its target audience reach and frequency
- The motion pictures that are released day and date, as well as those within three weeks before and after
- The theatrical release pattern (including which theaters and which screens within the multiplex are booked and how many)
- The season in which the picture is released (not only the time of year but the weather during play)
- Of course, the picture's audience satisfaction for each target group
- Critical reviews

Consequently, all these aspects are important tracking considerations in analyzing why pictures succeed or fail to the extent they do. These aspects should be considered during all of the phases of development, production, distribution planning, and execution of each picture. In addition to these aspects, producers are well served, when tracking other story and production-related elements that affect both grosses and profits, if they are aware of the following:

- Each picture's target audiences, their sizes, and consumption profile for each major distribution window
- The use of star power for their earnings effect, compared with star cost
- The overall earnings effect of using a major director as compared with the director's cost
- The effect, if any, of a picture's genre
- Its rating
- The effect of the running time of a picture

Data on several pictures, side by side, tell a story that can wonderfully still speculation. Knowledge really is power, and, to know each picture's inherent strengths and weaknesses, allows both producers and distributors to mount an approach in which they can view each picture's several audiences for maximum success patterns.

The Most Successful Motion Pictures Ever Released in the United States

A limited profile of some important characteristics of the 35 most successful motion pictures ever released in North America is shown in Figure 14.1. To measure these pictures fairly, each picture is positioned according to the quantity of theatrical

Figure 14.1

The Most Successful U.S. Motion Picture Releases of All Time

The Most Successful US Motion Picture Releases of All Time
As of December 31, 2004

++ Includes re-releases, using ticket prices current during each release.
* Grosses estimated from film rental
^ Marquee star at the time of original release.

Position	Picture	Symbol	Tickets Sold In Millions	U.S. GBO Adjust'd to 2004 Value	Prdctn Bdgts Adjst'd to 2004	Prdctn Bdgt To GBO Ratio	U.S. Studio	Producer	Director	Star Power^
1	GONE WITH THE WIND	++	204.64	$1,096.4	$51.78	21	MGM	David Selznick	Victor Fleming	Clark Gable, Vivien Leigh
2	STAR WARS	++	178.10	$954.2	$33.16	29	FOX	George Lucas	George Lucas	
3	THE SOUND OF MUSIC	++,*	142.40	$763.0	$47.10	16	FOX	Robert Wise	Robert Wise	Julie Andrews, Christopher Plummer
4	E. T.	++	136.00	$728.6	$19.18	38	U	Stvn Spielberg	Stvn Spielberg	
5	THE 10 COMMANDMENTS	*	131.00	$701.8	$91.58	8	PARA	Cecil B. DeMille	Cecil B. DeMille	Charlton Heston, Yul Brynner
6	TITANIC		130.86	$701.0	$232.14	3	FOX/PARA	James Cameron	James Cameron	
7	JAWS	++	128.00	$686.2	$40.48	17	U	Richard Zanuck	Stvn Spielberg	Roy Scheider, Richard Dreyfuss
8	DOCTOR ZHIVAGO		110.00	$586.8	$64.76	9	MGM	Carlo Ponti	David Lean	Julie Christie
9	SNOW WHITE	++,*	109.00	$584.0	$19.35	30	BV/RKO	Walt Disney	David Hand	Animated
10	MARY POPPINS		108.00	$576.9	$30.01	19	BV	Walt Disney	Rbt Stevenson	Julie Andrews, Dick Van Dyke
11	101 DALMATIONS (Original)	++,*	105.21	$563.6	n/a	n/a	BV	Walt Disney	Geronimi / Luske	Animated
12	THE EMPIRE STRIKES BACK	++	98.11	$525.6	$39.06	13	FOX	George Lucas	Irvin Kershner	Mark Hamill, Harrison Ford, C. Fisher
13	BEN-HUR	++,*	98.00	$525.2	$95.52	5	MGM	Sam Zimbalist	William Wyler	Charlton Heston
14	RETURN OF THE JEDI	++	97.98	$524.9	$60.06	9	FOX	George Lucas	Richard Marquand	M. Hamill, H. Ford, C. Fisher
15	THE STING	*	91.21	$488.7	$21.82	22	U	Tony Bill, &	George Roy Hill	Paul Newman, Robert Redford
16	RAIDERS OF THE LOST ARK		87.19	$467.1	$39.83	12	PAR	George Lucas, &	Steven Spielberg	Harrison Ford
17	THE EXORCIST	*	87.00	$467.0	$48.63	10	WB	Wlm Ptr Blatty	Wllam Friedkin	Ellen Burstyn, Max von Sydow
18	THE ROBE		87.00	$466.1	$34.80	13	FOX	Frank Ross	Henry Koster	Rchrd Burton,Jean Simmons,V Mature
19	JURASSIC PARK		86.19	$461.7	$80.90	6	U	Stvn Spielberg,&	Stvn Spielberg	
20	THE GRADUATE		86.00	$458.4	n/a	n/a	AVCO	Mike Nichols	Mike Nichols	Anne Bancroft, Dustin Hoffman
21	STAR WARS: PHANTOM MENACE		84.86	$481.8	$128.53	4	FOX	Lucas, Rick McCallum	George Lucas	Neeson, McGregor, Portman
22	FANTASIA	++,*	83.04	$444.9	$30.27	15	BV	Walt Disney	Algar/Armstrong	Animated
23	THE GODFATHER	*	79.35	$425.2	$26.43	16	PAR	Albert Ruddy	Francis Coppola	Marlon Brando, Al Pacino
24	BAMBI	++	79.26	$424.6	n/a	n/a	BV	Walt Disney	David Hand	Animated
25	FOREST GUMP		78.87	$422.5	$66.29	6	PAR	Wndy Fineman, &	Robert Zemeckis	Tom Hanks
26	THE LION KING		75.00	$401.0	$53.15	8	BV	Don Hahn	Allers, Minkoff	Animated
27	GREASE		71.43	$382.7	$16.60	23	PAR	Aln Carr, Rbt Stigwood	Randal Kleiser	John Travolta, Olivia Newton John
28	GHOSTBUSTERS		71.00	$380.4	$56.90	7	COL	Ivan Reitman	Ivan Reitman	Bill Murray,Dan Aykroyd,Sigrny Weaver
29	BEVERLY HILLS COP		70.00	$374.3	$24.89	15	PAR	Bruckheimer,Simpson	Martin Brest	Eddie Murphy
30	SHREK 2		69.95	$436.5	$75.00	6	DrmWrks	Lipman, Warner, Williams	Adamson, Asbury, Vernon	Animated
31	PINOCCHIO	++,*	69.62	$373.0	$34.52	11	BV	Walt Disney	Luske, Sharpsteen	Animated
32	SPIDER-MAN		69.48	$417.8	$143.87	3	COL	Ian Bryce, Laura Ziskin	Sam Raimi	Maguire, Dafoe, Dunst
33	INDEPENDENCE DAY		69.00	$371.0	$88.54	4	FOX	R. Emmerich	Dean Devlin	Animated
34	BUTCH CASSIDY & THE SUNDANCE KID		68.00	$362.2	$49.66	7	FOX	John Foreman	George Roy Hill	Paul Newman, Robert Redford
35	HOME ALONE		67.70	$362.7	$24.49	15	FOX	John Hughes	Chris Columbus	

Figure 14.1 continued

The Most Successful U.S. Motion Picture Releases of All Time

Kids: 5-11
Youth: 12-17

Position	Picture	Target Audiences	Genre	U.S. Rating	Opened U.S. Theatrical	Running Time In Hours	Tagline
1	GONE WITH THE WIND	Women, men	Romantic drama	G	12/15/1939	3.7	The most magnificent picture ever!
2	STAR WARS	Youth,kids,men,wmn	Ac Adv, Sci Fi	PG	5/25/1977	2.0	A long time ago in a galaxy far, far away . . .
3	THE SOUND OF MUSIC	Women,men,families	Mscl Rmntc drma	G	3/2/1965	2.9	The happiest sound in all the world!
4	E. T.	Kids, youth,men,wmn	Adv, Drama, SciFi	PG	6/11/1982	1.9	He is afraid. He is alone. He is 3 million light years from home.
5	THE 10 COMMANDMENTS	Women, men, families	Drama	Not Rated	11/9/1956	3.7	The greatest event in motion picture history.
6	TITANIC	Youth, women, men	Rmntc drma, Ac	PG-13	12/19/1997	3.2	Collide with destiny.
7	JAWS	Men, youth, kids	Ac, Thrlr, Horror	PG	6/20/1975	2.1	She was the first.
8	DOCTOR ZHIVAGO	Women, men, youth	Romantic drama	PG-13	12/22/1695	3.3	A love caught in the fire of the revolution.
9	SNOW WHITE	Kids, Families	Ani Chldrns Fntsy	G	12/21/1937	1.4	Walt Disney's first full length feature production.
10	MARY POPPINS	Kids, families	Chldrns Mscl Cmdy	G	8/29/1964	2.3	It's supercalifragilisticexpialidocious!
11	101 DALMATIONS (Original)	Kids, families	Anim Chldrns Adv	G	1/25/1961	1.3	It's 'arf comedy. . .'arf mystery. . .and it's howlarious!
12	THE EMPIRE STRIKES BACK	Youth,kids,men,wmn	Ac Adv, Sci Fi	PG	5/21/1980	2.1	The adventure continues. . .
13	BEN-HUR	Men, youth, women	Ac Adv Drama	G	11/19/1959	3.5	The world's most honored motion picture.
14	RETURN OF THE JEDI	Youth,kids,men,wmn	Ac Adv, Sci Fi	PG	5/25/1983	2.2	The Empire falls. . .
15	THE STING	Men, youth, women	Crime Drma Cmdy	PG	12/25/1973	2.2	All it takes is a little confidence!
16	RAIDERS OF THE LOST ARK	Youth,men,kids,wmn	Action Adventure	PG	6/12/1981	1.9	Indiana Jones—the new hero from the creators of Jaws and Star Wars.
17	THE EXORCIST	Men, youth	Horror	R	12/26/1973	2.0	That man is The Exorcist.
18	THE ROBE	Men,women,families	Drama	Not Rated	9/16/1953	2.3	The modern miracle you see without glasses!
19	JURASSIC PARK	Youth, men,kids,wmn	Ac,Ad,SciFi, Thrlr	PG-13	6/11/1993	2.1	An adventure 65 million years in the making.
20	THE GRADUATE	Women, men	Romantic Drama	R	12/21/1967	1.8	This is Benjamin. He's a little worried about his future.
21	STAR WARS: PHANTOM MENACE	Youth,kids,men	Ac Adv, Sci Fi	PG	5/23/1999	2.3	Every generation has a legend. Every journey has a first step. Every saga has a beginning.
22	FANTASIA	Kids, families, youth	Anmtd Mscl Fntsy	G	11/13/1940	2.0	Walt Disny's technicolor FEATURE triumph.
23	THE GODFATHER	Men	Crime Drama	R	3/15/1972	2.9	
24	BAMBI	Kids, families	Cldm Anim Fntsy	G	8/13/1942	1.2	A great love story.
25	FOREST GUMP	Men, women, youth	Drama,Rmnc,Adv	PG-13	7/6/1994	2.4	The world will never be the same once you've seen it through the eyes of Forrest Gump.
26	THE LION KING	Kids, families, youth	Anim Mscl Fntsy	G	6/15/1994	1.5	Life's greatest adventure is finding your place in the Circle of Life.
27	GREASE	Youth,wmn,kids,men	Mscl Cmdy Rmnc	PG	7/7/1978	1.8	Grease is the word.
28	GHOSTBUSTERS	Youth,men, women	Comedy, Horror	PG	6/8/1984	1.8	They're here to save the world.
29	BEVERLY HILLS COP	Men, youth, women	Ac Crime Cmdy	R	12/5/1984	1.8	The heat is on!
30	SHREK 2	Youth, kids, men, wmn	Animated Comedy	PG	5/23/2004	1.5	In the summer of 2004, they're back for more.
31	PINOCCHIO	Kids, families	Chldrns Ani Fntsy	G	2/9/1940	1.5	For anyone who has ever wished upon a star.
32	SPIDER-MAN	Youth, men, women	Ac Rom Fntsy	PG-13	5/3/2002	2.0	With great power comes great responsibility.
33	INDEPENDENCE DAY	Men, youth, women	Action SciFi War	PG-13	7/3/1996	2.4	EARTH take a good look. It could be your last.
34	BUTCH CASSIDY & THE SUNDANCE KID	Men, women, youth	Ac Wstm Cmdy	PG	10/24/1969	1.8	Not that it matters, but most of it's true.
35	HOME ALONE	Kids, youth, families	Comedy, Drama	PG	11/16/1990	1.8	A family comedy without the family.

Authored by Entertainment Business Group, this report's data sources are from Exhibitor Relations Company, the National Association of Theatre Owners (NATO) Encyclopedia of Exhibition, Internet Movie Data base, the Motion Picture Association of America (MPAA), participating studios and production companies.

admissions, since a theater ticket in 1949 was about $.39, compared with 2004 ticket prices that average approximately $6.25.

Because pictures on this list range from 1937 to 2004, our evaluation should be tempered by the vast changes in the entertainment universe during this time. In 1937, television was not a theatrical competitor, whereas in 2004, 98.3 percent of U.S. households had at least one color TV. VCRs did not reach 50 percent U.S. household penetration until 1986, but by 2004, they were at 91 percent penetration, DVD players were at 51 percent penetration, and telling the future of product delivery (as computers naturally merge to become the home entertainment data storage device), PC penetration in 2004 was 64.96 percent, on its way to a forecasted 90 percent by 2010. Basic cable television with its broad channel selection didn't reach 50 percent U.S. household penetration until 1987, and by 2004, cable television was at 68 percent and satellite was an additional 19.8 percent. On the other hand, the U.S. population had grown well over 50 percent during this period of time, to 110 million households in 2004.

Although there are many more important revelations to be discovered in analyzing this document, we will consider a few that are the most beneficial to producers and distributors.

Box Office Weighted by Gross Profit Figures

This report, in keeping with the industry standard of ranking each picture by its box-office dominance, places *Gone with the Wind* in first position. For producers, this report would be misleading if it did not also show each picture's production cost, and its box-office-to-production-cost ratio, adjusting these budgets to a 2004 currency value. Using this gross-profit perspective, *E. T.*, *Snow White and the Seven Dwarfs*, and *Star Wars* are the leading three pictures, with *Gone with the Wind* slipping to sixth position.

One very important element is readily evident here: A picture's earnings capacity does not increase with its production cost. *E.T.* yields stunning box office earnings that are 38 times its negative cost. *Titanic* yielded a very similar gross, but it yields a comparatively sparse three times its negative cost. What is to be learned here? Certainly not that *Titanic* overspent. It should be assumed that the cost of this highly successful picture was approximately correct for its story. What we can learn is that, unlike most other consumer products, motion pictures are valued by the entertainment dynamics of their stories and that of two stories with equal entertainment power, one may be substantially less expensive to produce than the other. Respecting this phenomenon has motivated the strongest independent producers to analyze each of their picture's negative-cost-to-earnings ratios; and some of them to establish minimum thresholds for their pictures to pass their internal greenlight.

The Studios

All seven of the major studios are represented in the report, plus DreamWorks and Avco. Fox has more pictures represented than any other studio, with nine (including its shared credit with Paramount for Titanic), followed closely by Buena Vista and Paramount with seven.

It should be remembered that throughout this period, the studios, as a group, released 200 to 500 pictures each year. These 35 are a small sampling and do not represent the dominance in studio earnings. For instance, as referenced earlier, Warner Bros. has sustained a leading earnings position among the studios during this period, although it has just two pictures represented on the list.

Producers and Directors

This is one of the most telling aspects of the report. The producers and directors responsible for these pictures are the powerhouse icons of their time. Walt Disney produced six of the seven Buena Vista pictures listed, George Lucas produced four pictures and directed one, and Steven Spielberg produced two pictures and directed four. Most of these producers and directors, even if listed only once, are unquestionably industry legends.

A great lesson here is to see the close correlation between the greatest pictures ever made and the most skilled producers and directors in the industry. This is clearly the single most consistent element among the successful pictures.

Star Power

There is a strong argument for looking at a star-caliber cast when examining such pictures as *Gone with the Wind, The Ten Commandments, Ben Hur,* and *The Sting.* On the other hand, 10 of the 35 pictures, including *Star Wars, E.T.,* and *Titanic,* use no "star" actors. Clearly, many leading producers and directors use talent that lend themselves to the picture, rather than primarily attaching star power for the sake of the marquee.

Target Audiences

Understanding each picture's target audiences and their entertainment consumption characteristics in each major territory is essential to understanding the earnings potential of each picture.

Studying the picture's target audiences reveals some compelling and valuable characteristics. By number of target audiences, 27 of the pictures have three or more. Producers discovering pictures with three or more primary target audiences should be encouraged with these pictures' higher earnings potential, simply because the audience universe being drawn upon is substantially greater.

Number of target audiences	Number of pictures
1	1
2	8
3	17
4	10

The pictures are closely divided between their most significant target audiences, with kids, youth, and men dominating ten pictures each.

Most significant target audience	Number of pictures
Kids	9
Youth	11
Men	10
Women	5

The primary target audience is youth, then men and kids, with women again standing out as an obviously underserved, though high entertainment-consuming audience. The most prominent target audience overall in these films is men, with women and youth close behind and kids last.

One of the target audiences	Number of pictures
Men	26
Women	24
Youth	24
Kids	18
Families	10

Genre

"Sci-fi is in and cop shows are out." Commentary on this and every other combination of genres continues to be bantered about as if genre is a crucial picture-selection criterion for audiences. These pictures support the position that great stories well produced is the common success formula and genre has little effect on either success or failure. For these pictures, *action* is the most dominant genre category, and *drama* is the next most prominent genre category. A solid story driven with action is the dominant genre mix of these most successful pictures.

Genre	Number for which it is lead genre	Number for which it is one genre used
Action	12	13
Drama	3	12
Adventure	1	9
Romance	4	8
Animation	5	7
Comedy	2	8
Children	3	5
Science fiction	0	6
Musical	2	4
Fantasy	0	5
Crime	2	3
Horror	1	3
Thriller	0	2
War	0	1

MPAA Rating

We can clearly see from the large television-audience shares of motion pictures that have a restricted-audience rating during their theatrical release that they appeal to audiences who are restricted from viewing them at theaters and for youth, buying, or renting them on home video/DVD. Nevertheless, because of this restriction, all the kids, most of the youth, and most of the family audience earnings are lost during the theatrical release and significantly from home video/DVD. This reduces profits as evidenced by the sparse four restricted-audience pictures on this list. The 10 general-audience pictures are primarily pictures for kids or kids and family.

MPAA rating	Number of pictures
G	10
PG	12
PG-13	6
R	4
Not rated	3

Theatrical Release Date

So, do these pictures evidence a particular film industry golden age? On the contrary, the industry has been graced with great filmmakers throughout its brief history. Of the 35 most successful pictures, there were two pictures in the 1930s, three in the 1940s, four in the 1950s, six in the 1960s, six in the 1970s, six in the 1980s, six in the 1990s, one in 2002, and one in 2004.

And what about releasing pictures in off-season? For these pictures, as with most others, there is never a bad time to release a great picture. Some of these pictures were released in the traditionally off-season months of January, February, March, August, and September.

Year of release	Number of pictures	Year of release	Number of pictures
1937	1	1973	2
1939	1	1975	1
1940	2	1977	1
1942	1	1978	1
1950	1	1980	1
1953	1	1981	1
1956	1	1982	1
1959	1	1983	1
1961	1	1984	2
1964	1	1990	1
1965	1	1993	1
1966	1	1994	2
1967	1	1996	1
1969	1	1997	1
1972	1	2002	1
		2004	1

Running Time

The average running length for these pictures is 2 hours and 12 minutes. This includes five pictures running over three hours and four under one-and-a-half hours. Though longer pictures tend to have a higher production cost, there is no correlation between a picture's time and its grossing capacity. Consider the stronger earning *E.T.* at a sprightly 1 hour, 55 minutes, compared with *Titanic* at 3 hours, 17 minutes, or *The Ten Commandments* at 3 hours, 40 minutes.

Running-time category	Number of pictures
3 hours or more	5
2:30–2:59	2
2:00–2:29	14
1:30–1:59	10
1:00–1:29	4

Tagline

The taglines often capture a sense of the theatrical release campaign used by the studios. These can be useful in developing a sales strategy for pictures with similar audiences and stories.

Theater Attendance and Earnings by Target Audience

This report, shown in Figure 14.2, is essential for balanced producers. This report efficiently reveals the audience universe using the four major targets.

Attendance Percentages

Youth are 50 percent more frequent in their regular attendance than their closest target, 18+ men. Youth are more involved attendees of movies as a group, with only 5 percent never attending, compared with 27 percent men and 32 percent women.

Populations of Target Audiences

As population numbers are considered in the analysis, the audience and commensurate earnings potential slips away from youth. By sheer size, adult men and women are the largest theater attendees.

Annual Admissions

Men slightly lead women in tickets purchased, and together, they spend over five times more than the youth audience.

Box Office Earnings

Each target audience demonstrates an impressive earnings vitality. However, the production of pictures that strongly appeal to all three of these targets represents the ultimate wisdom.

Figure 14.2

Theater Attendance and Earnings by Target Audience

U.S. Theater Attendance and Earnings by Target Audience
2004

Attendance Percentages of Target Audiences					
Audience	1 Per Month	2 - 6 / Year	1 / Year	Never	Totals
Kids 5 - 11	26%	41%	16%	17%	100%
Youth 12 - 17	54%	34%	8%	4%	100%
Men 18 +	28%	33%	12%	27%	100%
Women 18 +	24%	34%	13%	29%	100%

Populations of Target Audiences, in Millions					
Audience	1 Per Month	2 - 6 / Year	1 / Year	Never	Totals
Kids 5 - 11	7.8	12.3	4.8	5.1	30.1
Youth 12 - 17	13.7	8.6	2.0	1.0	25.4
Men 18 +	29.5	34.7	12.6	28.4	105.3
Women 18 +	27.1	38.4	14.7	32.7	112.8
Total Target Audiences Populations					273.6

Annual Admissions of Target Audiences, in Millions					
Audience	1 Per Month	2 - 6 / Year	1 / Year	Never	Totals
Kids 5 - 11	107.0	56.3	5.5	0.0	168.8
Youth 12 - 17	187.6	39.4	2.3	0.0	229.3
Men 18 +	403.3	158.4	14.4	0.0	576.1
Women 18 +	370.3	174.9	16.7	0.0	561.9
Total Target Audiences Admissions					1,536.1

Approximate Box Office Earnings of Target Audiences, in Millions					
Audience	1 Per Month	2 - 6 / Year	1 / Year	Never	Totals
Kids 5 - 11	$664.8	$349.4	$34.1	$ -	$1,048.3
Youth 12 - 17	$1,165.1	$244.5	$14.4	$ -	$1,424.0
Men 18 +	$2,504.4	$983.9	$89.4	$ -	$3,577.7
Women 18 +	$2,299.5	$1,085.9	$103.8	$ -	$3,489.2
Total Target Audiences Populations					$9,539.2

This analysis was prepared by EBG. The data sources for this report are from The Motion Picture Association of America, the National Association of Theater Owners (NATO), Exhibitor Relations Company, Inc. and the U.S. Census.

Information Sources

As business owners and creators, producers ought to keep current on creative, business, technology, and related information. This information allows them to more effectively weave and bob along with the changing industry landscape, taking advantage of opportunities and avoiding the new challenges that will continue to appear with ever-greater regularity.

Fortunately, data have never been more available and convenient to access. Most sources are available on the Web, by e-mail, or by fax.

Some of the most respected and constructive sources used by entertainment executives are as follows.

Exhibitor Relations Company, Inc.
15760 Ventura Blvd., Suite 806
Encino, CA 91436
818-784-2380

This is one of the oldest and most used sources in the industry, providing historical and weekly box office information, trade screening reports, development and production reports, and many special statistical and narrative reports, including:

- Weekly box office/trade screenings/issuance of MPAA ratings/special report updates
- Bimonthly motion picture release schedules for all major and minor studios, by picture, showing primary cast, director, and release date (there is an e-mail version of this sent weekly that includes release patterns)
- Reports on motion pictures in development, including their relative detail
- Reports on pictures in production, with creative and distribution detail
- Reports on pictures in production without distribution
- The "Alpha List," which details pictures in comatose development, active development, and production
- Special research on demand

MovieBiz.tv
moviebiz.tv

This Web service delivers all fundamental Greenlight Analysis worksheets, data and campaign copies. It also delivers powerfully enabling business products including The Entertainment Banking, Distribution, and Business Resource Guide, and a series of highly beneficial online resources that include, among others:

- Production Funding Planner and Bank Loan Calculator
- Picture Target Audiences and Campaign Signature Matrix
- Greenlight Analysis and Global Producer's Share Forecast
- Single and multiple picture development entity and production entity business plans
- (7) Global Audience Forecaster

NATO Encyclopedia of Exhibition
natoonline.org
4605 Lankershim Boulevard, Suite 340
North Hollywood, CA 91602
818-506-1778

This book is published annually and contains several extremely helpful reports. These are not always in the ultimate final form for analysis by producers, and are for the pictures released a year prior to the one just ended, but the data are accurate and, in the main, complete.

Consider the following information, combined from two of these reports, which reveals MPAA (CARA)-rated motion pictures that received no U.S. theatrical distribution. Various estimates from festivals and other sources indicate that there are five to 10 times more feature length pictures that are not rated, and so do not appear on these reports. If that is true, that increases the annual number of produced but unreleased pictures to more than a thousand. This is a tragic waste of resources and sobering motivation for producers to collaborate with global distributors from the earliest beginnings of their pictures, and for investors to mitigate risk through making this an essential initial, if not benchmark, criteria.

MPAA (CARA)-Rated Pictures with No U.S. Distribution

Year	CARA-rated pictures	Pictures released by all U.S. distributors	Pictures not distributed
1993	605	440	165
1994	635	410	225
1995	697	370	327
1996	713	420	293
1997	673	458	215
1998	686	509	177
1999	677	461	216
2000	762	478	284
2001	739	482	257
2002	786	467	319
2003	940	473	467

The NATO Encyclopedia annually reports on the number of theater tickets sold, total box office take, average ticket prices, average major motion picture production costs (which were $63.8 million average per picture in 2003), average studio theatrical release print and advertising costs (which were $46.9 million average per picture in 2003), a report on each studio's theatrical grosses by picture, among several other excellent reports.

Hollywood Creative Directory
hcdonline.com

This is one of the best sources for information on studio and network executives and production companies. Though available in published form, this is most useful as an online service.

The Studio System
inhollywood.com

This fee-based service is an industry standard providing extensive search and retrieval contact information for entertainment executives and professionals at the studios, production companies, talent agencies, and PR firms; as well as motion picture and television talent, agents, projects in development, company client rosters, literary sales, special reports, and research.

Nielsen Media Research
Nielsen.com
11150 West Olympic Boulevard, Suite 1000
Los Angeles, CA 90064,
310-966-4900

This is perhaps the most complete and accurate source for television-viewing information, in a broad array of published reports and custom-designed research.

Daily and Weekly **Variety**
variety.com

The Hollywood Reporter
hollywoodreporter.com

These provide daily news and maintain archives on everything entertainment in the industry. They each also have research capacities.

National Cable Television Association
ncta.com
1724 Massachusetts Avenue, NW
Washington, DC 20036
202-775-3550

This is the best initial source for understanding the 300-plus cable television network landscape. Their *Cable Television Developments* book lists all the networks, their primary executives, contact information, programming and audience focuses, and subscribers.

Paul Kagan Research
pkbaseline.com

This one of the most respected and reliable entertainment industry research firms. They publish reports and perform sophisticated research and analysis.

Internet Movie Database
imdb.com

This is a powerful, user-friendly, free and fee-based motion picture information Internet service.

Showbiz Data
showbizdata.com

This data resource has an especially useful, free Internet news update that reports opening box office figures, tracks the top U.S. pictures for the year, updates the 10 U.S. studios by their grosses, and summarizes some of the week's top stories. The site also offers an excellent fee-based service for U.S. and international box office data and other industry information.

The Independent Film & Television Alliance (I.F.T.A. or the Alliance)
afma.com

This is the resource for international motion picture and television sales information, forms, procedures, referrals to member companies, research, and instruction. The alliance conducts AFM, the premiere annual sales event. It also operates what may be the entertainment industry's finest arbitration tribunal.

Producer Success Principles

These principles are especially for motion picture producers, but they are also profitably applied by producers of television narrative and documentary programming, commercials, and even student film productions.

1. Story. Discovering, developing, and producing quality stories is the core focus. Story is the single most essential, important, and powerful asset upon which creative and financial success rests. This is where investments of time, study, review, hyper-polishing, and money will return the greatest overall benefits. This is where the answer should always be, "Yes, we will wait and further invest until we have it worked out and completely wired."

2. Target Audiences. Every story appeals to specific target audiences more than to others. Producers should know who these audiences are, where they are, how many there are, what their entertainment consumption profile is, and what drives their motion picture passions. With the majority of audiences and income sourced outside the United States, this audience understanding should also be understood for, at least, the seven leading international territories. Where appropriate, cover shots should be produced to deliver seamless pictures to these international territories. Knowing each picture's target audience universe is the most fundamental information for determining its earnings potential. This question is typically one of the first asked by distributors. The audience is the most important participant in the industry. Cater to them.

3. Balance. Sustaining a balance between each picture's story, targeted audiences, and potential producer's share of profits is the most predictable approach to ensure each picture's successful development, production, and global distribution.

4. Talent. The strongest evolution of producer/talent relationships begins with meetings that allow each to test the other's creative affinity for the story, then continues with deal-making meetings involving the talent's agent, manager and/or attorney. The producer's research, planning, and preparation all help render talent attachment a predictable and even pleasant experience.

5. Global Distribution. Producers should exclusively develop and produce motion pictures for which they have first engaged development-level collaborative relationships with a distributor in the United States and at least four of the seven major international territories. Distributors do what producers cannot do. They make each unknown picture a household name to its target audiences. They set up and manage each picture within their marketplace. They do the impossible. Though they occasionally underperform, they are the independent producer's inseparable partners.

6. Development. Producers should plan and finance each picture's development in a fashion as well defined and complete as the manner in which they plan and finance each picture's production. This planning, risk-mitigated approach, and compelling deal-construct will appeal to private investors, who should be the initial primary, if not exclusive, provider of development capital.

7. Financing. Development investors should substantially, if not completely, recoup their investment before production and should participate in the long-term income of the picture(s). Producers should use banks as their primary, and where possible exclusive, production financing source. Accordingly, producers should understand entertainment banking sufficiently to submit funding packages that they know will be accepted.

8. Entertainment Law. The development, production, and liquidation of motion pictures consistently engage the producer in the process of representation, negotiations, and documentations. Contract language does not always correlate with contemporary language interpretation. In negotiations, producers should be decisive, but *always* agree on basic terms only, with these being subject to their attorney's review.

9. Production Company Team. A producer's sustained solidarity is largely assured by the production company team. These members must be skilled, dedicated, and largely self-managed. Consequently, they must be carefully selected, refined, empowered, advanced, and allowed to monetarily participate in the team's successes.

10. Living a Full Life. In addition to skilled imagineering, producing, and releasing successful motion pictures, producers need the full symmetry of participation with their family, use of contemplation and study, and participation in the arts. If these are kept in mind as producers plan and schedule their time, they will enrich and fulfill their lives.

Index

A

ADR (Alternative Dispute Resolution), 97
agents, 101–102
   attorneys as agents, 102
   as creative resources,
     105
   relationships with producers, 166
airlines/ships as ancillary movie market,
     64–65
Alliance (Independent Film & Television
     Alliance), 186
Alternative Dispute Resolution (ADR), 97
American Film Market, 41
American Film Marketing Association's
     Arbitration Tribunal, 97
ancillary media as motion picture industry
     participant, 15
Arbitration Tribunal of American Film
     Marketing Association, 97
attorneys. *See* entertainment
     law/negotiations, attorneys/law firms
     audiences
   age demographic categories, 3
   distribution windows
     audience characteristics, 52–56
     effects of theatrical releases on
       ancillary distribution, 51–52

most successful motion pictures in
     U.S., 178–179
motion picture industry participant, 1–4
orientation, 3–4

B

balanced independent producers, 10–12
   international territories markets, 42
     guidelines for success, 42–45
banking. *See* entertainment
     banking/financing

C

cable television distribution. *See*
     syndicated television distribution
Cannes Film Festival, 41
CARA ratings, 184
completion guarantees/guarantors
   completion bond packages, 79–80
   completion bond provisional
     acceptance letters, 80–81
   engaging, 159
   insurance cost, 81
   perceived and real values, 78–79
   relationships between participating
     parties, 79

completion guarantees/guarantors
[*continued*]
  relationships with producers, 166–167
  responsibilities, 77–78
consumer brands as ancillary movie
      market
  establishing picture's brands, 5–7
  motion picture industry participant, 15
  picture branding process, 161–162
  premium tie-ins, 15–16, 62–63
  product placement, 15–16, 62
  production company brand presence,
      167–169

D

day and date theatrical releases, 50
deal documentation, 95
  deal memos, 94–95
  deal reviews/line-outs, 95–96
  letter agreements, 95
  long form agreements, 95
deal points, 22–23
development companies, 108–109
  financing, 110–111
  forms of company structures, 111–112
  interrelationships with production
      and producing companies, 110
  investment risk evaluation, 110–111
  and production companies
    development plan activities, 145–146
    emphasis on development, 142
    interrelationships, 110
    predirector development, 152–153
  team members, 132, 135–136
    guidelines for optimization, 136–137
    necessity of complete team, 131–132
    producer-team member relationships,
      137–138
development deals
  fair deal preparation, 104–105
  negotiations, 103–104
  planning, 102–103
development financing. *See also*
      entertainment banking/financing
  basics, 113–114
  motion picture development and
      production schedules, 114
  process of securing financing
    develop plans, 118
    formulate investments, 125, 130
    make presentations, 130
    prepare activity projection, 118–124

    prepare cash flow projection,
      124–125, 126–129
    prepare investment's documentation,
      130
    select development team and
      advisors, 125
  sources
    coproduction companies, 117
    government agencies, 117–118
    investors, 115–117
    production companies, 115
    studios, 115
direct distribution expenses (DDE)
  international territory gross, 31
  network television gross, 30
  theatrical distribution, 28
directors
  attaching to production companies,
      153–154
  most successful motion pictures in
      U.S., 178
  profit points participation, 104
  relationship with producers, 154–155
dispute resolutions, 97
distribution/distributors
  ancillary markets, 162–163
  announcements, 146–147
  international territories, 31, 162
  major and minor distributors, 19–20
  motion picture industry participant, 4–8
  net earnings share analysis, 31–33
  operating perspective, 7–8
  presales, 158–159
  sales agent fees, 30
  subcontractors, 15
  U.S. studio agreements, 158
distribution-only relationships
  independent producers with studios,
      24, 25–27
distribution windows in U.S.
  airline/ship showings, 64–65
  consumer brands
    premium tie-ins, 15–16, 62–63
    product placement, 15–16, 62
  games, retail and electronic, 13, 64
  hotels/motels, 65
  miscellaneous schools/institutions, 65
  network television, 13–14, 30, 59–60
    audience characteristics, 53–56
    audience sizes, 52–53
  novelization/paperbacks, 13–14, 61
  premium cable television, 13–14, 29–30,
      58–59

audience characteristics, 53–56
audience sizes, 52–53
sound tracks/music publishing, 63–64
syndicated television, 13–14, 30, 59–61
audience characteristics, 53–56
audience sizes, 52–53
theatrical, 13, 28
audience reaction's effect on other
windows, 51–52
audience sizes, 52–53
earnings analysis, 56
toys and merchandising, 64
video/DVD (home entertainment),
13–14, 28–29, 57–58
audience characteristics, 53–56
audience sizes, 52–53
earnings analysis, 56
DVDs distribution. *See* video/DVD
(home entertainment) distribution

E

entertainment banking/financing.
See also development financing
completion guarantees/guarantors
completion bond packages, 79–80
completion bond provisional
acceptance letters, 80–81
insurance cost, 81
perceived and real values, 78–79
relationships between participating
parties, 79
relationships with producers, 166–167
responsibilities, 77–78
loans
approval process, 71
bank financing worksheet, 71–74
basics, 67–68
gap financing, 73, 74, 75
lending decisions, criteria, 68–69
loan memorandum contents, 69–71
timing in production for approaching
banks, 75–76
types, 74–75
motion picture industry participant, 15
production companies
coordinating financing, 157
engaging bank loans, 159–160
engaging completion bonds, 159
raising financing, 143–144
relationships with banks, 166–167
entertainment law/negotiations
attorneys/law firms

attorneys as agents, 102
basics, 83–84
contract-relative communications,
85–86
producers as attorneys, 84–85
role in communication with
concerned parties, 96
role with talent proposals, 105
selection criteria, 84
deal documentation, 95
deal memos, 94–95
deal reviews/line-outs, 95–96
letter agreements, 95
long form agreements, 95
dispute resolutions, 97
literary concerns
greenlight reviews, 92
literary releases, 87–89
literary releases, example letter,
89–90
literary rights option/acquisition,
92–94
step deals, 90–92
negotiation basics, 86–87
Exhibitor Relations Company, Inc., 183

F

feasibility analysis, 2–3
financing. *See* entertainment
banking/financing

G

games (retail and electronic) as ancillary
movie market, 13, 64
gap financing, 73, 74, 75
gross box office, 28

H

Hollywood Creative Directory, 184
The Hollywood Reporter, 185
home entertainment distribution.
See video/DVD
(home entertainment) distribution
hotels/motels as ancillary movie
market, 65

I

in-house studio production, 23, 25–27
Independent Film & Television Alliance,
186

independent producers
  advancing team vitality and allegiance,
      171–172
  balanced producers, 10–12
    international distributors relationships,
        41–45
  as business owners, 16
  creative protectionist producers, 8–10
  deal points, 22–23
  library picture management, 170
  most successful motion pictures in
      U.S., 178
  motion picture industry participant, 8–12
  multiple picture management, 165–166
  principles for success, 186–187
  relationships with agents, 166
  relationships with banks, 166–167
  relationships with completion
      guarantors, 166–167
  relationships with international
      distributors, 41–45
    global day and date theatrical
        releases, 50
    global production of American style
        pictures, 50
    international sales departments, 49–50
    license timing and documentation,
        46–49
    maintaining relationships, 45–46
  relationships with studios, 22–23, 166
    distribution-only, 24, 25–27
    in-house studio production, 23,
        25–27
    negative pickup, 23–24, 25–27
    output relationships, 34–35
    split negative pickup, 33
    studio acquisition of renegade
        pictures, 33–34
  sustaining balance, 169–170
international territories
  box office statistics, 38–41
  distribution agreements, 158–159
  distribution gross, 31
  global popularity of U.S. motion
      pictures, 37–38
  leading motion pictures, 41
  motion picture industry participant, 14
  relationships with independent
      producers, 41–45
    global day and date theatrical
        releases, 50
    global production of American
        style pictures, 50
    international sales departments, 49–50
    license timing and documentation,
        46–49
    maintaining relationships, 45–46
Internet Movie Database, 185
investments in motion pictures
  investment memorandums, 143
  offering preparation, 142
  partner communications, 144–145
  risk evaluation, 110–111

L

law firms. See entertainment
        law/negotiations, attorneys/law firms
licensed media as motion picture industry
        participant, 12–14
licensees as motion picture industry
        participant, 15
limited liability companies (LLCs), 112
literary/story concerns
  creative aspect of production, 16–17
  greenlight reviews, 92
  internal greenlights, 147
  literary releases, 87–89
    example letter, 89–90
  literary rights option/acquisition, 92–94
  search for, 140–141
  selecting, 147–152
  step deals, 90–92
loans for movie production
  approval process, 71
  bank financing worksheet, 71–74
  basics, 67–68
  gap financing, 73, 74, 75
  lending decisions, criteria, 68–69
  loan memorandum contents, 69–71
  production stage to approach
      banks, 75–76
  types, 74–75

M

motion picture industry participant
  ancillary media, 15
  audiences, 1–4
  consumer brands, 15
  distribution subcontractors, 15
  distributors in U.S., 4–8, 12–14
  financing participants, 15
  international territories, 14
  licensed media, 12–14
  licensees, 15

producers, 8–12
  production talent and subcontractors, 15
  retailers, 12–14
motion picture statistics and reports,
      173–174
  elements affecting earnings, 174
  most successful pictures released in
      U.S., 174–182
    information sources, 182–186
motion picture studios
  distribution arena, 21–22, 22
  distribution-focused, 20
  executive arena, 21–22
  integrity, 21
  most successful pictures released in
      U.S., 177–178
  production arena, 22
  relationships with independent
      producers, 22–23
    comparisons, 24–28
    deal points, 22–23
    distribution-only, 24, 25–27
    in-house studio production, 23, 25–27
    negative pickup, 23–24, 25–27
    output relationships, 34–35
    split negative pickup, 33
    studio acquisition of renegade pictures,
        33–34
MovieBiz.tv Web service, 183
MPAA ratings, 180, 184

N

National Cable Television Association, 185
NATO Encyclopedia of Exhibition,
      183–184
negative pickup, 23–24, 25–27
negotiations. *See* entertainment
      law/negotiations
network television distribution, 13–14,
      30, 59–60
  audience characteristics, 53–56
  audience sizes, 52–53
  gross sales, 30
Nielsen Media Research, 185
novelization/paperbacks as ancillary
      movie market, 13–14, 61

P

paperbacks and movie distribution.
      See novelization/paperbacks as
      ancillary movie market

Paul Kagan Research, 185
post-production, 161
premium cable television distribution,
      13–14, 29–30, 58–59
  agreements, 158–159
  audience characteristics, 53–56
  audience sizes, 52–53
preproduction, 160
principal photography, 160–161
producers. *See also* independent producers
producing companies, 108–109
  forms of company structures, 111–112
  interrelationships with development
      and production companies, 110
production companies, 108–109
  brand presence, 167–169
  deal planning, 102–103
  defining, 140
  and development companies
    development plan activities, 145–146
    emphasis on development, 142
    interrelationships, 110
    predirector development, 152–153
  directors
    attaching, 153–154
    relationship with producers, 154–155
  distributors/distribution
    ancillary markets, 162–163
    announcements, 146–147
    international territories, 162
    presales, 158–159
    U.S. studio agreements, 158
  establishing, 140
  final preproduction, 160
  financing
    coordinating, 157
    engaging bank loans, 159–160
    engaging completion bonds, 159
    raising, 143–144
  forms of company structures, 111–112
  investment memorandums, 143
  investment offering preparation, 142
  investment partner communications,
      144–145
  investment risk evaluation, 110–111
  marketing materials, 157
  physical production preparations, 156
  picture branding, 161–162
  post-production, 161
  principal photography, 160–161
  shooting scripts, 155–156
  stories
    internal greenlights, 147

search for, 140–141
selecting, 147–152
talent attachments, 156
team members
  advisors, 132, 133–134
  assembling, 143
  complete team necessity, 131–132
  executive committee, 132, 134–135
  guidelines for optimization, 136–137
  producer-team member relationships,
    137–138
profit points participation, 104

R

renegade pictures, 33–34
retailers as motion picture industry
  participant, 12–14

S

sales agent fees, 30
shooting scripts, 155–156
Showbiz Data, 185
sole proprietorships, 111
sound tracks/music publishing as ancillary
  movie market, 63–64
split negative pickup, 33
stories. *See* literary/story concerns
The Studio System, 184–185
syndicated television distribution, 13–14,
  30, 59–61
  audience characteristics, 53–56
  audience sizes, 52–53

T

talent
  attaching, 156
  initial selection steps, 100–101
  most successful motion pictures in
    U.S., 178
  motion picture industry participant, 15
  profit points participation, 104
  secondary talent offers, 105
television distribution. *See* network
    television distribution; premium
    cable television distribution;
    syndicated television distribution
theatrical distribution, 13, 28
  audience reaction's effect on other
    windows, 51–52
  audience sizes, 52–53
  earnings analysis, 56
  theatrical rereleases, 170–171
toys and merchandising as ancillary
  movie market, 64

V

video/DVD (home entertainment)
    distribution, 13–14, 28–29, 57–58
  agreements, 158
  audience characteristics, 53–56
  audience sizes, 52–53
  distributor's home entertainment net, 29
  earnings analysis, 56
  gross income, 28–29
  video duplication and general
    expenses, 29